THEATER AS LIFE

THEATER AS LIFE

PRACTICAL WISDOM DRAWN FROM GREAT
ACTING TEACHERS, ACTORS & ACTRESSES

by

Paul Marcus, Ph. D.
with Gabriela Marcus

MARQUETTE
UNIVERSITY

PRESS

 # 748812796

LIBRARY OF CONGRESS CATALOGING-IN-PUBLICATION DATA

Marcus, Paul.
Theater as life : practical wisdom drawn from great acting teachers, actors & actresses
/ by Paul Marcus ; with Gabriela Marcus.
   p. cm.
Includes bibliographical references and index.
ISBN-13: 978-0-87462-069-6 (pbk. : alk. paper)
ISBN-10: 0-87462-069-4 (pbk. : alk. paper)
1. Acting—Psychological aspects. 2. Self-realization. 3. Acting—Study and teaching. I. Marcus, Gabriela, 1987- II. Title.
PN2071.P78M37 2011
792.02'8—dc23

2011033396

cover design - coco connolly

www.marquette.edu/mupress/

♾The paper used in this publication meets the minimum requirements of the
American National Standard for Information Sciences—
Permanence of Paper for Printed Library Materials, ANSI Z39.48-1992.

Association of American
University Presses

MARQUETTE UNIVERSITY PRESS
MILWAUKEE

The Association of Jesuit University Presses

"My goal is, to the extent of my powers, to make clear to the present generation that an actor is a teacher of beauty and truth. ... A love of the theatre has been born in you. Begin now to make sacrifices to it, by which I mean that service to art consists in the ability to make selfless sacrifices to it."

Constantin Stanislavski, Letter to a Young Student

FOR IRENE,

A WONDERFUL WIFE AND MOTHER

The lessons of another teacher in this book, Viola Spolin, reflect a certain genius. Her *Improvisations for the Theater* link feeling to form through the spontaneity of play and the sequencing of the body. Spolin's simple exercise on being seen is a psychological masterpiece. The actor is asked to stand in front of the class for three minutes and is prompted to "Do nothing." Three minutes is a long time to stand before a group of people (an audience) and be witnessed doing nothing.

Spolin's improvisational exercise can take on deep resonance. The actor begins to ask herself about the experience of being seen, offers various attempts at manipulating the relationship with the audience, seeks different personas through which to filter the experience, and ultimately understands the nature of being seen as an actor out of role. Spolin's lesson leads us to question, "Is there an actor if there is no role to play?" and "Is it only through role that we can be seen in life?" Being seen, for Spolin, is to understand the limitations we face in controlling how others perceive us in the artist's negative space that is outside of role. Or, even, if we can/do exist in that empty space at all.

The compelling obligation of the actor to the role and the role to the person is evidenced in contemporary playwright, David Mamet's drama, *A Life in the Theater*. It is his love poem, of sorts, to his chosen art form. In a poignant moment, the actor leaves the theater struggling to locate a self out of role, seeking a part to play in the choice of a mundane meal.

The beauty and the value of this volume are found in the ways the authors have derived lessons from the artistic and the psychological for a more rewarding living of life. The greatest lessons I learned from Stella Adler were about living. She was a larger than life figure. Her message to actors was that great acting comes from strong choices.

And yet, for Stella, it is not only in the place of strength where the artist engages with her creative process. She writes, "The actor has a built-in broken heart, which helps him to understand, but it doesn't help him win. There's no actor who looks like a banker at the end of life. He looks distinguished, but not as if he's won. The actor pays a price, and that price is his heart" (2000, p. 251).

The nobility of the actor is the willingness to consider existence through the inter-subjectivity of role, action, intention. It is a willingness, psychotherapist Irvin Yalom suggests, to live an *examined* life. It is a willingness, as Cassavetes father said, to be "truthful."

Nobility is a form of servitude. Acting is a form of servitude. Therapy or psychology is a form of servitude. Stella Adler taught me how to be a good servant.

This book offers us a guide to some self-care through the "rules" and properties of the theater. We understand our own nobility as we learn to be good servants to ourselves.

The actor—like the analysand—like the person of faith—like the human being—can learn the value of living life with the "broken heart" to which Stella refers. When we operate from this place of deep understanding of our situation and compassion for it and for those places in others, the inner critic—Stanislavski's "small actor"— is silenced. There are, indeed, no small parts. And upon this stage, we can find a life that celebrates our humanity with a simultaneously humble and dignified sense of our own being.

For Paul Marcus, locating the deeper psychological meaning within the craft of acting brings him onto the *stage* with his daughter. For Gabriela Marcus, this dramatic process reveals the dynamic magnificence of her father's peopled world, its perils, its pleasures, its enchantments, and its tempests. Shakespeare's Miranda, the daughter, cries out to and on behalf of her father, Prospero,

> O, wonder! How many goodly creatures are there here! How beauteous mankind is! O! Brave new world that has such people in't! (p. 1394)

In its essence, the book before you reflects a simple yet profoundly moving transaction. A father and his daughter listened deeply and with great respect to each other. They combined the great teachings of their worlds, their arts. This rich and practical book is the result.

Professor Maria Hodermarska
Drama Therapy Program
New York University, Steinhardt School
Licensed Creative Arts Therapist, Registered Drama Therapist

CHAPTER TWO

EMOTION RECOLLECTED
IN TRANQUILITY

LEE STRASBERG'S "METHOD"

"This is why acting is an art. For it is when we are able to create reality, truth, and beauty out of such seemingly adverse conditions, out of a void so to speak, and do it with just the basic implements of life around us, with just ourselves and nothing else to work with, then and only then, have we transformed the theatre and its works into an art form."

–Lee Strasberg

LEE STRASBERG (1901–1982) WAS UNDOUBTEDLY one of the most influential directors and acting teachers in modern theater. His "Method" technique of acting (known as "The Method") was in part responsible for producing some of the greatest American actors like Montgomery Clift, Paul Newman, Al Pacino and Dustin Hoffman.[1] According to Strasberg, his Method was strongly influenced by the immortal Stanislavski, "everything we deal with in these exercises—relaxation, concentration,

---

1   It is mistakenly believed that Marlon Brando was successfully trained by Strasberg: "Lee Strasberg tried to get credit for teaching me how to act. He never taught me anything...To me he was a tasteless and untalented person...I went to the Actor's Studio...because of Elia Kazan...But Strasberg never taught me acting. Stella [Adler] did—and Kazan." Brando, *Songs My Mother Taught Me* (New York: Random House, 1994), p. 85.

sense memory, emotional memory—was defined by Stanislavski."[2]
While Stanislavski rejected a central aspect of Strasberg's Method,
particularly his claim that "emotional memory" is the core of generating
truthful and believable emotion, the basis of great acting (Stanislavski
gave up the concept he invented), Strasberg stubbornly and boldly de-
fied the master. Affective memory is "the process of contacting one's
memories of emotions in order to channel them into a role."[3] Strasberg
further elaborates the lynchpin of his Method:

> The basic idea of affective memory is not emotional recall but that
> the actor's emotion on the stage should never be really real. It al-
> ways should be only remembered emotion. An emotion that hap-
> pens right now spontaneously is out of control—you don't know
> what's going to happen from it, and the actor can't always maintain
> and repeat it. Remembered emotion is something that the actor can
> create and repeat: without that the thing is hectic.[4]

When discussing Strasberg, perhaps more than any other acting
teacher, we are dealing with something of a lay "master psychologist,"
for many of his important insights about acting that have bearing on
the non-actor's search for the "good life" are centrally concerned with
the conscious and unconscious vicissitudes of the emotions and their
mastery, on and off the stage. As Strasberg noted, "exploration [ex-
tending the actor's range of imagination and expression] tries to open
new galleries and tunnels in the unconscious levels of the instrument
[the actor] where most actors' creation takes place. It attempts to mine
levels never before employed. Thus as he extends his range, the actor
also extends his technique."[5]

In this chapter we will discuss some of Strasberg's key concepts, such
as relaxation, concentration, sense memory, affective memory, justification and imaginative personalization and substitution. These core
concepts, and a few others, constitute the main thrust of Strasberg's

2   Lee Strasberg, *A Dream of Passion. The Development of the Method.*
    Evangeline Morphos (Ed.) (New York: A Plume Book, 1987), p. 124.

3   Quoted from Jeremy G. Butler, *Star Texts: Image Performance and
    Television* (Detroit: Wayne State University Press, 1991).

4   Quoted in Richard Schechner in *Working With Live Material*, from the
    Tulane Drama Review (1964): 9.1: 96.

5   Robert H. Hethmon, *Strasberg at The Actor's Studio* (New York: Theatre
    Communications Group, 1965), p. 252.

teaching system.[6] Each one of these concepts also has bearing on how to live the "good life."

RELAXATION

Relaxation, the process of becoming less tense, tight, regulated and restricted, is for Strasberg a key pre-condition of great acting. Unlike Suzuki, who saw tension as positive, Strasberg and most other Western actors regard tension as the nemesis of acting. As Strasberg noted, "tension is the occupational disease of the actor. Relaxation is the foundation on which almost all actors' work is based."[7] Strasberg approvingly quotes Stanislavski who believed that in relaxation "lay the whole secret, the whole soul of creativeness on the stage..."[8] Of course, a certain amount of tension and anxiety is needed to act, as it is motivating and enlivening. As Jerzy Grotowski noted, "He who is totally relaxed is nothing more than a wet rag." However, for the most part, as nearly every actor and actress will tell you, tension, nervousness and the like is lethal for performers, while relaxation is a fundamental condition of possibility for a great performance. As Strasberg

---

6   Edward Dwight Easty, *On Method Acting* (New York: Ivy Books, 1981), p. ix.

7   Robert H. Hethmon, editor, *Strasberg. At the Actors's Studio. Tape-Recorded Sessions* (New York: Theatre Communications Group, 1965), p. 89. While Strasberg used improvisation in his training system, we will not be discussing this subject in this chapter as the topic has been examined in great detail in the chapter on Viola Spolin, "the high priestess" of improv. Suffice it to say that Strasberg believed that "improvisation is essential if the actor is to develop the spontaneity [and reasoning power] necessary to create in each performance 'the illusion of the first time.'"; "To stimulate a continuous flow of response and thought within the actor is the primary value of improvisation"; "Improvisation leads not only to a process of thought and response, but also helps to discover the logical behavior of the character rather than encouraging the actor 'merely to illustrate' the obvious meaning of the line" (Strasberg, *The Dream of Passion*, pp. 107, 108, 110); "Improvisation is the only means that helps the actor to break the grip of the cliché, the conventional and mechanical form of expression which still rules the stage as in the past and must always be fought." S. Loraine Hull, *Strasberg's Method as Taught by Lorrie Hull. A Practical Guide for Actors, Teachers and Directors* (Woodbridge, CT: Ox Bow Publishing, 1985), p. 237.

8   Strasberg, *The Dream of Passion*, p. 50.

noted, about 75% of giving a great performance depends on one's ability to relax.

For Strasberg, as in ordinary life, tension is a hugely destructive feeling, for it undermines one's internal life, including one's sensory awareness and creativity. Tension, said Strasberg, eradicates the actor's ability to think clearly and feel deeply: "The actor cannot achieve a real relation between what he is thinking and the expression which should be part of that thought or experience. The expression becomes contaminated."[9] "Tension is the presence of unnecessary or excess energy which inhibits the flow of thought and sensation to the required area."[10] Without tension, says Strasberg, the actor's (and the non-actor's) natural expressiveness can emerge. Taking his lead from Stanislavski who felt that relaxation was a preliminary pre-condition for almost all acting work, Strasberg developed a set of exercises that were meant to calm the actor, to reestablish a mental and physical equipoise. As Edward Dwight Easty pointed out, to release tension, one must be mindful that it exists and one needs to be able to locate the place and source of tension.[11] Strasberg emphasized that tension is always a mind/body experience and one can conceptualize and reduce the tension from either or both points of entry. For example, "an actress who has tension in her legs will enter the stage with a stiff, artificial, 'stagey' walk. An inflexible spine will affect the whole back and possibly the shoulders and arms with its rigidity. Tension can even settle in the hands and fingers causing them to become clumsy and to shake."[12] Strasberg's relaxation exercises were part of a sequence of training that tended to focus on three major areas, the side of the temples, the bridge of the nose and the muscles. The goal of these exercises was to remove the "unnecessary tension" (as we said, some tension is "positive") so that the actor can be liberated to do the things he needs to do on the stage with a greater sense of ease and effortlessness.[13] As Strasberg summarized it,

---

9   Ibid.
10   Ibid., p. 125.
11   Easty, *On Method Acting*, p. 65.
12   Ibid., p. 69.
13   Richard Brestoff. *The Great Acting Teachers and Their Methods* (Lyme, NH: Smith and Kraus Book), pp. 97-99.

the actor becomes completely responsive. His instrument gives forth a new depth of resonance. Emotion that has been habitually held back suddenly rushes forth. The actor becomes real—not merely simple or natural. He becomes fully concentrated. He unveils totally unsuspected aspects and elements of himself, but with such a degree of ease and authority that he seems literally to have taken off a mask, to have emerged from a disguise that previously smothered and concealed his true personality. Yet all he did was relax.[14]

What Strasberg is getting at in his emphasis on relaxation is an insight that also has bearing on the non-actor: Relaxation, as Donald Curtis noted, "means releasing all concern and tension and letting the natural order of life through one's being." In a state of relaxation we are most ourselves. In fact, sadly, so many of us mainly experience ourselves through a palpable tension and anxiety-ridden filter that facilitates confusing one's authentic self with an inauthentic self. It also makes life utterly miserable. As a famous Chinese proverb says, "Tension is who you think you should be. Relaxation is who you are." Relaxation is not a luxury; it is a necessity, especially for making contact with one's most genuine and true self.

Strasberg's way of looking at relaxation has a similarity to the Taoist concept of "wu–wei," usually translated as "non action," but which implies much more, just as Strasberg is getting at something more than relaxation as simply a state of rest, inactivity and tranquility. Wu-wei, says Burton Watson, "is not a forced quietude, but rather the renunciation of any action that is occasioned by conventional concepts of purpose or achievement, or aimed at the realization of conventional goals."[15] Wu-wei, in other words, does not mean taking no action, but rather means doing nothing that is not natural and spontaneous. Wu-wei requires a passive receptivity and flexible attitude toward oneself

---

14   Ibid., pp. 92-93. Strasberg's exercise, called "private moment," is a useful way of cultivating relaxation. It is a physical exercise in which the actor generates a sense of solitude, while in reality he is in with other people, such as the classroom audience. The goal is to allow the actor "to feel private in public," that is, to feel greater freedom, less inhibition and self-consciousness, and thus be able to focus on what he is actually doing with enhanced concentration. Strasberg was clearly influenced by Stanislavski's notion of "public solitude" in his "privae moment" exercise.

15   Burton Watson, *The Complete Works of Chuang Tzu* (New York: Columbia University Press, 1968), p. 468.

and others; it requires a patient waiting for the spontaneous transformation of things; and it involves a respect for restraint and limits.
Wu-wei, as Alan Watts noted, is thus best translated as "don't force
it;" the idea is to feel intuitively the kind of action that is required in
a particular context. "Through non-action, no action is left undone,"
Lao Tsu famously said. The deeper point that Strasberg is making is
that relaxation, as it applies to the actor and real life, involves renounc-
ing the inordinate need to control that which cannot be controlled,
and by doing so, paradoxically one gains greater control. In a word,
we are in control of control. Such an outlook on relaxation requires
that the actor and ordinary person relinquish, or at least dramatically
reduce, their inflated narcissism and grandiosity, their selfish motives
and unrealistic desires. Instead, the goal is that they must comfortably
respond (not react) spontaneously to all things as they come, flowing
with the natural currents of the world. For Strasberg, as with many
other acting teachers, this, in part, means giving way to an "unself-
conscious self-surrender, a relinquishing of control,"[16] to the creative,
impossible to pin down, repository of the unconscious.

CONCENTRATION

Relaxation, the bedrock of great acting, creates the conditions of possibility for the actor to concentrate—to focus all of his thoughts and
mental activity on the subject or activity he is engaged in, usually in
silence. For Strasberg, following Stanislavski, "actors concentrate best
when they are relaxed and relax best when they are concentrated."[17]
Strasberg's notion of concentration is not only tied to relaxation but
also a robust imagination, the latter being a pre-requisite for being a
great actor. As Strasberg noted, "concentration on the object implies
believing it, seeing it so precisely that you really do become convinced,
so that the senses come alive as they do in life when you see a real
object."[18] [Remember, on the stage everything is actually "make believe."] Objects, continues Strasberg, "can be mental or thought objects,
or fantasy objects. They can be situations, or events, or relationships,

16   John R. Suler, "Paradox," in *The Couch and the Tree. Dialogue in
     Psychoanalysis and Buddhism,* Anthony Molino (Ed.) (New York: North
     Point Press, 1998), p. 326.
17   Brestoff, *The Great Acting Teachers,* p. 100.
18   Hethmon, *Strasberg. At the Actor's Studio,* p. 96.

or characters—or elements of these things—as created by the play-wright." Most importantly, "through concentration the actor brings these things alive for himself" and the audience.[19] Bill Russell, the famed basketball star, caught the gist of Strasberg's point when he said, "concentration and mental toughness are the margins of victory," the basis of a great performance on the stage and in real life.

The creative dynamic among relaxation/concentration/imagina-tion is fueled by "sense memory," this being Strasberg's key, though controversial, concept. Sense memory is the potentiating basis for all great acting. It can be simply defined, says Easty: "It is a remembering of the five senses...[it] brings a feeling of life to every object that is associated with these five senses." Moreover, without a finely tuned sensory memory, it is near impossible to generate the motivation that facilitates the response to objects on stage in a manner that is truthful, real and persuasive.[20] In other words, it is through the senses—sound, touch, sight, smell and taste—fully responding to the imagined ob-jects and other stage stimuli, which bring about a sense of compelling reality to the performance. Strasberg developed a number of exercises that are meant to develop the actor's "instrument," that is, the mind/body/heart attunement. If one consciously concentrates on generating the sense for which one is aiming, say hearing about a sad happening, the physical expression of the sense will emerge fairly spontaneously and naturally, i.e. the face will appear sad. Likewise, if one convincingly imagines that one is drinking a glass of wine during a performance, even though one is actually drinking some grape juice, the audience will experience the actor as expressing a truthful and believable emo-tion. In real life, such responses are usually enacted on an unconscious level, this being a main difference between the make believe world of the stage and real life.

Thus, for Strasberg, by being mindful of sensory aspects of one's experience, one's focus inevitably shifts from oneself in the narcissistic sense to the imaginary reality of the stage. One's psychic and physical energy has been transferred, as it were, away from observing oneself in an obsessive self-referential manner, to the imaginary world around

---

19   Ibid., pp. 96, 98.
20   Easty, *On Method Acting*, p. 24.

oneself. As a result, deeper, wider, and most importantly, controlled and repeatable emotion is accessible to the actor.

What a fine-tuned sense memory has to offer the average person is at least two things: first, it teaches one to be more mindful of the present moment, to cut through the psychological patterns that disconnect one from one's experience. Training the senses to be more sensitive helps one to experience the world with the fullness of one's being and this almost always increases one's sense of happiness. Second, and this perhaps speaks more to Strasberg's deeper point, when one has developed an enhanced imagination, one is able to recognize the insubstantial and ephemeral nature of one's thoughts—that is, one can, for better or worse, create one's inner and, to a lesser degree, one's outer world as one would like it to be. To some extent, one can socially construct one's world as one wants, which is liberating to the spirit. Thus, our claim is that what is true on the stage is, in a sense, also true in real life. The art of living requires a highly developed capacity to apply one's imagination in a context-sensitive and psychologically truthful manner to human and non-human interaction—and to the larger world— as life circumstantially unfolds in consciousness. To accomplish all of this requires not only a finely tuned capacity for relaxation, concentration and sensory memory, and we would add, emotional intelligence, but also, the expansion and deepening of one's capacity for creative visualization via greater mindfulness of one's sensory world, a key element in great acting and living.

AFFECTIVE MEMORY

We have already defined affective or emotional memory in the beginning of this chapter, but a restatement is warranted as it is a central concept in Strasberg's thinking. According to Strasberg, "affective memory is not mere memory. It is memory that involves the actor personally, so that deeply rooted emotional experiences begin to respond. His instrument awakens and he becomes capable of the kind of living on the stage which is essentially reliving."[21] Affective memory, in other words, "is the conscious creation of remembered emotions which have occurred in the actor's own past life and then their application to the

---

21   Hethmon, *Strasberg. At the Actor's Studio*, p. 109.

character being portrayed."[22] Affective memory involves sense memory, which is the "reliving sensations that were experienced through the
five senses." It is, Strasberg emphasizes, "reliving, not just remembering, the difference is between knowing something and truly recreating
it."[23] Following Stanislavski's formulation (which he ultimately aban-
doned), by recreating the sense memory of an emotional happening,
the emotion would necessarily emerge. "The real memory involved
then is sensory not emotional. The actor does not focus on the feeling,
but on the physical circumstances surrounding the emotional event."[24]
Strasberg often cited Wordsworth's famous formulation about what
constitutes great poetry, "emotion recollected in tranquility" (a spontaneous upsurge of compelling feelings) to point out that affective memory animates all of the arts—musical, literary, visual—but it most often operates on an unconscious level.[25]

The point of affective memory, finding one's own past emotions that
correlate to the character the actor is playing, is to make a character
come compellingly alive on stage, yet in a controlled and repeatable
manner. Emotion, for Strasberg, cannot be reproduced merely by
thinking of or remembering the emotion itself. Emotion can only be
reproduced by a concentrated and focused "effort to remember each
circumstance and each sensory step" that generated the emotion in the
first place.[26] Obviously, to accomplish such mastery over one's emotional life is not easy. There are many mistakes one can make, including engaging in forms of superficial and inordinate narcissistic display
and other kinds of indulgences and/or tapping into overwhelmingly painful and/or traumatic memories that one cannot handle, that
cheapen and/or distort the emotion one is trying to express. The goal
of Strasberg's affective memory exercises is to train the actor to be able
to produce genuine emotion that is in sync with the character one is
playing at a given moment and circumstance, and that can be repeated
at will. "Recreating and reliving an intense emotional experience at will
was at the core of our work," says Strasberg.[27] In a word, "the actor

22   Easty, *On Method Acting*, p. 44.
23   Hull, *Strasberg's Method*, p. 38.
24   Brestoff, *The Great Acting Teachers*, p. 111.
25   Ibid., p. 83.
26   Easty, *On Method Acting*, pp. 45, 48.
27   Strasberg, *A Dream of Passion*, p. 114.

has learned to stimulate and control his physical, mental, sensory and emotional behavior," this being the condition of possibility for a great performance. (It is also axiomatic for living the "good life.")[28] While Strasberg has been criticized that his training system de-emphasizes "actions, given circumstances, objectives and characterization," without a doubt, there is no acting teacher that so perceptively stressed the noble goal of honest psychological self-exploration.[29] Moreover, his Method has undisputedly produced some of the greatest American actors, which gives validity to the usefulness of his acting theory and performance techniques.

Strasberg's discussion of affective memory has important insights that are useful to the non-actor, namely the importance in real life of "working through" (i.e., of psychologically metabolizing) one's memories, especially the painful ones, in order to make them more controllable, containable and bearable. For he who denies, deflects and in other ways, inordinately defends against painful and other memories, almost always pays a dear price in terms of cutting himself off from his experience and personal history, this often being the basis for the development of neurosis. Moreover, as Strasberg and for that matter, Freud has pointed out, recovered memories and other forms of one's experience that have been sequestered, repressed and in other ways defended against, when "released" and are part of conscious awareness, can become the basis for much creativity and other forms of personal growth and development. Such expansion and deepening of one's consciousness can also become the impetus, if not basis, for greater pleasure in one's life. Strasberg has thus provided a technology of memory and emotional recall that can help the non-actor make contact with parts of himself that he has long forgotten or jettisoned, to his detriment. Through affective memory, for example, the average person can find "true" or genuine emotion, to help color and deepen his experience of life. That is, the person is able to more easily draw from his emotional experience in the service of his well-being and flourishing. Moreover, and this is an important point, by being more capable of summoning one's emotional memories and previously defended against inner experience, the person becomes more emotionally available and receptive

---

28   Hull, *Strasberg's Method*, p. 102.
29   Brestoff, *The Great Acting Teachers*, p. 116.

to others. That is, he becomes better able to respond mindfully, in the moment, as well more expressively, with intensified feeling, even passion, to the reasonable needs and desires of the other. This too enriches one's experience of living the "good life."

JUSTIFICATION

Following Stanislavski, justification is a well-known term in acting theory. Indeed, Strasberg applies this concept in his theorizing and technique with some fine-tuning. Justification can be defined as the reason an actor behaves the way he does, that is, says Strasberg, "what would motivate me to do it that way is the principle of justification."[30] According to S. Loraine Hull, "an actor uses his imagination to justify whatever is comfortable or whatever he himself would not normally do in a particular manner. An actor tries to justify necessary behavior, thinking or movement for the role."[31] One way for justification to be implemented, especially when there is difficulty finding a compelling reason for the actor's behavior, is for the actor to use an analogy, by saying to himself something like "it is as if" to justify what needs to be done. More specifically, he can say to himself, "If I were in this particular situation in real life, what would I do, what would I say, how would I say it, and why?"[32] According to Hull, this technique tends to facilitate an actor's conviction in what he is doing and fosters his confidence and faith in himself. In a nutshell, says Easty, if an actor is to communicate his tasks to a "logical, consistent, and realistic" endpoint they must be justified by the beliefs and valuative attachments of the play as put forth by the playwright. The actor must have "real" reasons, authentic motivations that are meaningful to the actor's instrument, and they must be justified for happening as they do. "We must learn to act the reasons for a character's behavior"[33] in a truthful manner that is sensitive to circumstance.

Justification, a reason or circumstance that rationalizes an action or attitude, is of course what most of us are consciously and unconsciously doing as we live our lives. We give reasons to ourselves to justify why

---

30   Hull, *Strasberg's Method*, p. 327.
31   Ibid.
32   Easty, *On Method Acting*, p. 119.
33   Ibid., p. 116.

we do what we do, and why we do it the way we do. Actors, according
to Strasberg and others, have the added task that they have to justify what they are actually doing in the context of "make believe," the
illusionary world of stage performance. What Strasberg's notion of
justification has to offer the average person is the need for a greater
awareness that to live the "good life," one needs to have a reasonable
rationale for one's choices and actions. Otherwise, one's behavior is
likely to be "off track," out of sync with what is necessary to do in the
context in which one finds oneself, and can even be self-destructive. In
addition, Strasberg highlights the idea that one needs to make sense
of one's actions so one doesn't feel so conflicted and troubled. For the
actor, an effective justification for his behavior feels and looks right.
In real life this is also crucial, otherwise one feels a jarring sense that
one's rationale for one's behavior and the actual behavior is not con-
gruent, which creates dissonance and an awkward and/or dishonest
presentation of the self. Indeed, Leon Festinger's famous theory of
cognitive dissonance indicates that when a person feels dissonance, a
lack of consistency or compatibility between one's actions and beliefs,
he feels tension and is motivated to reduce the dissonance. He can,
for example, modify one of his thoughts, which reduces the perceived
significance of the dissonant thoughts and/or add further tension-re-
ducing justifying thoughts. Either one of these tactics has the effect of
neutralizing the person's sense that his rationale for his actions and his
actual behavior are unpleasantly discordant. Strasberg's discussion of
justification also stresses the fact that to generate a modicum of happiness requires that there be a high degree of what Freud called ego
syntony—that is, experiencing one's thoughts, feelings and actions as
consistent and harmonious with the total personality (ego dystonia is
when one experiences one's thoughts, feelings and actions as dissonant
with the total personality).

Strasberg's formulation of justification reminds one that one can
justify oneself and one's actions in an untruthful manner. One can dis-
honestly justify one's behavior to suit one's wishes at the expense of
properly dealing with reality, including respecting the needs and rights
of others. In psychoanalytic parlance, this is called rationalization, "the
process by which a course of action is given ex post facto reasons which

not only justify it but also conceal its true motivation."[34] Whether on the stage or in real life, the use of rationalization is responsible for some of the biggest mistakes one makes in how one conducts oneself.

IMAGINATIVE PERSONALIZATION AND SUBSTITUTION

Imaginative personalization can be defined as "a process in which the actor recalls an actual person he knows as a model for his partner or for what he is visualizing, talking or thinking about in a scene." Substitution, a related notion, is "a process in which the actor recalls from his own life an object or situation he knows for the actual or imaginary object or situation onstage or seen offstage."[35] Substitution can sometimes involve what Strasberg called "particularization," a process in which "the actor recalls an incident or occasion in his own life," one that can be used in a role. For example, "if the writer has a character refer to an incident that evokes certain feelings, the actor can choose a particular event from his own life that evokes similar feelings. He uses the words of the writer but with those words he describes his own secret, personal memory."[36] Through particularization, "the actor defines the things that he speaks of so they have for him the significance that the author dictates."[37] The point is that personalization is a technique that the actor summons "if the thing isn't going on strong enough," that is, if the required emotion is not available to the actor. Continues Strasberg, "the most important thing is to use the other actor"[38] as a catalyst for generating the appropriate emotion that is truthful to the circumstance of the role he is playing. In other words, personalization provides the actor with a keen sense of focus and concentration through recalling in an exacting and concrete way,

---

34 Charles Rycroft, *A Critical Dictionary of Psychoanalysis* (London: Penguin, 1995), p. 151.
35 Hull, *Strasberg's Method*, pp. 328, 330.
36 Ibid., p. 156.
37 Hethmon, *Strasberg At The Actors Studio*, p. 131. (We are quoting the editor, not Strasberg.)
38 Ibid.

a real life person as a template for the character the actor is playing, or is speaking about, or is responding to as acted by a fellow thespian.[39]

Strasberg's discussion of personalization and substitution has significance for the non-actor in at least three important ways. First, Strasberg is highlighting the need for empathy, insightful awareness, as it relates to one's own personality as well as toward others. In the acting context, accurate empathy is necessary for the actor to reach deeply into himself and make contact with aspects of himself—meaningful persons and situations that are at times painful or disturbing to recollect. However, if one is incapable of engaging these important people and situations from the past in fantasy (i.e., in one's imagination), then one is doomed to a superficial and bland presentation on the stage and in real life. For unless one can face one's "otherness," the disavowed, alien, disturbing and unfamiliar in oneself, one cannot call forth the necessary images and emotions to give a compelling performance on the stage or in real life. In other words, a person—actor or non-actor—can productively take himself only as far as his self-awareness allows him.

Second, Strasberg is highlighting the need for the non-actor to be able to metabolize and contain one's disturbing memories and the like, in order to use them for the sake of being more effective at one's tasks and to gain pleasure. In the acting context, being effective means playing the role properly; in real life, it means using one's emotions to positively animate one's general comportment in the world, a kind of sublimation, as Freud called this. Strasberg has mentioned that when one uses personalization, substitution and affective memory, it is important not to dredge up memories that are too painful and unwieldy to use in one's consciously conceived acting task. That is, the non-actor needs to refine his ability to access his emotions in a way that they are manageable and workable, so as to improve the quality of one's experience of oneself and others.

Third, Strasberg's formulations suggest that it is not enough to simply recollect and feel memories from the past, but in addition, the feelings need to be enacted. In the theater context this means feelings should be acted in a truthful and circumstance-sensitive manner. In real life, this means that feelings must be given a concrete expression

---

39   Ibid., p. 131. (We are quoting the editor, not Strasberg.)

in a real and reasonable way and not just reside in one's fantasy and imagination. Enactment, to perform or relate something using acting, is a healthy sublimation of one's feelings in a way that has productive, tangible ramifications for oneself and for others. Enactment is not to be confused with "acting out," when a person engages in activity which can be understood as a substitute for recollecting past experiences. The essence of "acting out" is the substitution of thought by action.[40] In the acting context, this means that one is physicalizing one's role but without a compelling justification or reason, hence the behavior comes across as contrived, superficial or boring. In real life, "acting out" expresses unconscious emotions in actions rather than words, often leading to harmful ramifications for oneself and for others.

THE FRUITS OF THE VOYAGE

Strasberg noted the two main problems of the actor, problems that concerned him throughout his long teaching career: "How can the actor both really feel, and also be in control of what he needs to do on stage?....How can the actor make his real feeling expressive on the stage," especially to obtain the "heightened expressiveness" that leads to an inspirational performance?[41] How does the actor "create in each performance the same believable experience and behavior, and yet include what Stanislavski called 'the illusion of the first time'"?[42] In a nutshell, says Strasberg, quoting Francois Joseph Talma's definition of acting at its best, the answer is, "a warm heart and a cool mind."[43] Indeed, Strasberg developed a novel acting training system to help the actor to know how to "stimulate the heart to be warm," this being the master key to giving a great stage performance.[44] As we have suggested, the capacity to have a "warm heart," to strike the right equilibrium between "calculation and warmth" as Strasberg describes it, is also the master key to living the "good life." Strasberg emphasizes this point when he approvingly quoted Denis Diderot's essay on acting, "The Paradox of Acting": "[W]hat makes the human being of supreme excellence is

---

40 Rycroft, *Dictionary of Psychoanalysis*, pp. 1-2.
41 Strasberg, *The Dream of Passion*, pp. 6, 19.
42 Ibid., p. 35.
43 Ibid., pp. 35-36.
44 Ibid., p. 36.

a kind of balance between calculation and warmth. Whether on the stage or in ordinary life, the man who displays more than he feels affects ridicule rather than sympathy." Freud pithily made a similar insight when he wrote that "anyone who gives more than they have is a rogue." That is, there must be a strong correspondence between truth and reality in one's general comportment to live authentically, to live the "good life."

As we have seen, Strasberg developed a number of pragmatic exercises in relaxation and the like, but what was always the most important element in his Method "was the use of the soul of the actor as the material for his work—the necessity for the study of the emotions and the analysis of simple and complicated feelings."[45] Strasberg's main ways of evoking the actor's emotions, imagination and inspiration were through concentration and affective memory. Affective memory is composed of sense memory, the recollection of physical sensation and emotional memory, which is the recollection of more powerful personal responses.[46] Whether on the stage or in real life, to the extent that one can master one's emotional life, to be comfortably conversant with what one is feeling both consciously and unconsciously in the moment, one is more likely to be able to love deeply and widely and work effectively and productively.

This capacity for what is often called emotional intelligence in the popular press is critical to giving a great performance on the stage and in real life. Emotional intelligence, Mayer, Salovey and Caruso, claim, is the capacity to discern emotion, assimilate and integrate emotion to assist thought, comprehend feelings, and to control feeling to bring about personal growth and development.[47] A developed sense of emotional intelligence, Mayer and colleagues say, involves discerning emotions in oneself, others and in objects (like a beautiful painting); it involves comprehending emotions in a nuanced manner, especially the ability to create some intelligibility to the ambivalent, ambiguous and complex nature of, and relationships among, feelings. It involves managing feelings effectively, the capacity to adjust and harmonize

---

45   Ibid., p. 62.

46   Ibid., pp. 69-70.

47   J.D. Mayer, P. Salovey, and D.R. Caruso, "Emotional Intelligence: New Ability or Eclectic Traits," *American Psychologist* (2008): 63.6: 503-517.

emotions in oneself and with others, in order to accomplish what one wants, including simply to enjoy oneself. Goleman also suggests that emotional intelligence requires a high degree of self-awareness, the ability to perceive one's emotions and to understand their impact on oneself and others, especially as it relates to decision-making. Self-management means being able to properly regulate and adapt one's emotions to one's context; social awareness is the capacity to comprehend other's feelings, a kind of empathic attunement, while grasping social networks; and finally, relationship management is the capacity to assist others amidst conflict and difficulty. Obviously, these descriptions of emotional intelligence have tremendous overlap with what Strasberg has written about in the theater context, though what Strasberg has provided was a detailed, psychologically sophisticated model about "how to" increase one's emotional intelligence, what we prefer to more aptly describe as a "technology of the self," to quote Michel Foucault, a way of achieving a high degree of autonomy, personal integration and self-mastery over one's emotional life. Strasberg clearly had this wider and deeper description in mind when he wrote, "the fundamental nature of the actor's problem [is]: the actor's ability to create organically and convincingly, mentally, physically, and emotionally, the given reality demanded by the character in the play; and to express this in the most vivid and dynamic way as possible."[48]

The obvious, though often overlooked, point we are making in this "appearance is all," "external behavior is everything," action-based culture is that in order to make one's life a "work of art," in order to master the "art of living," what is required, following Strasberg, is "the fundamental work of the actor"—"the training of his internal skills."[49] While the actor's instrument is himself, says Strasberg, "he works with the same emotional areas which he actually uses in his real life."[50] Likewise, the non-actor can derive enormous benefit by engaging Strasberg's oeuvre as he perceptively and artfully explains and demonstrates how to work with ordinary human emotions to create a truthful, circumstance-appropriate, passionate, and beautiful reality on the stage—and we believe, on the stage of real life.

---

48   Strasberg, *The Dream of Passion*, p. 105.
49   Ibid., p. 116.
50   Ibid., p. 122.

CHAPTER THREE

THE MIRACLE OF THE
IMAGINATION

STELLA ADLER

"Ninety-nine percent of what you see and use on the stage comes from imagination....The imagination is what animates the instrument [the actor], keeps it in tune. It's the ignition key. Without it, nothing else works."

—Stella Adler

STELLA ADLER (1901–1992), AN ACCLAIMED ACTRESS AND TEACHER, was steeped in the theory and technique of Stanislavski. In fact, she was the only American to have been taught by him when she went to train in Paris for about five weeks in 1934. After her training with Stanislavski, Adler returned to New York and spread the Stanislavski "gospel," a viewpoint that radically altered acting theory and practice in America. In particular, citing chapter and verse from the Master, Adler indicated that Stanislavski rejected "affective memory," the idea that the actor draws from a similar emotional experience in his life to facilitate him experiencing the necessary believable, truthful emotion on the stage (especially as practiced by Strasberg, who, as we demonstrated in chapter two, strongly believed that affective memory was the foundation of great acting). Instead, as Brestoff pointed out, Stanislavski and Adler emphasized "imagination, circumstances and actions" to bring out the best in actors. In particular, Adler believed

that the "right" emotion will naturally emerge if the actor properly
physicalizes, that is, physically exemplifies the desired emotion ("anything you do is physicalizing," said Adler). In other words, the physical
characteristics will call to mind the necessary emotion, or at least, they
will assist the actor in locating and creating the "emotional tone that is
appropriate to the character" he is playing.[1] It is important to note that
Adler was not simply a clone of Stanislavski; she put her own "spin" on
his concepts just as did other great American acting teachers who were
heavily influenced by Stanislavski (like Strasberg). Adler was an amazingly compelling acting teacher, attuned, caring, direct and appealingly
flamboyant in her effort to bring about visual theatrical poetry in her
trainees. Indeed, Marlon Brando, her most famous student (she also
taught Anthony Quinn, Robert De Niro and Warren Beatty), wrote
in his foreword to Adler's *The Technique of Acting* (1988),

> To me Stella Adler is much more than a teacher of acting. Through
> her work she imparts a most valuable kind of information—how to
> discover the nature of our own emotional mechanics and therefore
> those of others. It is troubling to me that because she has not lent
> herself to vulgar exploitations, as some other well-known so-called
> "methods" of acting have done [Brando is probably taking a swipe
> at Strasberg, Adler's main stage director rival, whom he disliked],
> her contributions to the theatrical culture have remained largely
> unknown, unrecognized, and unappreciated.[2]

Thankfully, Brando's characterization of Adler as unknown and un-
appreciated has long been corrected, for Adler's teaching methods and
reflections on performance and the like have influenced actors and acting teachers the world over. Adler was a tough critic of her students
though she also generated great loyalty from them as they felt deeply
inspired by her acting and "life-conduction" wisdom. As Adler said
to her students in one of her master classes, "you act with your soul.
That's why you all want to be actors, because your souls are not used
by life." Elsewhere, she elaborated, "life beats down and crushes the
soul and art reminds you that you have one."

1   Richard Brestoff, *The Great Acting Teachers and Their Methods* (Lyme,
    NH: Smith and Kraus, 1995), pp. 118, 119.
2   Stella Adler, *The Technique of Acting* (New York: Bantam Books, 1988),
    p. 1.

In this chapter we will review some of Alder's main concepts that she taught her students, for example, her view of imagination, circumstances, actions, justification, character and a few others. While all of these concepts are by now somewhat familiar to the reader, Adler had a unique elaboration of their Stanislavski-based meanings that we want to make known. Most importantly, there was a deep humanism that animated Adler's thinking and teaching style. For instance, she points out that the first notion that the actor must master, one that we believe underlies all of her other insights about acting (and living), is that

> Acting means the elimination of human barriers. You must knock down the walls between yourself and the other actors. This will give you a sense of freedom on the stage.
>
> The actor shows special generosity in saying to the audience:
>
> "I am going to give you ideas."
>
> "I am going to give you pleasure."
>
> "I am going to dance for you."
>
> "I am going to tell you the aches of my heart."
>
> All of this is a form of artistry, of giving. It is a love affair with the audience. But, in order to carry on this love affair, you must begin to think and act in new ways.[3]

The remainder of this chapter will in part unpack Adler's theories of acting performance and the profound implications her insights have for living the "good life." For Adler, as with other acting teachers, acting and real life growth and development are intimately co-mingled, "the actor's mind, heart and soul are involved in his profession....You're here to learn to stretch yourself in life, and in so doing on the stage as well."[4]

IMAGINATION

Imagination, roughly defined as the ability to form images and ideas in the mind, especially of things never seen or never experienced directly, is the bedrock of Adler's acting theory and performance technique.

---

3   Adler, *The Technique of Acting*, p. 7.

4   Ibid., p. 47; Adler, *The Art of Acting*, Howard Kissel (Comp. & Ed.) (New York: Applause, 2000), p. 207.

The "imagination consists of your ability to imagine things you have never thought;" on the stage, "every circumstance [the "place," "where am I?"] you find yourself in will be an imaginary one." Moreover, says Adler, "an enormous wealth of material exists in the mind of the actor, never to be tapped except in plays."[5] This is a form of self-awareness and self-knowledge that can be used in one's real life. Rotte, one of Adler's students and colleagues, wrote that for Adler, accessing the imagination centrally involves drawing from the unconscious, a domain which Adler described as "the life within." The imagination, said Adler, includes "everything that you know consciously, and at least ten billion times more that you know unconsciously." In other words, the actor must be able to use his conscious awareness to evoke unconscious processes that constitute and superbly feed his imagination which, ideally, also strongly animates his performance.[6]

For Adler, the main function of the imagination on the stage is that it "can alert the actor toward immediate reaction. He can see fast, think fast and imagine fast." It is the "instantaneous reactions from the actors to whatever objects they are working with" that Adler tried to facilitate in her imagination exercises. The ability to have an imagination that comes quickly requires that the actor be open and receptive to his external and internal worlds, a kind of free, flowing and unrestrained consciousness: "all the actor has to do is let it happen."[7]

Adler describes what it means to be "seeing imaginatively," for example, in one exercise she asks her students to imagine a scene in which "snow has fallen" or they are "looking into a pot." Continues Adler, "now that you have seen it, you can accept the imaginative scene. It is true for you." Most importantly, "imagination refers to the actor's ability to accept new situations of life and believe in them. From your imagination comes your reactions to the things that you like and dislike. If you cannot do this, you had better give up acting."[8]

Adler also notes that the actor must develop his capacity for "seeing and describing." The gist of this skill is to "take in a specific image

5   Adler, *The Technique of Acting*, p. 17.
6   Joanna Rotte, *Acting with Adler* (New York: Limelight Editions, 2000), p. 59.
7   Ibid., p. 18.
8   Ibid., p. 20.

carefully," say "an apple tree" or "a wooden fence." The actor must be able to visualize the images vividly, intensely and exactingly prior to him being able to describe what he has seen. It is only after the actor does this that he can convince his fellow thespians and the audience that he has seen what he has seen, as instructed by the playwright. Adler distinguishes what she is getting at, between "taking an image in and giving it back," versus "reporting," finding so-called facts and objects and telling people about them. According to Adler, the finely tuned capacity of taking "an image in and giving it back" is "what makes you an artist."[9]

Adler further notes that there are many ways that an actor sees. For example, an actor must be able to see specifically and rapidly. He must also be able to mindfully see what grabs his attention, as well as see "everyday activities in life and place them in circumstances." Finally, the actor must be able "to see the simple, eternal scenes of human behavior in its historical setting."[10] What Adler is getting at is the need for the actor to greatly sharpen his observational skills, skills that have important bearing for the non-actor: "you must be continually aware of the ongoing changes in your social world." In particular, continues Adler, "go to things that are forever, like a particular tree or a particular flower."[11] The idea here is that to the extent that you can view things as vividly unique (you must take nothing for granted that you observe), then the apt feeling is likely to be evoked that can be conveyed to one's fellow actors and the audience in a believable and truthful manner: "the feeling evoked by the description is more important than the description [the words used] itself."[12] Adler is being extremely literal when she insists that the actor perfect his observational skills. She quotes the American novelist Thomas Wolfe who wrote, "This week I'm looking at noses. That's good."

Adler indicates that there are many resistances in the actor (and the non-actor) to imaginatively and vividly engage the world via one's observational modality, especially if the situation being imagined requires a strong response, say "a boy being beaten by a policeman."

---

9   Ibid., pp. 20, 21.
10   Ibid., p. 22.
11   Ibid., p. 24.
12   Ibid., p. 25.

Holding back, that is, defending oneself against the experience of what one is imagining leads to an inhibited and muted performance, and in real life to a blunted self-presentation. The actor must be able to be mindful of what he is experiencing in the moment, with the fullness of his whole being, that is, in a free, flowing and unrestrained manner. Anxiety about revealing oneself, of being vulnerable, of looking stupid or unskilled, for example, is quite common. Adler's straight talking advice is: "I say to you, do not push, but be able to let go." Most importantly, to live imaginatively, continues Adler, the actor must make the correct choices, choices that will make the actor strongly react. These choices are crucial to a great performance: "in your choice is your talent." Living imaginatively, according to Adler, thus requires seeing and acting in imaginative circumstances, emotionally and intellectually embracing everything the actor imagines as believable and truthful. The actor's task "is to defictionalize the fiction." Adler gives a simple example,

> If you need a lemon tree but have never seen one, you will imagine some kind of lemon tree. You will accept it as if you have seen it. You have imagined it, therefore it exists. Anything that goes through the imagination has a right to live and has its own worth.[13]

Elsewhere Adler notes,

> As you imagine the scene, there will be many facts. Don't leave them dead. As actors you must create for us the miracle of life, not the fact. This life is what is called 'the actors creation.' If you can create the play ['fire your own imagination,' including 'to push toward... the illogical'], you will know why you want to act. If you don't create it, you will not want to act.[14]

Adler's discussion of the imagination has tremendous bearing on how one creatively lives one's everyday life. As Adler has suggested and Irish poet, philosopher and Catholic scholar John O'Donohue has elaborated,[15] the imagination brings "wonderful gifts" to those who mindfully nurture and use it, including accessing the truth, beauty and

---

13   Ibid., p. 26.

14   Ibid., p. 28.

15   John O'Donohue, *Beauty: The Invisible Embrace* (New York: Perennial, 2004). We have liberally drawn from O'Donohue's writings and lectures in our discussion of the imagination.

goodness in the world. The poet W. H. Auden felt similarly when he wrote that for the romantic poet the "imagination is a power of vision which enables man to perceive the sacred truth behind sensory phenomena and therefore the noblest of all mental faculties." For example, says O'Donohue, the imagination is "like a lantern" that illuminates new "inner landscapes" and "regions of the mind" that help create an openness to the transcendent, that is, it allows one possibly to glimpse what is *not* said in words, but is critically important and meaningful in an experience. For the person with a rich imagination, the mind is not dulled and the heart is not blunted; in psychoanalytic language, such a person is not trapped in the endless thicket of neurosis, including rigidly relating only to surface reality. Rather, he "engages the world visually in an imaginative way," and thus he notices that new things around him have a vibrant "life," a deeper "reality" to them than he ever realized. Adler insinuated this enhanced consciousness when she wrote about using props on the stage, saying "you cannot use a prop unless you give it dignity and unless you have a liking for it."[16]

A robust imagination, as Adler describes it, also requires what O'Donohue calls "grace of innocence." This refers to the notion that the imagination does not easily give way to the blast of facts, detached analysis and explanations that constitute the received wisdom about a particular thing or experience. It is not persuaded by that which is considered settled, finished, fixed or framed by authoritative knowledge and authoritative figures. As Adler said to her students, whom she wanted to be autonomous and separate from her, "Write this down. 'My aim is to be independent from Miss Adler or anybody else. I know this as well as you do, and in the sense that I know it as well as you do, I don't need you.'"[17] In other words, the imagination believes that there is "more" than what meets the eye, there are "secret worlds" and "hidden treasures"—similar to what Levinas calls "otherness"—concealed in the simplest and clearest things, if only, as the Buddhists say, one mindfully engages the world, develops the mental skill of attentiveness and emotional openness to one's moment to moment awareness of what one is experiencing. For the robust imaginer, for the non-actor and actor at their best, reality is not closed, but continuously offers

16 Adler, *The Technique of Acting*, p. 59.
17 Adler, *The Art of Acting*, p. 13.

new possibilities and hope, especially for self-transformation and
self-transcendence. According to O'Donohue, "the imagination is the
faculty that bridges, co-presents, and co-articulates the visible and invisible;" it "creates and constructs your depth experience."[18] Put differently, the imagination is the organ of fresh perception for discerning
manifestations of the "more" and the "beyond" that we associate with
the transcendent (or with God) on and off the stage.

For O'Donohue, a related aspect of the imagination is that it has a
"passion for freedom." The nature of the imagination is to press ahead
beyond the usual frontiers. It wants to roam freely beyond the well-
traveled borders without using the usual maps of experience and understanding to make sense of things. In the essay "Fate," Emerson says
that "the revelation of thought [i.e., the imagination] takes man out
of servitude into freedom." Moreover, the imagination paradoxically
waits to be surprised, for it knows that there is something about the
unforeseen and unanticipated that powerfully touches us, just as it
provides insights into what really matters. Thus, the robust imaginers,
both non-actor and actor, have much in common. Both want to engage
the world with a "dishabituated eye," "defamiliarizing the familiar," in
order to better apprehend the wonders of ordinary life.[19] It is, in part,
this inner readiness to be intrigued, surprised and "disrupted" by the
otherness and strangeness of people and things (e.g., fellow actors, the
circumstances, the props, the script), that is a distinguishing feature of
the robust imaginer.

The robust use of the imagination also provides us with a renewed
sense of youthfulness, especially playfulness of spirit. One is enlivened
through one's playful imaginative use of mind and heart and, by doing so, one reclaims the depth and intensity of experience, as well as
the "urgency, restlessness and passion," "the wildness of heart," most
frequently associated with youth. Psychoanalyst Donald Winnicott
famously located this imaginative capacity in a magical realm he called
"transitional space," the psychic place where a young child uses a "transitional object," like a loved doll or piece of cloth, as a way of being

18 John O'Donohue, *Anam Cara; A Book of Celtic Wisdom* (New York:
Harper Perennial, 1997), pp. 51, 95.

19 M.H. Abrams, *Natural Supernaturalism: Tradition and Revolution in
Romantic Literature* (New York: W.W. Norton & Company, 1971), pp.
384, 379.

midway between himself and his mother in the service of separating from her and further individuating, yet still being connected to her: "it is within the space between inner and outer world, which is also the space between people—the transitional space—that intimate relationships and creativity occur." Art (and religion and philosophy), for example, represents an adult form of this imaginative dwelling in this transitional space. Such a creative use of the imagination, at its best, allows the non-actor and actor to be able to relate to others and the world as sources of deepening personal growth and development, enlivening, and interconnectedness to people, things and animals. Adler implicitly acknowledged this point when she taught her students "animal movement." The purpose was to eliminate the social mask of the actor and to free him of his anxieties and inhibitions.

Finally, the robust imaginer, similar to the God-seeker, is open to what in religious language is called "revelation." By revelation we do not only mean the showing of divine will or truth, as the religious usually characterize it. We also mean the disclosure, especially the surprising disclosure, of something previously hidden or secret, often in one's everyday life, which is judged as extremely valuable and good. As theologian Paul Tillich noted, life-altering existential questions, especially in the theological context, are asked on the basis of "ultimate concern," and they are best answered through revelation. The imagination is the psychic vehicle for receiving such revelations (e.g., the so-called "x" factor in performance that in part distinguishes the great actor), and it usually does so, says O'Donohue, not in a flash, as popular culture would have it. Rather, he says, the imagination gently coaxes us into new situations, new questions and new possibilities, more analogous to how one looks at a beautiful painting than a dramatic unfolding, though that too can be part of revelation. As we look at the painting, as we gradually engage its otherness, its loveliness and splendor emerge. The same gradual process often characterizes the love relation, whether to a person or to God. As we gradually engage the Other, her summoning nature, her mysterious layering and deep presence moves us, just as her beauty of spirit, mind and body captivates us. The imagination, as Adler and O'Donohue suggest, thus often operates according to a principle of suggestiveness and insinuation, even seduction. As

Rotte wrote, Adler's "spiritual standard was to extend oneself outward
to the maximum degree...she was advising us to open ourselves up to
the experience of love..."[20]

CIRCUMSTANCES

Circumstances, living in a particular state or set of conditions, affects what happens or how somebody reacts in a particular situation.
According to Adler, "in life, every human being knows what place he
is in," that is, "everyone is somewhere. The place is called the given
circumstances of life," such as being in a theater, a lecture hall, or in
one's kitchen.[21] For an actor, to be "thrown" into an unfamiliar place
like a new theater is disorganizing and inhibiting of one's performance
capability. Thus, says Adler, before he goes to the playwright's script
it is imperative that the actor literally familiarize himself to the new
circumstances in which he finds himself; he must actually physically
explore the new space he is in, such as the set. Such physical movement
facilitates the "relaxation, the sense of truth and the self-confidence"
that the actor needs to begin work on a new script.[22]

Adler was frequently quoting to her students Stanislavski's performance axiom, that "the truth in art is the truth of your circumstances."
This is the first question the actor has to ask himself when he performs, "where am I?" The idea here is that in order to be able to properly imagine in the imaginary setting of the stage, you have to be able to
relax and unself-consciously embrace the truth of circumstances with
which the playwright provides you. Relaxation, says Adler, "comes
from the truthfulness of the circumstances the actor creates."[23] Adler
aptly summarizes the matter, "As an actor you are always in given circumstances. It is your responsibility to fill the place. Take the fiction
out of the circumstances by letting the place tell you what to do."[24]
Moreover, she says,

> when we let the circumstances dictate what we do, everything
> will have a reason [a compelling justification], will seem perfectly

---

20   Rotte, *Acting with Adler*, p. 37.
21   Adler, *The Technique of Acting*, p. 30.
22   Ibid., p. 30.
23   Adler, *The Art of Acting*, p. 80.
24   Ibid., p. 31.

natural, truthful. It's only when we don't understand the circumstances that we have to "act," that we have to fake it. And believe me,
the audience knows that instinctively.[25]

Thus, says Rotte, for the actor (and we would add, for the non-actor),
to grasp what he is talking about, he must comprehend "the logic of
the place and nature of everything in it," what Adler called "managing
the circumstances."[26]

This discussion of circumstance would not be complete unless we
mention Adler's famous disagreement with Strasberg about "substitution" and "affective memory," a subject touched upon in the previous
chapter. As Marlowe summarized the controversy, after her trip to
study with Stanislavski in Paris in 1934, Adler challenged Strasberg's
use of substitution and affective memory, the practice of accessing
one's personal history and experiences to generate a believable and
truthful result. Instead, with Stanislavski's blessing, she argued for a
technique of "living in the moment, using your partner and a belief in
the imagined circumstances to create an emotional result." Moreover,
says Marlowe, according to Adler, "if an actor studied the text and
stayed 'present' in the imaginary conditions of the play, the emotions
in the script would eventually surface organically."[27] Adler made her
objections to Strasberg's approach known in no uncertain language,
sometimes being a bit hard-hitting:

> A great disservice was done to American actors when they were
> persuaded that they had to experience *themselves* on the stage in-
> stead of experiencing the play. Your experience is not the same as
> Hamlet's—unless you too are a royal prince of Denmark. The truth
> of the character isn't found in you but in the circumstances of the
> royal position. The action of Hamlet, to decide whether to live or
> die, has to match his circumstances, not yours. Your past indeci-
> sion on who to take to the prom won't suffice....whatever you re-
> construct from your emotional memory is no substitute for putting
> your imagination to work.[28]

---

25   Ibid., p. 82.
26   Rotte, *Acting with Adler*, p. 61.
27   Jenny Marlowe, "Stella Adler and Her Technique of Acting," http://
www.loveacting.com/stella_adler.html, p. 1.
28   Adler, *The Technique of Acting*, p. 32; Adler, *The Art of Acting*, pp. 65, 83.

Adler is making an important distinction about performance technique, but also about how one lives an authentic life. She is staking out a specific position about the art of acting and living in which the "truth" of an experience, such as becoming a character on the stage, is not to be mainly found in its correlation with one's personal life (though obviously this is true to some extent: remember Adler's comments about the need to let one's unconscious animate one's imagination). Rather, in Adler' view, "the truth is always the truth in the circumstances of the character." In other words, her technique prioritizes doing over feeling, though to be sure, Adler agrees that personal memories of experiences and things can give you "clues" about how to play a character, "but only clues."[29] Thus, for Adler, in contrast to how many people conceptualize their emotional lives, emotion emanates from the actor's dedication to the circumstances, which firstly includes the "where," but also includes the "when," "what" and "who" questions. Brestoff continues, "if the actor can make the situations in which characters find themselves vivid and believable [remember that the circumstances are always changing on and off the stage], then emotion should flow naturally. So a clear and deep understanding of the given circumstances is critical for the actor's expressive truthfulness."[30] The same, we believe, is often true in real life. If one learns to experience the world in a context-sensitive manner, that is, in a rich, detailed and deep way, such that one's whole being, including one's actions, are engaged in, and in sync with, the changing circumstances, then the emotions evoked are likely to be more believable, and most importantly, truthful to oneself and to others.

ACTIONS

"To hell with the emotion. Rather, technically steal the essential doing of the action," said Adler.[31] For Adler, more than beautifully uttering the words contained in the script, more than creating the apt emotion to fit the circumstance, it is doing the pertinent action that is the basis

---

29   Adler, *The Art of Acting*, p. 83.
30   Brestoff, *The Great Acting Teachers*, pp. 120–121.
31   Rotte, *Acting with Adler*, p. 111.

for great acting. Action is "what I am doing most which involves where I am doing it."[32] In other words, as Rotte notes,

> every group of words, phrases, or sentences that makes up a sequence of thought has behind it some able-to-be physicalized intention. This physicalized intention is what Adler called the action....the actor's language is action—the result of the life behind and under the words.[33]

Thus, for Adler the objective of her acting technique is to help the actor find, or rather, create the actions in a scene or play. Adler straightforwardly indicates what she means by an action in practical terms: "An action is something you do. To read; An action has an end. I'm reading the newspaper; An action is done in circumstances. I'm reading in the subway; An action is justified. I'm reading to follow the stock market."[34] For Adler there are "strong and weak actions." Strong actions require a clear objective, for example, "I'd like to drink coffee." A weak action is "I'd like to drink something." The idea is that to the extent that the actor can perform an action with a clear and definite end within the circumstances of the scene, the action's meaning becomes more compelling and therefore, it is likely to be more believable and truthful.[35] This includes, says Rotte, the "doable nature of emotion." For example, "sadness—to disconnect from, not taking in, the cause of the sadness;" "anger—to face, to try and control or even to annihilate something, not by means of the anger but by a tremendous power which angered people feel they have;" "joy—to explode out toward the source of joy." Once the doable nature of an emotion has been located in life and comprehended, it can be transposed to any set of circumstances of stage.[36]

Adler also points out that to do a strong action the actor must be mindful of "*What* you do. Have dinner. *Where* you do it. In the dining room. *When* you do it. At dinnertime. *Why* you do it. To feed the family after work" (our italics). Adler reminds her students that the "how" question is not part of her explanation of action. This is because

---

32   Ibid.
33   Ibid.
34   Adler, *The Technique of Acting*, p. 35.
35   Ibid.
36   Rotte, *Acting with Adler*, pp. 130-131.

the "how" is supposed to be a spontaneous, natural and unforeseen creation of the actor.[37]

Adler further indicates that the actor must be mindful of the fact that every action done has its nature, its living reality or truth: "In order to be truthful onstage you must know the nature of what you are doing and it must be truthfully done." Adler calls the things one does to achieve one's actions "activities." For example, when setting a table, the placing of the silverware on the table. The idea here is the need to literally physicalize one's actions. Moreover, every action has to be in sync with the playwright's overall action, or what Stanislavski described as the "ruling idea." That is, continues Adler, all actions of a character in a play are in a sense interrelated and unified, and the actor's actions must be compatible with the ruling idea. To achieve this intellectual and emotional objective often requires that the actor break up an action into steps, into smaller actions. These smaller steps must, however, "be for and needed by your action."[38]

To accomplish all of the above requires justification of the action, a concept we have discussed in our chapters on Stanislavski and Strasberg. Briefly, for Adler, justification, the reason for doing something, was the "heart of acting." According to Rotte, justification energizes "the action into circulation, it gets it going. Having said that real acting is not playing the play but needing the play, Adler offered justification as the means to really act."[39] Justification, as Adler views it, is mainly an imaginative rather than a logical process; it arouses the actor's creativity, which emanates from the actor's understanding of the nature of the circumstances. Through the right justifications, the right choices—"your talent is in your choice," says Adler—the actor can make contact with the meaning behind and beyond the mere words of the text. In this way, the actor experiences himself, and the audience experiences the actor, as imaginatively creating situations in a personal, vivid and enlivening manner, not as simply mouthing his lines.[40]

---

37   Adler, *The Technique of Acting*, p. 36.

38   Ibid., p. 38.

39   Rotte, *Acting with Adler*, p. 103.

40   Ibid., pp. 103, 104, 105. Adler also advocated the use of Stanislavski's "as if" to help stimulate the actor.

Adler's discussion of actions on the stage makes a profound point that is often overlooked in real life. In addition to physicalizing the action in a way that is truthful to the circumstances on stage, as in real life, it is not "who I am" that matters the most, but rather "what I do." According to Adler, "the measure of my worth and the secret of success" depends on one's actions, "all the rest is showiness, arrogance, and conceit,"[41] a reflection of self-deficits, or what psychoanalysts call inordinate or pathological narcissism. Indeed, as Howard Kissel points out,[42] for Adler acting was expressed in actions, which evoke the appropriate and natural emotions in the performer and the audience. If the actor comprehends the structure of the actions he performs he is assisting the spectator to comprehend his own behavior (and motivations) more profoundly. Adler's emphasis on doing as opposed to self-referential stirring up of emotions may well be rooted in her Jewish background, says Kissel (she grew up in the world of Yiddish theater; her father, Jacob P. Adler, was one of the greatest actors in the genre). As Adler noted, her Jewishness was a major influence on her acting career: "I'm a Jewish broad from Odessa. I'm deeply understanding of being a Jewish child, a Jewish woman, which has given me my talent and my standards."[43] In Judaism, for example, it is emphasized that God is not a mere impersonal abstraction that one prays to or meditates over, but rather he is a God who makes exacting demands in terms of one's moral behavior. Loving God is best expressed in ethical behavior, especially in being for the other before oneself. On the stage this is personified in inhabiting the character as the playwright instructs, it means playing with, and off of, one's fellow actor and giving him his due, it means being mindful of honestly connecting with the audience rather than narcissistically "playing to the crowd" and other forms of self-serving pretension.

CHARACTERIZATION

Characterization is a subject which Adler always regarded as tremendously important for the actor. Says a provocative Adler, "the actor

---

41   Adler, *The Technique of Acting*, p. 41.
42   Kissel, "Afterword," *The Art of Acting*, pp. 265, 266.
43   Barry Paris (Ed.), *Stella Adler on Ibsen, Strindberg and Chekhov* (New York: Vintage Books, 2000), p. ix.

doesn't exist; only the character exists." In other words, "characterization is the ability to understand what goes on in other people and
identify with it." There is a paradoxical quality in the history of acting
when it comes to characterization, in that "nobody has played himself....When the actor plays himself he is less interesting than when he
plays a certain person."[44] In other words, insists Adler, the actor must
understand that there is a serious difference between the character you
are playing and your own life. Skillful characterization is what gives
emotional depth and intensity, or "disciplined emotion," as Adler calls
it, to the actor's performance.

Adler's approach to characterization is complex and elaborate and
we can only here discuss some of the major features that make for
great characterization on the stage. The actor must understand what
the playwright wants to convey to the audience, what his message is to
the world. "Acting," says Adler, "is human behavior assembled in novel
and interesting ways" and it is imaginative and creative characterization that distinguishes one role from another, one play from another.[45]

In order to play a character well the actor needs to fully grasp the
circumstances with which the playwright provides him. These circumstances include the social situation (e.g., religion, education, political
context), the class from which the character comes (e.g., aristocracy,
upper middle class, middle class, working class), the character's profession or the way in which he makes a living (e.g., tailor, bank teller,
prostitute), the history of the character ("the five W's: Who are you,
What is your action, When is it happening, Where is it happening,
Why are you there"), the character's unique elements (e.g., carefree, responsible, scholarly) and the character's approach and outlook toward
his partner (i.e., you must know your partner's action, the way he looks
and what he does).[46] Moreover, says Adler, the best way of inhabiting a character is to understand the nature of the character's mind,
temperament and will, that is, how the character's faculties differ from
one's own. For example, does the character's mind work more quickly
or slowly, what is the character's temperament, are his feelings warmer

---

44 Adler, "Foreword." *Creating a Character. A Physical Approach to Acting*
     (Moni Yakim with Muriel Broadman) (New York: Applause, 1990), p. xii.

45 Adler, *The Technique of Acting*, p. 66.

46 Ibid., pp. 67-78.

or colder, is the character's will weaker or stronger? To discern all of this involves getting into the character's daily life by "doing simple actions in the character's imagined circumstances," his "imagined vision of reality,"[47] or learning the character's rhythm, as Adler calls it.

Adler did not have a formula for characterization, only practical suggestions on how to most effectively inhabit the character in a way that was truthful to the imaginary circumstances of the play. Most importantly perhaps, Adler is emphasizing that characterization means modifying and adjusting oneself to be in sync with the character, the other; it does not mean changing the character to fit oneself, which is essentially an act of interpersonal violence on the stage and in real life. What Adler is stressing is that for the actor to portray both the inside and outside of a character (like Marlon Brando, who worked from the inside to the outside, versus John Gielgud, who worked the other way around), it is required that one get away from oneself and get into the unique individuality of the character one is playing. Only in this way, insinuates Adler, can one get to the universality of the character as opposed to exhibiting the expected, usual aspect, which is usually boring. In real life this translates as transforming one's self-directed, self-obsessed subjectivity to one where empathy for the other is paramount. As Adler indicated, acting via the imagination and intellect is not fundamentally self-centric, rather it gets one into the character and is firstly directed at the audience. Likewise, in real life imagination and intellect guided by accurate empathy leads one to making a stronger, more comprehensive mutual connection to others, one based on generosity of spirit and high-mindedness, not a mainly self-serving "what's in it for me" attitude.

ADLER'S PHILOSOPHY OF LIFE

As we have suggested earlier, Adler's conceptualization of acting and performance was deeply connected to her philosophy of life in which the actor resides. Like Suzuki and other great acting teachers, Adler's philosophy of the life is not clearly explicated but is implicated in her training method and occasional digressions in her writings. By way of concluding this chapter, we want to suggest some of the elements of

47   Rotte, *Acting with Adler*, pp. 141, 142, 148, 158.

CHAPTER FOUR

THE REALITY OF DOING

SANFORD MEISNER

"An ounce of behavior is worth a pound of words."

—Sanford Meisner

S ANDFORD MEISNER (1905–1997) WAS ONE OF THE ORIGI-NAL MEMBERS of the influential Group Theater, having collaborated in the 1930s with three other great acting teachers, Harold Clurman, Lee Strasberg and Cheryl Crawford, who passionately believed that Stanislavski's acting theory and techniques were revolutionary and would radically transform acting in America. At the time Meisner was involved with the Group Theater, he, Stella Adler and Robert Lewis, two other master acting teachers, began to oppose the strong influence that Strasberg's interpretation of Stanislavski's oeuvre had on the group, particularly Strasberg's emphasis on "emotional memory" as the main thrust of great acting. After Adler returned from Paris in 1934, having done five weeks of daily training with the Master, she showed the members of the Group Theater that Stanislavski had, for the most part, rejected digging into one's personal history, one's past memories, as the main source of authentic emotion on the stage. Rather, Stanislavski emphasized the creative use of the imagination within the context of the given circumstances of the script as the best way of depicting what a character truthfully felt and thought. While Adler took Stanislavski's lead and focused on seeing and acting in imaginative circumstances, i.e., emotionally and intellectually embracing everything the actor imagines as believable and truthful, Meisner took a somewhat different direction, ultimately creating what is known as the Meisner Technique. Meisner has had a major influence on American acting theory, including having taught Gregory Peck, Joanne Woodward and Diane Keaton, among others. Meisner was a sought after acting teacher but apparently he could be very tough on his students, rather opinionated and even arrogant. According to Peter Von Berg writing in the *New York Times* in 1998, he was "appalled" at Meisner's teaching methods: "Gregory Peck nearly throttles his acting partner. Meisner 'liked that one.' Joanne Woodward runs out of the room in tears. Meisner said to her, 'that's the best thing you've done in six months.' Dianne Keaton never acts on stage because of a remark by Meisner."[1] Meisner rather provocatively wrote about one of the giants of the English-speaking stage, "See, I maintain, and will continue to maintain, that Laurence Olivier is not a great actor."[2] Finally, as Meisner reports saying to one of his students, "I told Lee [Strasberg]...You introvert the already introverted... Needless to say, he didn't pay any attention to me, but that's the reason I'm a better teacher than he was."[3]

Like Strasberg and Adler, Meisner more or less "cherry picked" aspects of Stanislavski's system that he felt were especially illuminating and helpful to the actor. It is apparent that all three of these acting teachers used similar Stanislavski-based concepts, though the emphasis and the particular "spin" they gave them differed. In this chapter we will discuss the main aspects of the Meisner Technique, including, for example, his emphasis on being in the moment, the reality of doing, the Word Repetition Game and living truthfully under imaginary circumstances. The Meisner Technique alleges that by being in the moment with one's partner, a kind of "communion,"[4] as Stanislavski

---

1   Peter Von Berg, (1998, January 25). Sanford Meisner, *The New York Times*, http://www.nytimes.com/1988/01/25/magazine/l-sanford-meisner-166502.html, section 6, page 8.

2   Sandford Meisner and Dennis Longwell, *Sanford Meisner on Acting* (New York: Vintage, 1987), p. 121.

3   Ibid., p. 59.

4   Communion is a concept that Stanislavski spent a long chapter explaining in *An Actor Prepares*. Very briefly and simply, it is a form of "spiritual intercourse" in which there is a feeling of emotional closeness to one's fellow actor. It requires that the actor be mindful of the other actor's physical

called it, something unique, powerful and most importantly, truthful, spontaneously emerges between the actors, providing that the circumstances of the scene are aptly discerned. Meisner's technique stresses that rather than merely straightforwardly playing the action or emotion, to express an action truthfully and believably it is obligatory for the actors to allow emotion and subtext to organically develop and escalate according to the truth of the action and respond according to what the other characters in the scene are doing. It is the energizing dynamic between the actors that gives life to the scene and captivates the audience.

BEING IN THE MOMENT

The idea of "being in the moment" has become something of a mantra recently, especially in the self-improvement world, but also in spiritual and scientific circles. Most importantly, and most profoundly, it is through the popularization of the Buddhist idea of "mindfulness"—complete attention to the present moment without habitual responses—that being in the moment has become understood. As Salzberg and Goldstein further note, for the Buddha, "happiness beyond our ordinary experience of pleasure arises when we are mindful."[5] On the stage this translates as a great performance. While Meisner does not cite any Buddhist or other similar literature in his discussion of being in the moment—what he calls in passing, "moment to moment"[6] interaction between actors—he unknowingly applies many Buddhist and Buddhist-like insights in his use of the idea when he taught his acting students.

For Meisner, being in the moment is a pre-condition of a great performance. Without this capacity the actor cannot effectively work with his partner based on instinct (his "inner impulses," as Meisner calls it, or a spontaneous and natural manner) as opposed to intellect. "Acting is all a give-and-take of those impulses affecting each person," said Meisner.[7] Moreover, such an immediate experience is both

and psychological existence and to be certain that he hears and comprehends what you say to him and what he says to you.

5   Sharon Salzberg and Joseph Goldstein, *Insight Meditation. Correspondence Course Workbook* (Boulder, CO: Sounds True, 1996), pp. 10, 85.

6   Meisner and Longwell, *On Acting*, p. 101.

7   Ibid., p. 62.

self-stimulating to the actor and entrancing to the audience. As Larry Silverberg, one of Meisner's published students noted, "Watch out, living in the present is addictive."[8]

What exactly is the psychological structure of living in the moment on the stage as Meisner uses the concept? As we said earlier, Meisner does not explicitly explain the concept but it permeates his acting theory in his emphasis on the importance of "emotional aliveness," "inner impulses," emotion that "infects you and the audience," "the flow of the river which is your emotion" and other such phrases especially meant to describe, or at least evoke the action/reaction dynamic between actors that is essential for great acting.

Being in the moment, in the "flow" as it is often called, essentially involves being aware of what is going on in one's personal present experience. Like any experience it can be analyzed in terms of its process. According to Matt, there are at least three stages to getting oneself into the moment, which to some extent illuminate what the trained actor needs to be able to do to focus his full attention on his partner: one must "empty your head, engage your action mind and narrow your focus."[9]

Emptying one's head, the first stage, is another way of saying that one needs to clear one's mind of the endless flow of chatter or noise (what the Buddhists call the "monkey mind"), being less reactive to one's thoughts, emotions and conflicts in order to attain greater focus on what one is actually experiencing in the here and now. Emptying the head tends to refer to more long range concerns, like thinking about what one has to do after work or worrying about being home for a delivery on the weekend. Being able to skillfully rid oneself of such intrusive thoughts and anxieties both requires and leads to greater calmness. In the acting context, this skill usually refers to relinquishing, or at least greatly reducing, the obsessive worry pertaining to such nagging questions as, "will I ever make it as an actor or actress?" and "how long will it take for me to have steady work?"

Engaging your action mind is a related notion to emptying your head in that rather than referring to more long-term concerns, it involves

8   Larry Sliverberg, *The Sanford Meisner Approach. An Actor's Workbook* (Lyme, NH: Smith and Kraus, 1994), p. 130.

9   "Matt," *Being in the Moment Without All the Bullshit.* http://lifeofmatt. net/blog/2009/03/being-in-the-moment-without-all-the-bullshit/

relinquishing the more short-term babble and worries. In the acting context this translates as the actor not being hyper-reflective, or fixating on such questions as "how am I doing," or more specifically, "what does (or will) the teacher or spectator think of my performance?" Such doubts and uncertainties are the corrosive judgmental thought processes that undermine the actor as he does his craft, and the non-actor as he goes about his business of trying to live the "good life."

Stage two is engaging in free flow, a kind of exercise, says Matt, which imitates the actions of the instinctual mind, the impulsive mind that feels natural rather than reasoned. Free flow has two basic rules, "if you think about doing something, do it immediately" and "if you have any other thought, say it out loud immediately."[10] These are, in part, the main parameters of Meisner's Word Repetition Game that stresses reacting to the impulse emanating from one's partner and the circumstances of the scene. Free flow requires that one surrenders to the momentum of an experience; it means giving in to the felt power and ever-growing pace of the experience of the here and now. Censoring, guessing, editing and repressing must give way to full existential engagement with what you are doing. It means giving up the habitual ways of thinking, feeling and acting, including not fantasizing about the past and/or future, and venturing into the unknown present with an open and receptive mind and heart. In the acting context, it means not "exhibiting," "sketching," "over acting," "indicating" or other forms of phoniness on the stage but being truthful to the circumstances of the play.

Finally, we come to stage three, narrowing one's focus. Such a psychic process goes further than getting oneself going and giving in to the momentum of what one is experiencing. It requires, says Matt, harnessing the instinctual mind, the impulse, taming and focusing it on what one is supposed to be doing in the real world (or the "real" world of the stage). This has been called, in Buddhist circles, "relaxed alertness" and "controlled spontaneity;" "it's devoting every fiber of your being to one thing"—what you are doing on the stage, for example— "and basking in the sheer joy that comes from that."[11] For Meisner, the capacity to be in the moment, especially with one's fellow actors, is the

---

10   Ibid., p. 6.
11   Ibid., p. 8.

pre-condition to what he says is the basis of all acting: the reality of doing.

THE REALITY OF DOING

Perhaps more than any other acting teacher Meisner would agree with the English espionage novelist John le Carre who wrote, "In the beginning was the deed. Not the motive, least of all the word." When it comes to the "foundation of acting," including most importantly, generating authentic, strong emotion, "it is the reality of doing" that most counts; "The seed to the craft of acting is the reality of doing."[12] "Feeling and being come out of doing," says Alice Spivak, an acting teacher trained by the master acting coach, Uta Hagen.[13] "Doing" refers to performing an action, activity, or a task in a particular situation or (set of) circumstance(s) in order to change it and produce a particular effect or result. Put simply, according to Meisner and/or the devotees of Practical Aesthetics,[14] "an action is the physical pursuance of a specific goal" ("generality is the enemy of all art," said Stanislavski). It "is the main building block of an actor's technique because it is the one thing that…the actor can consistently do on stage" (as opposed to trying, often unsuccessfully, to find and/or conjure up specific emotions on demand, a technique Strasberg supports).[15] In particular, for Meisner, the actor's focus should be centrifugal, away from himself, and on his fellow actor, his response to our actions and our response to his actions, a kind of "action-reaction dance." [16] Put somewhat differently by one British acting teacher probably influenced by Meisner, though originally trained by Strasberg, "emotions are a by-product of, or response to, something that you want from the other characters in

12   Meisner, *On Acting*, p. 16; Silverberg, *The Sanford Meisner Approach*, p. 3.

13   Eva Mekler, *The New Generation of Acting Teachers* (New York: Penguin, 1987), p. 173.

14   Practical Aesthetics is an offshoot of Meisner's, created by playwright David Mamet, actor William H. Macy and director Gregory Mosher.

15   Melissa Bruder, Lee Michael Cohn, Madeleine Olnek, Nathaniel Pollack, Robert Previto, Scott Zigler, et al., *A Practical Handbook for the Actor* (New York: Vintage Books, 1986), p. 13.

16   Brestoff, *The Great Acting Teachers*, p. 132.

the play;"[17] it is a kind of "agonism of a relationship," as Michel Foucault called it in a different context. An *agon*, from the Greek word for "a combat," is a "relationship which is at the same time reciprocal incitation and struggle; less of a face-to-face confrontation which paralyzes both sides than a permanent provocation"[18] (no doubt Bertolt Brecht's "theatre of politics" and, to a lesser extent, Antonin Artaud's "theatre of cruelty" both resonate with this idea of agonism). Regardless of which formulation one likes, as Meisner and others have correctly noted, this intersubjective interplay generates a strong flow, if not surge of energy between the actors, one so intense that it is felt almost physically by them. As a result, for the audience such truthful intersubjective dialogue can be dazzling to watch.[19]

What this boils down to is that for Meisner, genuine emotion is not necessarily something one finds inside oneself or tries to summon or invoke as is conventionally thought; rather, says Silverberg, "emotions come freely, as a side benefit, a gift, when our attention is on something else and that something else is what we are doing. The great news here is that when our attention is not on being emotional, our emotions suddenly become much more available."[20] According to Bruder and colleagues, "Your emotions are the natural and inescapable by-product of your commitment to your action."[21] Most importantly, this action must be directed away from self toward the other, whether human, animal or inanimate: "Don't give a performance. Let the performance give you," advised Meisner.[22] Meisner advises that by un-self-consciously doing the action that is directed toward one's partner, not only is there likely to be a spontaneous upsurge of truthful emotion that is in sync with the circumstances of the scene, but "the possibility of transcending [an actor's] own sacred self,"[23] the ultimate basis of giving a great

17   Eva Mekler, *Masters of the Stage* (New York: Grove and Weidenfeld, 1989), p. 83.

18   Michel Foucault, "The Subject and Power," "Afterword," in Hubert L. Dreyfus and Paul Rabinow (Eds.) *Michel Foucault: Beyond Structuralism and Hermeneutics* (Chicago: University of Chicago Press, 1987), p. 222.

19   Brestoff, *The Great Acting Teachers*, 132-133.

20   Silverberg, *The Sanford Meisner Approach*, pp. 3-4.

21   Bruder et al., *A Practical Handbook for the Actor*, p. 73.

22   Meisner and Longfellow, *On Acting*, p. 128.

23   Ibid., p. 114.

performance, is also likely to occur. Interestingly, for Meisner and for other acting theorists, the way into a great performance is by jettisoning the self, especially the selfish self, through giving to the other. Said Stanislavski, "our first duty is to adapt yourself to your partner." As great actors will tell you, inspiration on the stage involves a greater focus on giving to one's fellow actor, the character one is playing, and/ or to the audience, rather than focusing on what one gets.

Meisner's message is clear as it pertains to the non-actor trying to live the "good life." To the extent that one can focus on what one is doing for the other—that is, "serving" the real or imagined, animate or inanimate other—rather than what one is feeling, one is more likely to give a better "performance" on and off the stage. As we have said throughout this book, other-directed, other-regarding action, along with the worldview of, "responsibility for the other," often before oneself, as Levinas puts it is, ironically, the "royal road" to achieving what one wants for oneself: a "great performance," whether on the stage or, most importantly, in our efforts to fashion the "good life."

THE WORD REPETITION GAME

Perhaps the best known exercise in the Meisner Technique is what he called the Word Repetition Game. In this exercise one actor spontaneously utters a remark based on his fellow actor, and his remark would be repeated back and forth (somewhat like a seesaw, metaphorically) between the two actors in the near identical way until it is modified on its own. The manifest goal is to react truthfully, allowing the repetition to change organically and naturally, rather than by conscious, intentional intervention or through some type of interpersonal coercion. For example, one actor may begin by saying, "You're frowning." "I'm frowning." "You're frowning." "Yes, I'm frowning." The idea is that the participants are required to closely watch and react to their partner's actions and the underlying meaning and message. If they are able to sense the underlying impulse and respond instinctively to how they are emotionally impacted by their partner's actions ("work from your instincts," Meisner says), then, theoretically, their own actions will come about straight (and genuinely) from their partner. In the broader sense this exercise was meant to assist an actor to "live truthfully under imaginary circumstances." As we will detail later, this catchy definition of acting that Meisner famously articulated refers in part to the capacity to apply one's imagination in a context-responsive and psychologically truthful manner to human (and non-human) interaction as it circumstantially unfolds in consciousness, as guided by the parameters of the script. The Word Repetition Game is a key exercise for developing this capacity for emotional dialogue.

The two guiding principles of the Word Repetition Game are clearly spelled out by Meisner: "Don't do anything unless something happens to make you do it" and "What you do doesn't depend on you; it depends on the other fellow."[24] As one of Meisner's students put it, "acting is not talking. It is living off the other fellow."[25] It should be clarified that this "living off" the other is not meant in a parasitic or symbiotic sense; by truthfully existing in the moment, responding to what the other stimulates in you, you are more likely to have an upsurge of emotional aliveness on the stage and, for that matter, in real life.

In terms of living the "good life," Meisner is actually making two very important and often underappreciated observations[26]: First, the Word Repetition Game stresses the need to pay close attention to the other—one must be able to listen with care, serious consideration and concentration. More generally, Meisner is suggesting that a precondition of being a great actor on and off the stage is the capacity to respond promptly and without any hesitation to the vibes and needs of the other (remember what Stanislavski said, "our first duty is to adapt yourself to your partner"). Availability, openness and accurate empathy are thus three of Meisner's interrelated core values of which the non-actor ought to be mindful and integrate into his way of being in the world. (As Freud, Buddhists and many others have shown, this is hardly easy to do given how neurotically "defended" most of us are.) Second, and this point follows from the first observation, the Word Repetition Game emphasizes that the focus should be mainly on the other individual, not on oneself. It is one's fellow thespians and the circumstances that will evoke authentic emotion. In this way, both on the stage and in real life, self-consciousness, reserve, embarrassment and

24 Meisner and Longfellow, *On Acting*, p. 34.
25 Ibid., p.42.
26 Brestoff, *The Great Acting Teachers*, p. 131.

other forms of social anxiety have little opportunity to get generated, for one is responding truthfully in the moment to the other. Such a way of being in the world is altogether more satisfying to one's acquaintances, friends and significant others as well as to oneself.

LIVING TRUTHFULLY IN
IMAGINARY CIRCUMSTANCES

Using familiar notions that we have discussed in previous chapters, Meisner defined acting in the simple but thoughtful phrase as "living truthfully in imaginary circumstances."[27] Being truthful means living the imaginary circumstances of the stage as if they were real, "to defictionalize the fiction" as Stella Adler described it. This, as we have said, involves the capacity to be in the moment with one's fellow actors and effectively work off each other in accordance with the script, i.e., the circumstances of the scene and the other players. However, perhaps more profoundly, it entails being able to reside in a different dimension of the spirit, to engage a different domain of one's personality than what one usually accesses in ordinary life. In a certain sense Meisner is correct when he says, "acting doesn't have anything to do with everyday life. It has to do with the truth."[28] As Silverberg noted, "you must work from this place of deeper meaning within yourself, it has to be that personal….there is a price to pay, if you want the real thing there is a very high personal cost…the rewards are great."[29] In other words, as Meisner said, "the truth of ourselves is the root of our acting….You know, my biggest job in teaching you actors is to bring you together with yourself. That's the root of creative acting."[30] What Silverberg and Meisner seem to be getting at is that for the actor to play his role truthfully requires a capacity that goes beyond simply imitating life; rather, he must perform his actions with a sense of urgency and meaning as if his life depended on it (in fact, ironically, his life as a working actor may well depend on it!). Only in this way, when the stakes are very high, can the actor play his role in a non-fraudulent

---

27   Meisner and Longfellow, *On Acting*, p. 15.
28   Ibid., p. 162.
29   Silverberg, *The Sanford Meisner Approach*, p. 101.
30   Meisner and Longfellow, *On Acting*, pp. 45, 160.

and convincing manner.[31] Meisner quoted George Bernard Shaw who aptly elaborated this point: "Self betrayal, magnified to suit the optics of the theater, is the whole art of acting." By self-betrayal Shaw meant complete self-revelation of one's personhood to the audience. To do this, to passionately want to do this, requires great courage, among other qualities. Sometimes the motivation to act is mainly neurotic, like the need for narcissistic display and to be loved, though this is not necessarily bad, says Meisner, "So essentially our talent is made up of our transformed troubles."[32] By "optics of the theater," says one of Meisner's students, is meant "that when you put the real situation on the stage you need to keep its reality so that it's believable both to you and to the audience, but you have to raise it to a level above real life. Otherwise, it doesn't communicate."[33] That is, it is not emotionally compelling, and without being emotionally alive, a performance on and off the stage is rather uninteresting, if not utterly boring.

Drawing from Stanislavski, what the above discussion about "living truthfully in imaginary circumstances" means is that both in acting and real life lived at its best, there needs to be a "union of the deep substance of the inner life and a beautiful, light, expressive form of it."[34] In Stanislavski's classic study, *An Actor Prepares*, he provides advice on how to be a great actor, though his words also apply to ordinary life:

> The actor must recreate his work each time he repeats his part, with sincerity, truth and directness. It is only on that condition that he will be able to free his art from mechanical and stereotyped acting, from "tricks" and all forms of artificiality. If he accomplishes this he will have real people and real life all around him on the stage, and living art which has been purified from all debasing elements.[35]

The main insight here can be easily and beneficially recast and transposed to real life. The "good life" involves the capacity to live with a high degree of "sincerity, truth and directness" in one's relationship to oneself and toward others. "Artificiality," or what is usually called

31   Silverberg, *The Sanford Meisner Approach*, pp. 99, 100.
32   Meisner and Longfellow, *On Acting*, p. 190.
33   Ibid., p. 146.
34   Sonia Moore, *The Stanislavski System* (New York: Penguin, 1984), p. 54.
35   Konstantin Stanislavski, *An Actor Prepares* (New York: Routledge, 1964), p. 122.

phoniness—putting on a false show of something such as sincerity or expertise to deceive—must be eliminated from one's self-con-
ception and comportment to the world. This centrally involves, as
any acting teacher will tell you, the loss of self-consciousness. Self-
consciousness—feeling acutely and uncomfortably aware of one's
failings when in the company of others and believing that others are
noticing them too, as well as being overly conscious of the impression one makes on others and trying to act in a way that reinforces
this impression—is lethal to the actor (and to the ordinary person in
real life). By being mindful of the urgency to be truthful in one's self-
presentation, one is more likely to feel "real" and to live with a sense of
a heightened, authentic experience.[36] In a word, what we are advocating is the greater need in life for the individual "to live truthfully under
the imaginary circumstances" in which he finds himself. As all circumstances are to some extent imaginary, that is, they are construed and
mediated through one's own imaginative, creative mind and therefore
can never be an exact perception or replica of what is "out there," then,
as David Mamet noted, the stage actor's goal, "to be what you wish to
seem," seems about the best we humans can do, or as Stanislavski says,
"play well or badly, but play truly."[37]

PREPARATION, PARTICULARIZATION AND CHARACTER

For an actor to be able to generate the truthful, believable and con-
text-appropriate emotion that makes a performance captivating to the
spectator is perhaps the main problem he faces during every performance. Whether his part is big or small, whether it involves speaking or not speaking, the goal of the actor is to create for the audience
a sense of energy and vigor in his role, an interesting, relevant and
vividly imaginable character for the audience. However, there are instances when a script or a role one is playing does not evoke much
or any notable feeling in the actor—it leaves him cold. "Preparation,"
says Meisner, is the antidote to this feeling of emotional blunting or
deadness. It "is the device which permits you to start your scene or

---

36   This sense of heightened experience of oneself on the stage can have an
      addictive quality to it, as some actors we interviewed have reported.

37   Bruder et al., *A Practical Handbook for the Actor*, p. xi.

play in a condition of emotional aliveness. The purpose of preparation
is so that you do not come in emotionally empty."[38] Meisner rejected
Strasberg's "emotional memory," reaching into one's personal past to
evoke this needed sense of aliveness. Meisner believed that one could
never fully get to the reality of a past experience because the meaning
of one's past memories keeps changing, especially as one gets older.
Therefore, the past conceived as a kind of accessible frozen moment in
time or time capsule is not a reliable source of inspiration for the actor. Meisner suggested that the actor *imagine* the reality, the emotion,
he is supposed to be expressing via his character and the given circumstances. It is a form of personalized self-stimulation: "I want you
to find in yourself that element which belongs only to you and to no
one else, which is stimulating for you and for no one else."[39] Meisner
further points out that this kind of imagining is a form of, or at least
is analogous to, daydreaming, a series of what is in ordinary life often
distracting and usually pleasant thoughts and images that pass while
awake. However, in the context of the actor who is going to perform
on a stage, such daydreaming is exploited to evoke relevant feelings in
a controlled and artistic manner. Most importantly, says Meisner, such
"daydreaming…causes a transformation in your inner life, so that you
are not what you actually were five minutes ago because your fantasy
is working on you. But the *character* of our daydream is taken from the
play"[40] (italics in original). This "fantasy of the daydream is the most
personal, most secret of the acting values…we use our imagination
in order to fulfill in ourselves what we have more or less determined
is our emotional condition before we begin the scene." Citing Freud,
Meisner continues, preparation is mainly a function of the actor's "am-
bitious or sexual imagination."[41] "There is," says Freud, "a path from
fantasy back again to reality, and that is—art."

Meisner also advocates using Stanislavski's "magic if," what the
former calls "particularization," to ignite the imagination to generate
authentic emotion. The "as if," says Meisner, involves describing "for
yourself a situation that would bring you personally to the emotional

---

38   Meisner and Longwell, *On Acting*, p. 78.
39   Ibid., p. 80.
40   Ibid., p. 84.
41   Ibid., p. 85.

place you need to be in for the sake of the scene."[42] Interestingly, says
Meisner, where his American (and Russian and German, he says)
approach focuses on "emotional creation," the British actor typically
plays his character very differently: "Unlike the English, who know
intellectually what the character should be feeling and indicate this
through the way they verbally handle the text, we work from the living
truthfully under imaginary circumstances."[43] According to Meisner,
"Character comes from how you do what you do....it reveals itself by
how you do what you do."[44] In other words, "character is behavior. It
is the 'how' of acting," and preparation and particularization is crucial
here.[45] Put simply, if an actor has perceptively and accurately analyzed
a scene for action, "the physical pursuance of a goal," he will be able to
effectively create his character, the "illusion created by words and given
circumstances supplied by the playwright and the physical actions of
the actor."[46]

Meisner is making two points that have bearing on the individual's
quest to live the "good life," points that Stella Adler and others have
also stressed. First, he is emphasizing the importance of using one's
imagination, the capacity to shape images and ideas in one's mind, particularly of things never viewed or never actually experienced. More
specifically, it is through the imagination that one can access the instinctual aspects or "inner impulses" of one's personality, the realm
that Meisner feels is crucial for the actor to energize himself before,
and himself and his partner during, a performance. Likewise, it is the
use of one's mind's eye, the place in the mind where visual images are
conjured up from imagination or memory, that one is better able to
both enliven one's everyday life, including charming, delighting and
captivating others.

Second, Meisner is making the point that it is the "right" action, not
fabricating or conjuring up feeling or other forms of inordinate in-
troversion, that is most important for effectively acting on the stage.
Similarly, in real life one needs to focus on the "right" action, behavior

---

42   Ibid., p. 138.
43   Ibid., p. 136.
44   Ibid., pp. 156, 188.
45   Brestoff, *The Great Acting Teachers and Their Methods*, p. 137.
46   Bruder et al., *A Practical Handbook for the Actor*, p. 74.

that is true to what is happening in the moment in the given circumstances that one finds oneself. As the saying goes, in real life "talk is cheap," what counts most is what one does as opposed to what one says one will do.

As Meisner stressed over and over again, it is mainly through focusing on the vibes and needs of one's partner that one will generate a truthful action and the apt emotion in the given context. Without having to initially and primarily worry about generating the right emotional response when with others, the focus shifts to a morally "higher" purpose, namely the willful "serving" of the other before oneself. Paradoxically, such a way of being tends to be enormously personally satisfying.

CONCLUSION

"In Chekhov's presence everyone felt in himself a desire to be simpler, more truthful, more one's self," Maxim Gorky said in passing. As we have tried to suggest, to some extent, the same could probably be said about Meisner. In his reflections on such topics as being in the moment, working from one's partner and serving one's partner first, reality as doing, and living truthfully in the imagined circumstances, we have seen a master acting teacher trying to convince his students of the most direct route to great acting: "Simplicity is essential. Don't clutter yourself;" "What I am saying is that the truth of ourselves is the root of our acting." As Silverberg reports, Meisner's advice to actors, advice that we believe has bearing on the non-actor in search of the "good life," can be reduced to a simple idea, though one that is hardly easy to instantiate on or off the stage: "Hold tight to your integrity! You'll be a radiant beacon of light in a very dark world."[47] Indeed, one of Meisner's guiding valuative attachments is "no bullshit," or as he says more elegantly, to achieve "organic creativity," requires the capacity to "funnel the instincts." Meisner, somewhat like Chekhov, saw the necessity to bring an actor back to his "inner impulses," this being the bedrock of truth of a person and playing a character. Meisner succinctly and aptly elaborated this point, this being a most fitting end to our discussion of this brilliant acting teacher:

---

47   Silverberg, *The Sanford Meisner Approach*, p. 127.

I'm a very nonintellectual teacher of acting. My approach is based on bringing the actor back to his emotional impulses and to acting that is firmly rooted in the instinctive. It is based on the fact that all good acting comes from the heart, as it were, and that there's no mentality in it.[48]

---

48   Meisner and Longfellow, *On Acting*, p. 37.

CHAPTER FIVE

ACT BEFORE YOU THINK

THE IMPROVISATION OF

VIOLA SPOLIN

"Focus dissolves ambivalence, time-lag, should I, shouldn't I? The whole thing is to get out of the head."

—Viola Spolin

T HEATER IMPROVISATION, GENERALLY DEFINED AS THE CREATIVE PROCESS of inventing and performing something without any preparation or set text to follow, is considered by most actors and actresses to be a critical skill to being a great performer regardless of the venue. As Marlon Brando noted, "If an actor can't improvise, perhaps the producer's wife cast him in that part." Indeed, "improv" or "impro," as it is often called, helps actors develop the essential skills of inspired acting such as "accessing playfulness," "expanding interpersonal trust," "experiencing spontaneity," "opening to creativity," "broadening sensory, emotive, and movement expressiveness," and "creating and co-creating new realities with others."[1] Most importantly for our concerns, as John Hodgson and Ernest Richards note, "the qualities needed for the best acting [e.g., improv] are also those qualities required for the fullest

---

1   Daniel J. Wiener, *Rehearsals for Growth. Theater Improvisation for Psychotherapists* (New York: W.W. Norton & Company, 1994), pp. xii-xv.

living,"[2] again emphasizing the main thesis of our book, that "theater is lifelike and life is theater-like."[3] More specifically, "improvisation is a means of training people to think," though very differently than they are accustomed to thinking in their everyday lives.[4] Unlike the detached intellectualizing, discursive reasoning and obsessive-like cerebral doings that are rooted in the empiricism and rationalism of the Western mindset, improv aims to fully engage the immediacy of the real-life human situation in its essential fluidity and changeableness. This is the place where "the unconscious delivers the goods," where spontaneous creativity emerges as does the beauty of the unknown.[5] Improv thus emphasizes the intuitive—what Viola Spolin (1906–1994), the "high priestess" of improv, famously called "the X-area." The "X-area" is "an area to be prodded and investigated by everyone," it is "unhampered knowledge beyond the sensory equipment (physical and mental)," it is "the area of revelation."[6] Intuition, explains Paul Sills, Spolin's son and the founding director of the famous Chicago's Second City and of Story Theater, is "the direct knowing of something without conscious use of reasoning … it is a way of knowing other than intellectual knowing."[7] Intuition, at least as Spolin uses it in the improv context, implies a highly attuned sense of empathy, concentration and spontaneity, imagination, expanded awareness, emotional intelligence, and the ability to be supportive and helpful to others. These and other such qualities of the mind and heart are of course some of the required properties for living the "good life," to love and work, as Freud described it. In this chapter, which mainly draws from the brilliant work of Spolin and Keith Johnstone (the latter is the author of the path-breaking book *Impro. Improvisation and the Theatre*), we will delineate some of the key insights drawn from the lively, humorous

2   John Hodgson and Ernest Richards, *Improvisation* (New York: Grove Weidenfeld, 1974), p. 11.

3   Wiener, *Rehearsals for Growth*, p. 3.

4   Hodgson and Richards, *Improvisation*, p. 22.

5   Irving Wardle, "Introduction," in Keith Johnstone, *Impro. Improvisation and the Theatre* (New York: Routledge/Theatre Art Books, 1992), p. 10.

6   Viola Spolin, *Improvisation for the Theater*. Third Edition (Evanston: Northwestern University Press, 1999), p. 362.

7   Ibid., p. ix.

and wise world of improv, insights that have bearing on how the average person can enhance their everyday life.

VIOLA SPOLIN'S THEATER GAMES

Spolin's improvisational games significantly changed the way modern acting is conceptualized and approached. Instead of the comparatively heady, psychological and realistic emphasis of Stanislavski and his disciples, Spolin focused on games meant to free the actor of tensions rooted in his long-standing defenses against spontaneous feeling and rid the actor of subjective preconceptions of the fixed meaning of words, actions and the like. Most importantly perhaps, Spolin reminds us that acting is fundamentally a form of play—a pleasurable activity done for the sake of enjoyment. "Playing," says Spolin, is "fun, enjoyment, enthusiasm, trust; heightening the object [i.e., that which "sets the actor in motion"]; moving relations with fellow players; involvement with the focus [i.e., the "moving energy"]; the physical expression of the life force."[8] Spolin thus developed hundreds of games and exercises that "are simple, operational structures that transform complicated theater conventions and techniques into game form. Each game is built upon a specific focus or technical problem and is an exercise that militates against the artifice of self-conscious acting."[9] A game is "an accepted group activity which is limited by rules and group agreement," it tends to be lots of fun, it evokes naturalness, passion and delight and is comparable to the theater experience—and we would argue, other life contexts.[10] Exercises with titles such as "Space Walk" and "Feeling Self with Self," and games such as "Swat Tag," "Mirror," "Playball" and "Gibberish" give a sense of the kinds of games Spolin used to help the player increase his or her sensitivity and self-awareness and improve group and interpersonal communication, among other benefits. However, what Spolin's theater games give the actor is a point of focus to create instinctively and spontaneously rather than being in the self-conscious, judging mind. As one critic noted, Spolin's games are "designed to almost fool spontaneity into being." Thus, the

8 Spolin, *Improvisation for the Theater*, p. 365.

9 D.E. Moffit, *Master Acting Teacher Biographies: Viola Spolin*. http://www.jbactors.com/actingreading/actingteacherbiographies/violaspolin.html, p. 2.

10 Spolin, *Improvisation for the Theater*, p. 360.

logical, rational brain is transcended by the theater game focus and
the actor is freer to tap into the right half of his or her brain, the
place where the intuitive emanates, the metaphoric mind. As Daniel
J. Wiener, following Jerome Bruner, has suggested, human thinking
and comprehension tends to be mainly "verbal and sequential," which
is helpful "for ordering through abstraction" in the quest for truth.
However, in contrast to this "paradigmatic mode" as Bruner calls it,
the "narrative mode"—the part of the mind that configures experience
metaphorically for creating a "believable reality"[11]—we believe, is often
deemphasized at great peril to individual functioning, creativity and
human happiness. Obviously, both modes of thought are necessary
to properly operate in everyday life, including enjoying one's life, but
Spolin, Johnstone and others from the improv world have provided an
important counterpoint to the prevailing emphasis in our technocratic
society. They have pointed us toward a realm of knowledge—a kind of
practical wisdom for the art of living—which in a certain sense, says
Spolin, "is beyond the restrictions of culture, race, education, psychology, and age; it is deeper than the survival dress of mannerisms, prejudices, intellectualism, and borrowings," that the majority of people
tend to live in their daily lives.[12] What then can Spolin and company
teach us about this other realm of knowledge, of practical wisdom—
that is, about adult play, in particular, about developing a playful way
of being in the world?

CULTIVATING ADULT PLAYFULNESS

"In every real man a child is hidden that wants to play," wrote
Nietzsche. Indeed, most adults, at least in Western culture, are too
bound, tied and gagged by societal and personal restrictions, if not
neuroses, to live playfully in their everyday lives. Instead, what is
called adult play is mainly restricted to watching and participating in
competitive games like basketball and baseball, and sports competi-
tions like the Olympics. Such activities are pleasurable sublimations
of childhood play and have important cultural functions. However,
what improv tries to develop for adults is something more rooted in

11   Wiener, *Rehearsals for Growth*, p. 22.
12   Viola Spolin, *Theater Games for Rehearsal. A Director's Handbook*
     (Evanston, IL: Northern University Press, 1985), p. 4.

re-finding the aliveness and joy associated with play activities engaged in for their own sake, for the pleasure they give, most often without any serious aim or end and without much conscious anxiety, inhibition and/or guilt.[13] For sure, such nonpurposive play (in contrast to, say, adult work), is not easily achieved, for most adults are overly concerned with their presentation of self, the negative judgment of others and a wide range of other inhibitions. Perhaps it is for this reason that psychoanalyst Donald Winnicott famously argued that in part, the goal of psychoanalysis at its best is to transform "the patient from a state of not being able to play into a state of being able to play....It is in playing and only in playing that the individual child or adult is able to be creative and to use the whole personality, and it is only in being creative that the individual discovers the self."[14] To be able to play is thus a sign of "mental health," that is, it is an expression of autonomy and integration. It is also self-healing and therapeutic, and yet sadly, for most people in our society it is regarded more as a luxury than a necessity. Finally, through play one can learn an awful lot about people if one knows for what to look. Sounding more like a psychoanalyst than the wise philosopher he was, Plato noted, "You can discover more about a person in an hour of play than in a year of conversation."

The particular aspect of adult play, at least as it is developed and nurtured in improv, that we want to focus on is how certain individuals have the capacity to take the spirit of childhood playfulness and use it to animate their adult way of being in the world. Such rare people are often striking in their comportment and are often described as charming. That is, they have an uncanny capacity to actualize the inconceivable, to delight and attract others, often gaining their admiration without coming across as narcissistic and self-serving. As Henri-Frédéric Amiel said, "Charm is the quality in others that makes us more satisfied with ourselves." It is in part this capacity to be charming when fully integrated into one's mode of being in the world that gives a person that lightness of being, that beauty and grace, that most people desire. The psychological elements of this charming comportment are precisely the qualities that make for good improvisation and enhanced

13   Charles Rycroft, *A Critical Dictionary of Psychoanalysis*. Second Edition (London: Penguin, 1995), p. 134.
14   Donald Winnicott, *Playing and Reality* (London: Tavistock, 1971), p. 10.

living. In this view, psychological health is roughly equivalent to being dramatically accomplished, that is, to have the kind of intense, gripping and/or humorous excitement, startling suddenness, and/or larger than life impressiveness associated with the theater. The goal of improv is to increase the player's capacity to enter a playful state at will and to broaden his or her capacity to think, feel and act beyond his or her habitual ways of being in the world. In order to unpack the nature of play as so conceptualized in the improv context, we will discuss some of the key psychological elements of improv mentioned earlier— the cultivation of interpersonal trust, spontaneity, creativity, sensory/physical/emotional expressiveness, and producing and co-producing new realities with others.

DEEPENING INTERPERSONAL TRUST

Most improv in the Spolin tradition[15] emphasizes that for great improv or a great scene to emerge requires the player to be able to work off of the other player in a way that is truly other-directed and other-regarding. In other words, for the utmost synergy to occur between and among players requires that one's ego be downsized such that one's priority is to make one's fellow player shine. Likewise, the other player is trying to do the same. If exhibitionistic wishes, the need to stand out or other self-serving inclinations take over, the improv will inevitably be flat and unimpressive. As Spolin noted, "Acting [and authentic living] requires presence. Being there....the very act of seeking the moment, of being open to fellow players, produces a life force, a flow, a regeneration for who participate....If our openness is more than just a hope, a sentiment, a word, certain conditions must be met. The first of these we would call mutuality or trust. True playing will produce

---

15   As Gary Schwartz has pointed out (personal communication, 5/26/09), in contrast to Spolin, Johnstone's work stresses an intellectual approach rather than a physical mind/body one. While it is true that both Spolin and Johnstone accentuate avoiding inordinate ego involvement (i.e., the selfish ego) during improv, Johnstone's work, curiously simply *asks* the ego to be ignored without giving clear ways to eradicate or reduce the ego's selfish operations. Spolin's focus, however, is to actively replace the selfish ego with strong mutual focus, each focus defined clearly in each game. To be fair, Johnstone's mask work lessens the selfish ego, but that does not significantly impact regular scene improv.

trust."[16] Such trust is not about being passive but rather receptive to the other player(s), in that one both allows and vigorously risks being completely in the moment together with the others, without the need to comprehend or be in command of the future. Moreover, since the improv context is a heightened emotional reality with all types of presentation anxieties often generated, social connectivity and solidarity occurs between and among players such that greater trust and self-trust is generated. As Johnstone noted, "if you enjoy working with someone, they're a good improviser."[17]

The point that needs to be emphasized is that for this kind of spontaneous and creative behavior to emerge both within the improv and everyday context, it requires that "one get out of oneself," that is, one needs to give the reasonable needs and desires of the other precedence over oneself, while at the same time remaining actively responsive to the other's otherness (e.g., being open and empathic to the other's unique self-comportment), and one's own otherness (e.g., "taking in" what is spontaneously stirred up in oneself). It is this internal capacity to respectfully welcome the other with the fullness of one's being, without having to return to the enclosed circle of the self-possessed self that is vital.[18] In a sense, paradoxically, the more one selflessly gives to the other, the more one tends to get in return and both people feel mutually enhanced. As Johnstone noted, "the improviser has to understand that his first skill lies in releasing the partner's imagination."[19] Thus, for the "play-inducing, creativity-releasing, growth-enhancing"[20] qualities we associate with great improv and enhanced living to emerge, "being for the Other" before oneself is axiomatic; it is the received practical wisdom emanating from the magical world of improv.

---

16   Spolin, *Theater Games for Rehearsal*, p. 3.

17   Wiener, *Rehearsals for Growth*, pp. xii-xiii, 18.

18   Ephraim Meir, *Levinas's Jewish Thought. Between Jerusalem and Athens* (Jerusalem: Hebrew University Magnes Press, 2009), pp. 16, 3.

19   Johnstone, *Impro*, p. 93.

20   Ibid., p. 247.

INCREASING SPONTANEITY

Spontaneity, roughly defined as behavior that is natural and uncon-
strained and is the result of impulse (in the positive sense), not planning, is a concept that is often referred to in popular media and the
like. In the world of improv, spontaneity is a key concept, perhaps the
bedrock of great improv. Spolin defines spontaneity as "a moment of
explosion; a free moment of self-expression; an off-balance moment;
the gateway to your intuition; the moment when, in full sensory attention, you don't think, you act!"[21] What is important to grasp in Spolin's
definition of spontaneity is the relationship between spontaneity and
intuition, the latter being the way the player can evoke that exquisite moment when one is creatively being in the world as an organic
whole, when "we are re-formed into ourselves."[22] Spolin notes, "intuition bypasses the intellect, the mind, the memory, the known. Using
intuition cannot be taught. One must be tripped into it."[23] In other
words, Spolin claims, intuition requires transcending the familiar categories of thought, feeling and action, and "to enter courageously the
area of the unknown, and to experience the release of momentary genius within themselves." As William James remarked, "Genius means
little more than the faculty of perceiving in an unhabitual way." Most
importantly, continues Spolin, "the intuitive can only be felt in the moment of spontaneity, the moment when we are freed to relate and act,
involving ourselves in the moving, changing world around us....[in-
tuition] comes bearing its gifts in the moment of spontaneity."[24] The
goal of this combustible mixture of spontaneity and intuition argues
Spolin, is what she calls "transformation"—"the heart of improvisation
is transformation." And the heart of transformation is creativity, not
rearranging what is already known as most of us usually opt for in our
ordinary lives, but a radical change in one's way of being in the world,
at least during the theater game. Spolin aptly defines transformation
in her teacher's handbook for theater games for kids:

> The effects of game playing are not only social and cognitive.
> When players are deeply focused on a game, they are capable of

21   Spolin, *Improvisation for the Theater*, p. 370.
22   Ibid., p. 4.
23   Spolin, *Theater Games for the Classroom*, p. 4.
24   Ibid.

transforming objects or creating them. Whole environments arise spontaneously out of thin air. Impossible to capture fully in words, transformation seems to arise out of heightened physical movement and of exchange of this moving energy between players. Change occurs not once but over and over again. Transformations are theater magic and an intrinsic part of most theater games.[25] [In other words, in transformation,] [c]reation momentarily breaks through isolation, and actors and audience alike receive (ahhh!) the appearance of a new reality (theater magic).[26]

What is crucial to understand about Spolin's theater games is that every game presents a problem that needs to be solved within the context of the agreed upon rules of the game. All the player's efforts, his or her focus—"directing and concentrating attention on a specific person, object or event with the stage reality....the point of concentration of a theater game that keeps the players in process"—must be intensely directed to playing the game.[27] Paradoxically, it is within the context of the structure of the game, that such a focus, to which every action must be directed, facilitates spontaneity: "In this spontaneity, personal freedom is released, and the total person physically, intellectually, and intuitively is awakened."[28] Moreover, and this is one of the implications of theater games for everyday life, such excitement and boldness often leads the player to transcend many of his or her anxieties and inhibitions—call it a transforming liberatory moment—and thus, the player is often better able to go out into the "real" world, "to explore, adventure, and face all dangers unafraid."[29] Indeed, there are many children who in psychoanalysis as adults have told me (PM) about moments of personal fearlessness and triumph while playing a game or sport, an experience that became a radically transforming, deeply positive metaphor for their lives.

Of course, the above described liberation of one's spontaneity, intuition and creativity via the theater game probably comes easier to kids who are less shackled by restrictions in self-expression. However, what Spolin is putting her finger on is a deep point about the art of living

25   Ibid.
26   Spolin, *Improvisation for the Theater*, p. 372.
27   Ibid., p. 360.
28   Ibid., p. 6.
29   Ibid.

the "good life"; namely, it is the cultivation of the capacity for spontaneity in one's everyday life that is an essential element to maximally enjoy one's life. As Germaine Greer aptly wrote, "the essence of pleasure is spontaneity." However, more than simply enhanced pleasure, spontaneity, as with following an unknown river through a mountain, opens up a whole new sensibility about life. Ralph Waldo Emerson made this point just right: "Men grind and grind in the mill of truism, nothing comes out but what was put in. But the moment they desert the tradition for spontaneous thought, then poetry, wit, hope, virtue, learning, anecdote, and all flock to their aid." For Spolin, the way into spontaneity/intuition/liberation is the theater game, though we think that the theater game, that is, the qualities it requires and evokes in the players are transferable in other contexts in which the theater game is the learning paradigm. For this release of one's personality to occur requires the overcoming of the major stumbling block to great improv and living the good life: namely, fear. For it is fear of how one is coming across to others and of one's own often irreverent and other hidden impulses, that leads improv players to expurgate and edit their responses, such as getting stuck in the future (by planning their actions in advance), or in the past (by doing the safe and familiar)— the antithesis to being in the moment. Johnstone has pointed out the socially threatening nature of improv in that it reveals the "real" self as opposed to the choreographed one (hence, one must be "tripped" into the intuitive, says Spolin). Whatever the specific nature of the fear one has doing improv, Spolin has caught its essential thrust when she wrote, "the fear is not of the unknown, but of not knowing," [30] which is probably in part rooted in the childhood fear of being amiss. It is the tension associated with fear, broadly described, that blocks "free open thought,"[31] the foundation of all improv and creative living. As Henry Miller wrote, "all growth is a leap in the dark, a spontaneous, unpremeditated act without benefit of experience."

EXPANDING CREATIVITY

Creativity—the capacity to use the imagination to develop new and original ideas or things—like spontaneity, is a term that is bandied

---

30   Ibid., p. xiv.
31   Hodgson and Richards, *Improvisation*, pp. 56, 57.

all over the place. However, creativity is a key notion in the world of improv, for it is one of the engines that drive the art form. Spolin defines creativity in a unique but technical way that is only intelligible in terms of her theory of improv: "Create (limited) plus intuit (unlimited) equals creation."[32] What Spolin is getting at with this rather elliptical definition is this: to create involves allowing what is consciously known (in her jargon, the "limited," that which is easily accessible from one's "head"), to be animated by what is not yet known, the region of revelation (the "unlimited," that which is accessible only by intuition).[33] Where drawing from what is consciously known is basically a reasoning process, the upsurge of intuition is mainly a spontaneous unconscious expression. As Paul Sills noted, "there is no technique. You just need a little respect for the invisible." Thus, the childlike playfulness, the free, flowing, unrestrained way of being which is necessary for theater games, including "excitement and enthusiasm [which] are a precondition to breakthrough,"[34] are the conditions of possibility for creativity to emerge. Carl Jung made a similar point when he wrote, "The creation of something new is not accomplished by the intellect but by the play instinct acting from inner necessity. The creative mind plays with the object it loves."

Creativity by definition requires a well-developed imagination. Indeed, improv requires the "unfreezing of the petrified imagination" as one commentator noted. Imagination centrally includes the use of unconscious non-verbal phantasy in the service of conceiving what is not yet known. In the world of improv, says Johnstone, "imagination is our true self."[35]

For Spolin, imagination is "creating one's own ideas of how things should be," though in the improv and theater context it requires not only individual creation, but more importantly, group creation. What makes the imagination for Spolin's theater games and exercises so central is that through the imagination one can overcome any restraining and inhibiting circumstances: "I could be bounded in a nutshell

---

32   Spolin, *Improvisation for the Theater*, p. 357.
33   We are grateful to Gary Schwartz for clarifying Spolin's definition of creation and for his critical reading of this chapter.
34   Spolin, *Theater Games for the Classroom*, p. 19.
35   Johnstone, *Impro*, p. 105.

and count myself King of the infinite space."[36] Joseph Murphy put the
matter just right: "the truth is you can acquire any quality you want
by acting as though you already have it." In other words, what Spolin
was trying to access was transformation through creative vision (as
opposed to rational intelligence, though of course this too plays a role
in creativity)—that is, activating "the mind at play, having nothing to
gain and nothing to lose," while inventively "playing around the limits
and resistances"[37] of the circumstances of the specific theater game.
Indeed, as Henry David Thoreau noted in another context, in the
world of improv, but also in ordinary life, "the world is but a canvas to
the imagination."

Spolin's notion of creativity/imagination in the improv context has
an important bearing on how the average person engages life at its
best. While the simple game was her main venue, the creativity developed via the unique context of improv has larger life-conduction
implications: "Creativity is an attitude, a way of looking at something,
a way of questioning, perhaps a way of life—it may well be found on
paths we have not yet traveled. Creativity is curiosity, joy, and communion. It is process-transformation-process."[38] In other words, creativity is not only a technical procedure of a sort with its own structure
and dynamics, but most generally, it is a way of being in the world that
can deeply enhance one's everyday life. Winnicott made a similar point
when he wrote, "It is creative apperception more than anything else
that makes the individual feel that life is worth living."[39] In order to
be able to make creative apperception one's way of being and doing in
the world, there are at least two underappreciated aspects of creativity
that we want to mention, aspects that are especially applicable to the
improv world and yet have bearing on other non-theater contexts.[40]

---

36   Hodgson and Richards, *Improvisation*, p. 58.

37   Stephen Nachmanovitch, *Free Play. Improvisation in Life and* Art (New
     York: Tarcher/Putnam, 1990), p. 87.

38   Spolin, *Improvisation for the Theater*, p. 264.

39   Winnicott, *Playing and Reality*, p. 65.

40   The nature of creativity is a huge and complex psychological subject and
     of course, this discussion in no way is meant to be comprehensive. A good
     psychoanalytic (i.e., self psychological) study of creativity and its related
     concepts is George Hagman's *Aesthetic Experience. Beauty, Creativity, and
     the Search for the Ideal* (New York: Rodopi, 2005).

Firstly, to embrace a creative way of being in the world requires the capacity to abandon inhibiting self-judgment, especially one of the greatest fears that most people have, the infantile fear of being in the wrong. Spolin discusses this resistance to creativity in terms of "approval/disapproval syndrome," of which success/failure is a subspecies. However, it was Albert Camus who pithily recognized the antidote to such self-consciousness and mind judging when he said, "All great deeds and all great thoughts have a ridiculous beginning." As psychoanalysis has taught us, to tolerate the ridiculous—that which is unreasonable and not at all sensible or acceptable—always requires the ability to tolerate (and ultimately creatively transform) conflict and tension, especially as it relates to one's sexual and aggressive wishes, as well as to overcome one's self-deficits and the like, all of which is a precondition of the creative apperception. Paradoxically, it also requires the ability to take seriously that which at first seems silly. Indeed, to accomplish all of this requires a robust sense of self, not egocentricity, which is probably one of the reasons most people are not creative in how they live their lives. Said Spolin, "games and story bring out self rather than ego." The self in Spolin's formulation "refers to the natural part of ourselves," the part of self-experience that is "free of crippling mores, prejudices, rote information, and static frames of reference," in other words, "that part of us capable of direct contact with the environment" and "that functions free of the need for approval/disapproval..."[41] In contrast, egocentricity is not simply being interested in the needs and wants of the self with no or very little interest in others; to be egocentric is to "fear no support from others or from the environment," it is a form of "mistaken self-protection."[42] The point is that playing helps find the self; in fact, the self needs to be found, or one might say created, before one can authentically play.

Secondly, to be creative in the Spolinesque sense requires a bountiful conscious and/or unconscious capacity to love the other, including the otherness of the world. Said Spolin, "Theater games do not inspire 'proper' moral behavior (good/bad), but rather seek to free each person to feel his or her own, out of which a felt, experienced, actual love

---

41   Spolin, *Improvisation for the Theater*, pp. 368-369.
42   Ibid., p. 358.

of neighbor will appear."[43] What is important to recognize here is that
to live creatively requires having the capacity to responsibly serve the
other, broadly described. The great Indian mystic, Osho, made this
point brilliantly when he wrote, "To be creative means to be in love
with life [i.e., the other]. You can be creative only if you love life enough
that you want to enhance its beauty, you want to bring a little more
music to it, a little more poetry to it, a little more dance to it." Put in
straightforward psychological terms, to be creative as described above,
is a generous effort at reparation of an obviously imperfect world (and
on the personal level, a way of putting things internally right by rees-
tablishing a "good object-world").[44] That is, it is an effort at restoring
the outside (and inside) world into good condition, what in Hebrew
wisdom is regarded as one of the hallmarks of one's humanity, engaging in acts of responsibility for the Other, of "tikkun olam"—repairing
the world.

DEVELOPING GREATER SENSORY, PHYSICAL AND EMOTIONAL EXPRESSIVENESS

In general, in our culture we are most tuned into people via the verbal
modality. That is, most of us get on in the world through spoken language and tend to underemphasize other communication modalities,
such as the non-verbal realm, what in acting theory is called sensory
and movement expressiveness. According to Spolin, the capacity to be
emotive, to express strong feelings in a truthful manner in sync with the
circumstances one is in, is rooted in one's ability to integrate the sensory and the physical with the emotional into a seamless organic whole.
An organic response says Spolin, is "a head-to-foot response where
mind (intellect), body, and intuition function as one unit," it is the region of the self where one is "functioning out of total humanness."[45] In

---

43   Ibid., p. xv.

44   As Rycroft defines it, in psychoanalytic theory, an object is "that towards
      which the" person "relates himself." Usually objects are "persons, parts of
      persons or symbols of one or the other." Thus, a "good object" is "an ob-
      ject whom the" person "loves, who is experienced" as kind. "A good object
      [like a 'bad object'] may be either internal or external." A "bad object" is one
      whom the person hates or fears, who is experienced as malicious (Rycroft,
      A Critical Dictionary of Psychoanalysis, p. 113).

45   Spolin, *Improvisation for the Theater*, p. 364.

Spolin's view, these modalities are always interconnected, interrelated and work together, though in many instances one is blocked, stuck, or in other ways out of sort, such that one of the three elements is not in sync with the others, which creates a kind of awkward imbalance. These are the moments when the audience (and sometimes the actor) feels the performance is unimpressive, worn, even lifeless.

The terms sensory (relating to the sensation and the sense organs), physical (relating to the body rather than the mind, soul or feelings) and emotion (a strong feeling about somebody or something), are concepts that have been studied by psychologists and others for hundreds of years. However, Spolin has defined and used these terms in a very straightforward and accessible way within the theater game context, but in ways that somewhat differ from the conventional psychological definitions given above. The sensory she defines as the "body and mind; to see, taste, hear, feel, think, perceive, to know through the physical as opposed to the intuitive," the "X-area," the region of revelation. The physical, or what she calls "physicalization" is "showing and not telling; a physical manifestation of a communication." It involves "using self to put an object in motion; giving life to the object." And finally, emotion she defines as "organic motion created by playing."[46]

Spolin's sensory games aim to demonstrate the importance of the sensory equipment and physical bodies as valuable tools in improv and in all types of acting. As Spolin noted, "In stage life…mashed potatoes are often served instead of ice cream…it is not convincing when actors merely behave as if the substitutes were real." Rather, it is through the use of one's physicality that the actor is able to convincingly "make visible for an audience what is not visible."[47] It is such a new kind of sensory awareness that is essential for the actor, and we believe, the ordinary person, to fully engage life. The primary problem is that most people are lodged mainly in the verbal realm, including in most forms of psychotherapy, and for the most part, they remain estranged from their senses. Thus, as Spolin points out, perhaps the main stumbling block to having greater sensory engagement with the world, to using the body as a tool, is that the average person is too self-involved with his or her own subjective world, leading to impairment in making con-

46   Ibid., pp. 369, 365, 359.
47   Spolin, *Theater Games for the Classroom*, p. 56.

tact with the environment and letting it unfold. In the theater game context, says Spolin, a player who is too self-preoccupied has difficulties in fully playing with others; in the "game of life," such a person is often "armored against contact with others" and "against ideas other than one's own." The point is that the further development of one's sensory and physical realms permits the direct experience of the world (i.e., "full-body perception" and "energy exchange"), greater relatedness to its otherness (not only to people but to animals and objects), and a feeling of self-enhancement.

A word about "physicalization" is warranted as it is a key concept for Spolin. Physicalization centrally involves the capacity to give "physical expression of an attitude," and "giving life to an object."[48] The idea here is that while most of us express our emotions mainly verbally, and live in the intellectual and psychological realms, it is the physicalization of the emotion that gives it an impressive intensity, depth and transformational quality. That is, physicalization in the improv context fosters greater engagement with the phenomenal world and the ability to personally experience it. This is the key carryover to one's everyday life. Said Spolin, "Physicalize that feeling! Physicalize that relationship! Physicalize that pinball machine, kite, fish, object, taste, etc.!"[49]

Physicalization gives the player "a personal concrete experience on which further development depends;" it fosters greater physical expressiveness, a vital capacity since it is the physical and sensory connection with improv that is the gateway to deeper insights (the role of the artist is "to give insight"). Such sensory/physical engagement with the world allows the actor, and ordinary person, to navigate his or her way to what is not yet known, to the intuitive. Physicalization, showing not telling, keeps the player in a developing "world of direct perception," an open self in relation to the external world, and it is from such a self/world relation that authentic emotion emanates.[50]

It should be clear that Spolin views emotion as rooted in the sensory and physical, as opposed to the actors' personal feelings and individual psychology (e.g., Lee Strasberg's "Method" acting). In improvisation as

---

48   Spolin, *Improvisation for the Theater*, p. 365.

49   Ibid.

50   Ibid., p. 16.

Spolin conceives it, "we are interested only in direct physical communication" ("a moment of mutual perceiving"). Spolin continues,

> When energy is absorbed in the physical object, there is no time for
> "feeling" any more than a quarterback running down the field can be
> concerned with his clothes or whether he is universally admired...
> insisting upon this objective (physical) relationship with the art
> form brings clearer sight and greater vitality to the student-actors.
> For the energy bound up in fear of exposure is freed (no longer
> secretive) as the student intuitively realizes that no one is peeping
> at his or her private life or cares where he or she buried the body.[51]

The impact of phsyicalization on the personal level, says Spolin, is that
it awakens the whole organism, it allows the actor to let the physical
expression take him or her where it will. In the improv context, where
there are very few or no props, costumes or set pieces, actors learn that
stage reality, and we would argue, real life, needs to have its mindfully
created "space, texture, depth and substance, that is, physical reality."
It is creating this rich reality out of nothing, or almost nothing, that
allows for "the actor to take the first step into the beyond," into what
is not yet known. These are the moments when theater reality feels
most summoning to the audience, and in ordinary life, when living
feels most joyful.[52] For what opens up are new energy exchanges, new
creations.

PRODUCING AND CO-PRODUCING NEW REALITIES

Perhaps the essence of improv is the ability to create new realities, to
actualize what is unthinkable and unimaginable, what is "not yet." In a
certain sense, all of us produce and co-produce new realities as we go
through our everyday lives, for most of what we say and do with others is not rehearsed, but is a function of responding in the moment to
what is happening. And yet, when we see great improv, we feel there
is something rather extraordinary going on, as if what is a normative
aspect of social interaction has morphed into something appealingly
otherwise, something new. In a word, great improv is fundamentally
great storytelling, or rather "storymaking."[53] It is the result of sponta-

---

51   Ibid., pp. 16-17.
52   Ibid., p. 17.
53   Wiener, *Rehearsals for Growth*, p. 89.

neous individual and group process—as Spolin noted, "a story is an epitaph; the ashes of the fire."[54]

It is mainly through stories that we live our lives, what in psychological parlance is called a narrative of self-identity. In other words, it is through "metaphoric redescriptions," as philosopher Mary Hesse noted, or what psychoanalyst Roy Schafer called "retellings" that new experiences and new insights can emerge, which is exactly for what improv aims. Richard Rorty, also a philosopher, has pointed out, a "new vocabulary makes it possible, for the first time, a formulation of its own purpose. It is a tool for doing something which could not have been envisaged prior to the development of a particular set of descriptions, those which it helps to provide."[55] It is via these "retellings," as in improv, that we are able to see the material in question from a different slant, in a "new" way which gives "reality" to, or puts into sharp focus what was previously not seen. This is precisely what Spolin meant when she wrote that the main goal of theater games and improv is transformation, that is creation, the emergence of a new reality.

As we have implied, to tell a great story in the improv context requires a number of creative skills. A good story, one that helps make an aspect of life more intelligible, meaningful and more pleasurable requires the ability to generate a "greater coherence in its structure, a greater universality in its message, and greater artistry in its performance."[56] To accomplish all of this, Spolin notes, requires the capacity to deal spontaneously with what is unforseen and new; in fact, this is one of the main reasons improv is so compelling to watch—we are curious to see if the player will succeed or fail in his boldness and fearlessness as he engages his fellow players and the emerging, often challenging, situation. The parallel to ordinary life is obvious—we are all thrown into situations and circumstances that require us to spontaneously manage, hopefully inventively, while at the same time generate a symbolic structure, that is a story, that makes better sense of what we are experiencing. As the Baal Shem Tov said, "Telling proper stories is as if you were approaching the throne of Heaven in a fiery chariot."

54   Spolin, *Improvisation for the Theater*, p. 371. We have generously drawn from Wiener in my discussion in this section.

55   Richard Rorty, *Contingency, Irony, and Solidarity* (New York: Cambridge University Press, 1989), p. 13.

56   Wiener, *Rehearsasl for Growth*, p. 90.

Perhaps the most important aspect of telling a good story in the improv context was captured by Johnstone when he wrote, "If you improvise spontaneously in front of an audience you have to accept that your innermost self will be revealed." Moreover, in order to enter domains that "would normally be 'forbidden,'" such "spontaneity means abandoning some of your defenses," not an easy thing to do by any means.[57] Indeed, continues Johnstone, when a player says that he or she "can't think up a story" it is not because of a lack of talent but rather a decision not to put oneself out there.[58] Johnstone describes the many types of defenses that players use to avoid spontaneous self-creation and self-revelation, especially in the group context, defenses that have their counterparts in real life. For example, there is "blocking," that which inhibits or stops action from progressing or that eradicates your partner's premise or offering; "sidetracking," offering up a side-plot instead of going with the main theme of the story; "being original," which acts as a diversion or interruption from the main mood or energy of the story; "gagging," which uses gags or jokes to change "the context away from the adventure within the story toward amusement at it."[59]

The upshot of all of this is an obvious, simple, but underappreciated truth: To be able to tell a great story in the improv context requires a feeling of emotional and spiritual closeness to one's fellow players, to the audience and toward oneself (e.g., openness to one's otherness). Indeed Spolin made this point when she wrote, "that improvisation is not exchange of information between players; it is communion."[60] That is, "Individual freedom (expressing self) while respecting community responsibility (group agreement) is our goal."[61] The implications of these insights derived from the world of improv have their obvious correlations for ordinary life, namely, in order to produce and co-produce new realities, realities that are spontaneously creative and enhancing, requires that one obtain a high degree of "openness to contact with the environment and each other and willingness to play."[62]

57 Johnstone, *Impro*, p. 111.
58 Ibid., p. 116.
59 We have drawn from Wiener's summary of Johnston's twelve ways that improvisers inhibit, if not prevent, narratives from evolving (pp. 92-93).
60 Spolin, *Improvisation for the Theater*, p. 45.
61 Ibid., p. 44.
62 Ibid., p. 25.

To achieve this kind of openness to the otherness of one's players, the audience, the material, and oneself, requires a diminution of one's narcissism, one's need for self-aggrandizement and the like. As Spolin noted, to fill a pail full of apples requires an empty pail, a kind of "unselving or transelving," a jettison of the selfish ego. It is only then, when one has generated a less self-centric subjectivity, that one is properly receptive to the other broadly described. Moreover, this inner state is a kind of waiting, an openness and accessibility that is different than ordinary waiting for something to happen: "the improviser is in waiting, not waiting for," says Spolin. As with the Queen of England who has "ladies in waiting," whose function is to attend to the Queen's needs as they arise, so the improviser must attend to the other, in service.

CONCLUSION

Our main claim in this chapter is that Spolin's brilliant theater games and general approach to improv have something very important to teach the average person about the art of living the "good life." As Arthur Morey noted in his introduction to one of Spolin's books, "These games...go beyond the theatrical to nurture skills and attitudes that are useful in every aspect of learning and life."[63] For example, embedded in Spolin's improv are important valuative attachments that we have discussed: improv gives great importance to developing interpersonal trust, spontaneity, creativity, sensory, physical and emotional expressiveness, and story making. However, if there was one valuative attachment that most underlies Spolin's improv and that people need to be reminded of, it would be deepening and expanding the capacity to play, to have fun. The notion of fun is almost never taken seriously in scholarly discourse, including in psychological discourse, though it is mentioned in passing in the literature on "play." Fun, as we are using the notion, is more than simply having a feeling of enjoyment or amusement. In addition, at its best, it refers to a way of being in the world in which one uses one's ingenuity and inventiveness in the service of life-affirmation. That is, the whole person is awakened and attentive to the problem of living—mind, body, intelligence and creativity, spontaneity and intuition are all utterly responsive to the moment, and we think, to the other and the otherness of life. Moreover, such a

---

63   Spolin, *Theater Games for the Classroom*, p. 1.

way of embracing life without reserve tends to enhance one's capacity to appreciate the sad ironies of life that are funny. What Spolin gave to us are not only practical tools to develop such a funny or playful way of being, but she also gave us the "permission" to treat fun and play not as footnotes to one's adult existence, but as some of its main resources to live the "good life." As Dr. Seuss noted, "If you never did you should. These things are fun and fun is good....Today was good. Today was fun. Tomorrow is another one."

CHAPTER SIX

REAL LIVING IS
POLITICAL

BERTOLT BRECHT

"Art is not a mirror held up to reality, but a hammer with which to
shape it."

—Bertold Brecht

ERTOLT BRECHT (1898–1956), GERMAN PLAYWRIGHT,
STAGE DIRECTOR AND POET, was one of the most important theater practitioners in the twentieth century.
Heavily influenced by Marxist theory, Brecht's approach
to acting and theater in general was an alternative to the
"stifling realism" connected to Stanislavski and the "fake pomposity"
associated with the classical English theater.[1] In contrast to these traditions, Brecht advocated a theater that emphasized political ideas,
often with a strong ideological focus, presented in a manner that
was meant to "disrupt" the audience from its passivity and complacency. His "parable plays," the "epic masterpieces," as Hugh Rorrison
called them, were meant to be just that, like *Mother Courage and her*

---

1   Richard Brestoff, *The Great Acting Teachers and Their Methods* (Lyme,
    NH: Smith and Kraus, 1995), p. 147. As we shall suggest throughout this
    chapter, Brecht was against Stanislavski's "transfigured actors, the emo-
    tionally windswept audience, the too, too solid settings, the rigid formal
    framework of the plot" of a play [John Willet, *The Theatre of Bertolt Brecht*
    (London: Methuen Drama, 1977), p. 207].

Children (1941), a play that shows the horror of war written in reaction to the Nazi invasion of Poland, *Life of Galileo* (1943), a critical evaluation of the role of science and scientists in society, including the clash between dogmatism and scientific proof and *The Good Person of Szechwan* (1943), which focuses on the nature of goodness, especially "the conflict between business efficiency and private morality." In all of these plays, says Rorrison, the political take-home points that are potentially liberating to the actors and audience are indirectly expressed and the communist assumptions are lodged deep within the structure of the play.[2] As Brecht said, "To live means to finesse the processes to which one is subjugated."

There is much in Brecht's conception of acting training and stage directing that has bearing on the non-actor and actor when it comes to the art of living the "good life." In fact, as Brecht wrote in *Life of Galileo*, "Don't be afraid of death so much as an inadequate life." In order to explore some of Brecht's ideas about acting training and performance, mainly as a vehicle for the dissemination of communist-inspired political ideas—the making of a "critical aesthetics of dialectical materialism" as it has been called[3]—we will discuss some of his most innovative artistic ideas that have relevance to the non-actor's and actor's quest for the "good life," namely dialectics, "epic theater," *verfremdung* ("defamiliarization") and "gestus" (gesture).[4]

---

2   Hugh Rorrison, "Brecht, Bertolt," in Martin Banham (Ed.), *The Cambridge Guide to the Theatre* (Cambridge, UK: Cambridge University Press, 1995), p. 129. For Brecht the appeal of communism was not only that it was a rational force against Nazism but "that it seemed identifiable with scientific skepticism, with the interests of the dispossessed, with the ways of thought (and art) proper to a highly industrial age" (Willet, *The Theatre of Bertolt Brecht*, p. 215).

3   http://www.absoluteastronomy.com/topics/Bertold_ Brechts#encyclopedia, p. 1.

4   We have used Peter Brooker's choice of "key words" in Brecht's work to, in part, organize this chapter. See "Key words in Brecht's theory and practice of theatre," in Peter Thomson and Glendyr Sacks (Eds.), *The Cambridge Companion to Brecht* (Cambridge, UK: 2006), pp. 209-224. Brecht's ideas about acting and performance changed over his lifetime, thus this chapter only deals with some of his key ideas which were important at a particular time in Brecht's life and have relevance to the focus of this chapter.

DIALECTIC MATERIALISM

As Peter Brooker pointed out, Brecht's version of Marxism was mainly based on his reading of Marx, Lenin and Mao Tse-tung. His teacher
was Karl Korsch (prior to Korsch it was briefly Fritz Sternberg), a
dissident communist who he chose as his teacher because Korsch was
not afraid to defy party lines. For Korsch, the main thrust of Marxist
theorizing was what he described as "the principle of historical speci-
fication" which maintains it is necessary "to comprehend all things in
social terms of a definite historical epoch." In other words, social experience is to be understood in its unique socio-economic context, not in
terms of so-called universal abstract principles. As Brooker explains,
in Brecht's "'interventionist' art" he wanted to present theater in ways
that were in sync with the ideas of dialectical materialism, the Marxian
concept of reality in which all things are material and are in the con-
stant process of change brought about by the tension between con-
flicting or interacting forces, elements, or ideas, "the struggle of opposites." What Brecht wanted to do, says Brooker, was "to historicize and
negate the commonplace and taken-for-granted, to prise open social
and ideological contradictions, and so both demonstrate and provoke
an awareness of the individual's place in a concrete social narrative."[5]
As we shall see, Brecht used a number of theatrical strategies and tactics to accomplish his aim of shaking an audience out of their slumber.
That is, of changing their conventional and normalized ways of thinking, feeling and acting in the real world to help bring about a more just
and compassionate society.[6] It is this goal, to win the audience's minds
and hearts in order to change them, that in part, constituted Brecht's
notion of "epic theater."

---

5   Ibid., p. 210.

6   Brecht respected the idea that living the virtuous life, like being kind to
     another person, was of value, but he did not believe that such individual
     behavior was enough to bring about the sweeping social, economic and po-
     litical transformations he wanted. In addition, and mainly, the mechanism
     of change to bring about social transformation and social justice was to dis-
     cern, analyze and deconstruct the underlying socio-economic and political
     conditions that made possible exploitation of the underclasses.

EPIC THEATER

"Epic theater," also called "dialectical theater," was in part a reaction
against the "ranting and pretentious" German and Austrian classical
stage.[7] It was also a reaction against Stanislavski's realism, the view
that the goal of great acting and theater was to reproduce everyday
real life for the audience, to present lifelike representation of people
and the world, without idealization. Moreover, the aim was to get the
audience to so empathize and emotionally identify with the realistic
presentation of reality, with the fictions and illusions they saw, at least
at the time they were watching a play, so that they believed they were
in fact real (i.e., a suspension of disbelief). The effect on the audience
by the end of a play was that they felt emotionally moved, amused and
in other ways satisfied, but indifferent to the social evils, the injustices
that pervaded their world.[8] Epic theater was meant to counteract all of
this, to develop a non-Aristotelian theater experience for the audience,
one that did not emphasize the catharsis of emotion as the main goal.
Epic theory, says Roswitha Mueller,

> aims at the unity of theory and practice in an attempt to change the
> spectators' attitude from a passive to a productive one. The criti-
> cal ability of the audience is sharpened to recognize the contradic-
> tions in bourgeois society and to hold their own experience up to

---

7 Brecht, *The Theatre of Bertolt Brecht*, p. 165. Willett defines "epic," as
Brecht used the term, as follows: "a sequence of incidents or events narrated
without artificial restrictions as to time, place or relevance to a formal 'plot'"
(Willett, *The Theatre of Bertolt Brecht*, p. 169).

8 Brestoff, *The Great Acting Teachers and Their Methods*, p. 148. Brecht
was not against stylization per se in the realistic theater: "Of course the
stage of a realistic theatre must be peopled by live, three dimensional self-
contradictory characters, with all their passions, unconsidered utterances
and actions. The stage is not a hothouse or a zoological museum full of
stuffed animals..." (Willet, *The Theatre of Bertolt Brecht*, p. 216). However,
according to Margaret Eddershaw, the most important difference between
Brecht and Stanislavski on acting theory was that "Brecht wanted his actors to 'distance' themselves from their roles; instead of embodying characters, they were to demonstrate them. A result of this is the reduction
of the actor's emotional involvement in the part and consequently of the
audience's empathy" [Margaret Eddershaw, "Acting Methods: Brecht and
Stanislavski." In Graham Bartram and Anthony Waine (Eds.), *Brecht in
Perspective* (Essex, UK: Longman Group Limited, 1982), p. 136].

comparison with the way these contradictions are presented. Thus norms of behavior and action and the resulting social relations are not taken for granted but are understood in their historicity.[9]

Brecht accomplished this detached critical attitude in the audience by using a number of devices or "tricks" (though not emotional tricks), as Jerzy Grotowski would disparagingly call them—devices meant to remind the audience that the play they were viewing was a fabricated image, a symbolic expression of a slice of life, in other words, a representation of reality but not actually reality. Drawing in part from the innovative techniques of Russian director, actor and producer Vsevolod Meyerhold, Brecht used such devices as "the direct address by actors to the audience, transposition of text to third person or past tense ["the text was always his primary concern in the theater"[10]], speaking the stage direction out loud, exaggerated, unnatural stage lighting, the use of song, and explanatory placards," all were meant to emphasize the socially "constructed nature" of the theatrical experience (that is, it was "made up").[11] By helping the audience to grasp that the play they were seeing, the "reality" of the stage performance, was in fact a social construction, the audience could then extrapolate that their personal and social reality was also constructed and therefore modifiable.[12] Brecht called such devices *Verfremdungseffekt* (the V-effect), translated as "defamilarization," "estrangment effect," or Brecht's actual term, "alienation effect." Their purpose was to "disrupt," destabilize and deconstruct the audience's sense of its taken-for-granted everyday reality so that they

9   Roswithat Mueller, "Learning for a new society: The Lebrstuck," in Thomson and Sacks, *The Cambridge Companion to Brecht*, pp. 107-108.

10   Willet, *The Theatre of Bertolt Brecht*, p. 214

11   While theater "reality" is socially constructed, so is so-called "reality" outside the theater. That is, it is impossible to get a non-mediated, objective "God's eye" view of "reality," "reality" is always perceived from a particular interpretative frame of reference that animates what one "sees." As Peter L. Berger and Thomas Luckman have brilliantly demonstrated in their landmark book, *The Social Construction of Reality. A Treatise in the Sociology of Knowledge*, all of social reality is socially constructed. In a certain sense, theater "reality" is not any less "real" than "reality" outside the theater—both are improvised interpretations. Put differently, a play is a play within the play of life.

12   http://www.absoluteastronomu.com/topics/Bertold_ Brecht#encyclopedia, p. 9.

could embrace a more critical, rational and socially responsible (i.e, communist and socialist versions of what is socially responsible) attitude toward the injustices of the world. As Brestoff succinctly notes, in terms of the theater experience, "this really means that a common event or moment is performed in such a way that it can be seen with fresh eyes." The key dilemma for Brecht was what can an actor do that would both defamiliarize and distance the audience and yet still maintain their interest, especially their interest to bring about decisive political and social transformations?[13] The critic Herbert Ihering hints at the solution to the actor's dilemma when he wrote in 1926 that Brecht "did not analyze the characters; he set them at a distance....He called for a report on the events. He insisted on simple gestures. He compelled a clear and cool manner of speaking. No emotional tricks were allowed. That ensured the objective, 'epic' style." The goal of such an approach was that the critical, judgmental and objective audience viewed the actor with the same alert attention as when evaluating "a sporting event," a "boxing ring attitude of 'smoking and observing.'"[14]

VERFREMDUNGSEFFEKT

As Brecht wrote, "The main business of the theatre," is "the exposition of the story and its communication by suitable means of alienation," a view that aptly states the relationship of epic theater to the V-effect. As Brooker further notes, "the task of the V-effect…is to reveal a suppressed or unconsidered alternative; to show the possibilities for change implicit in difference and contradiction."[15] In Brecht's own words, "Alienating an event or character means first of all stripping the event of its self-evident, familiar, obvious quality and creating a sense of astonishment and curiosity about them."[16] These various "making strange" devices mentioned earlier were developed with the V-effect in mind. What is dialectical about this V-effect conception is that by showing the contradictions, ambiguities and ambivalences connected

13   Brestoff, *The Great Acting Teachers and Their Methods*, p. 149.

14   Willet, *The Theatre of Bertolt Brecht*, pp. 144, 172.

15   Brooker, "Key words in Brecht's theory and practice of theatre," pp. 215, 218.

16   Ibid., p. 215. As Willet point out, this goal of defamliarization was exactly what Shelley had in mind when writing his poetry, "makes similar objects to be if they were not familiar" (Willet, *The Theatre of Brecht*, p. 177).

to a particular taken-for-granted reality, one is able to see other options, different ways to think, feel and act. Wrote Brecht, "What is obvious [i.e., taken for granted reality or accepted truth] is in a certain sense made incomprehensible, but this is only in order that it may then be made all the easier to comprehend."[17] In other words, through embracing a critical and historicizing outlook in and out of the theater, a person is able to discern the reasons for him taking social reality for granted, the basis for his passivity, complacency and emotional blunting as it relates to what Brecht called, "the great social task of mastering life,"[18] that is, socially responsible behavior that is meant to help radically transform the world, make it more just and compassionate.

What epic theater and the V-effects have to do with the real life of the non-actor as well as the actor is best captured by Michel Foucault's notion of "problematization," a necessary internal capacity, an attitude to develop in order to live the "good life." According to Foucault, problematization indicates "the ensemble of discursive and nondiscursive practices that makes something enter into the play of the true and the false and constitutes it an object of thought" [whether manifested, for example, in artistic standards, moral deliberation, political analysis or scientific knowledge].[19] Problematization is concerned with critically putting into sharp focus the "truth games" that permeate our experience of ourselves and the world. For example, "What truth game is the person playing who regards himself" as an actor or artist, or "as insane or sick?" Or "as a living, speaking, working being?" Or "as a criminal or the subject of sexual desire?"[20] The point is to grasp how one's identity is unconsciously shaped and how one's sense of taken-for-granted reality is played out in the real world, often to our and another's detriment. In a sense this is exactly what Brecht was trying to do in his conception of theater and performance, to create "a jarring element," to

17 Ibid., p. 216.
18 Ibid., p. 217.
19 Thomas Flynn, "Foucault's mapping of history." In Gary Gutting (Ed.), *The Cambridge Companion to Foucault* (Cambridge: Cambridge University Press, 1994), p. 37.
20 Ibid., p. 37.

"glimpse" social reality "in all its strangeness and incomprehensibility" so as to change it for the better.[21]

What Foucault, Brecht and, we would add, Freud were advocating was the need for individuals to understand the way in which they are fashioned into the sorts of individuals they are within the context of a normalizing, depersonalizing and oppressive society. What are those limiting conditions that subjectify individuals (make them who they are, "produce" their self-identity) such that their autonomy and freedom to invent themselves are undermined? In this view, freedom is not only an end of domination but a revolt, a form of resistance within its practices. As Foucaultian scholar John Rajchman wrote (sounding very similar to Brecht), for Foucault freedom is the capacity to "identify and change those procedures or forms of thought which our stories become true, because we can question and modify those systems which make only particular kinds of action possible."[22] That is, the awareness of freedom entails the dissolution or changing of those anonymous, depersonalizing, conformist practices that constitute our conception of ourselves that we take to be self-evident and "true" within the context of our imperfect and oppressive society. To accomplish such a consciousness of freedom requires internalizing a problematizing attitude toward oneself and others, to engage in what Foucault called the "practice of criticism."

For Foucault, Brecht and Freud, the goal of their respective disciplines was to apply critical thought to particular areas of modern experience in order to create an experience of what Foucault called their "intolerability." In other words, Foucault, like Brecht, hoped to fashion the space necessary for people to "think differently" about that which they viewed as self evident, "true" and "good"—but was, in his view, intolerable in terms of what he took to be our present danger, i.e., the normalizing, depersonalizing "disciplinary" society. This required that Foucault's readers feel radically disrupted, a transient "paralysis," as he called it. By inducing a temporary paralysis Foucault tried to "shake" the reader from his un-self-critical participation in taken-for-granted reality, "business as usual" practices that can have negative effects on

21   John Willet (Ed.), *Brecht on Theatre. The Development of an Aesthetic* (New York: Hill and Wang, 1996), pp. 28, 27.
22   John Rajchman, *Michel Foucault: The Freedom of Philosophy* (New York: Columbia University Press, 1985), p. 122.

others. Foucault, Brecht and Freud wanted to generate the possibility for experiencing that which is dangerous and intolerable about our discourses, practices and institutions. All three debunking thinkers tried to foster our thinking in a different way, and thus discover how we may be free to act differently, more justly, humanely, and true to ourselves. Like Foucault and Brecht, Freud in his development of psychoanalysis aimed at helping people recognize and change those personal limiting elements that constitute the taken-for-granted sense of ourselves, elements that truncate our personal freedom to be and do otherwise. Thus, all three of these great thinkers advocated what we believe is essential to live the "good life," what Foucault called a "permanent critique of ourselves" (which includes a permanent critique of our socio-economic reality). A permanent critique of ourselves refers to critical and analytic modes of self-reflection about the limits that make us the people we are. Such a relationship to oneself opposes the conformist aims of normalizing, depersonalizing disciplinary power and implies and promotes greater autonomy and individuality. It is this kind of investigative thinking, a continuous self-questioning that interrogates back into its own origins and historical conditions of emergence, which is crucial to make ourselves and the world better, to live the "good life."

GESTUS

Gestus is the key concept of Brecht's acting and performance theory, though he never clearly defined it:

> "Gest" is not supposed to mean gesticulation; it is not a matter of explanatory or emphatic movements of the hands, but of overall attitudes. A language is gestic when it is grounded in a gest and conveys particular attitudes adopted by the speaker towards other men. … Not all gests are social gests. The attitude of chasing away a fly is not yet a social gest, though the attitude of chasing a dog may be one, for instance if it comes to represent a badly dressed man's continual battle against watchdogs. One's efforts to keep one's balance on a slippery surface results in a social gest as soon as falling down would mean 'losing face'; in other words, losing one's market value.[23]

---

23 Willett, *Brecht on Theatre. The Development of an Aesthetic*, p. 104. Willett defines gestus as "at once gesture and gist, attitude and point" (Willet, *The Theatre of Bertolt Brecht*, p. 173).

Gestus, in other words, is not as Stanislavaki would have it, supposed to simply depict the character's internal life, but to add commentary on the social circumstances in which the character is situated
(Stanislavski regarded such commentary as appalling acting). As Meg
Mumford wrote, gestus is "the aesthetic gestural presentation of the
economic and socio-ideological construction of human identity and
interaction"....that which "finds ultimate expression in the corporeal
and intellectual work of the performer."[24] Brestoff gives a famous example of gestus from *Mother Courage and Her Children*, one of the
greatest anti-war plays of all time that takes up the theme of the horror of war and the notion that goodness is often not rewarded when
dishonesty and immorality are the rule of the day. The quoted passage
from Brestoff is clear and illuminating of the meaning and implemen-
tation of gestus by the masterful actress.

By way of context, says Brestoff, the character, the role of *Mother
Courage* is both as a sympathetic, feeling individual human being, and
a personification of the avarice of the capitalist class (showing the economic foundation of her role was crucial). The actress must portray
both of these sides of the character to the audience. The actress Helen
Weigel, Brecht's second wife, created an especially striking and eye-
catching gest with which to enact this. On one hand, *Mother Courage*
cannot be viewed as obviously responding to the killing, the shooting
of her son by soldiers because this would prevent her from conducting
her ongoing profit-making business. On the other hand, she cannot
be viewed as so heartless and uncaring as not to respond at all to her
son's death, after all, she is a feeling human being. This is the actress's
crucial performance dilemma—how to find a creative solution to the
emotional and practical conflict. Brestoff continues his description of
Mother Courage:

> In one astonishing moment, when the soldiers are looking away,
> Wiegel looks out at the audience, grabs her skirt, throws her mouth
> as far open as she can, and screams. Only she screams without
> sound. Her face is contorted with all the energy of shock and grief,
> but no sound comes from her throat. After a moment she composes
> her face, and collapses into herself. She has not given herself away;

24   Peter Thomson, "Brecht and actor training. On whose behalf do we
      act?" In Alison Hodge, (ed.), *Twentieth Century Actor Training* (New York:
      Routledge, 2006), p. 109.

she can go on. In one moment the audience sees *Mother Courage's* inner torment and her ability to disguise it from those who might threaten her pursuit of the Almighty Dollar. The moment is made even deeper because the audience begins to see that *Mother Courage* does not possess the ability to learn. Thus, a personal and social revelation are distilled into a silent scream.[25]

The pragmatic importance of the gestus to the actress is considerable, for the "right" gestus inspired the audience to not only appreciate the actress's inner world, but more importantly, through watching the actress's behavior the spectator was able to see the connection between what the actress was doing and the spectator's own life and struggles. Gestus, said an actor who worked with Brecht, was to be based on the social location, status, and history of the character one was playing, with particular focus on the many contradictions to be found and exposed in the actions and verbal script.[26] Brecht even once had Peter Lorre speak in a "broken and disjointed" way so as to express the character's contradictions.[27] The overriding purpose of gestus was to bring the scene as close to reality as was possible: "This may sound quite abstract, but it was achieved during rehearsal in a most practical, even playful manner."[28]

While Brecht's notion of gestus is specific to the theatrical context, it does bring to light an issue that is often taken for granted in human interaction, namely that the "trick" to compellingly relating to others, in part, depends on what is emphasized during the interaction. As F. Scott Fitzgerald wrote in the *Great Gatsby*, "Personality

25   Brestoff, *The Great Acting Teachers and Their Methods*, p. 151.

26   In contrast to Stanislavski who believed that the actor should aim for a constancy and evenness in the role he played, that all his actions should be an integrated whole, Brecht emphasized the inconstancy and disparities in character portrayal. Said Brecht, overstating his point, "The continuity of the ego is a myth. A man is an atom that perpetually breaks up and forms anew" (Willet, *Brecht on Theatre, The Development of an Aesthetic*, p. 15). What Brecht is overstating is the fact that an individual needs and has a degree of continuity of his self-experience, otherwise he would be utterly dysfunctional if not psychotic.

27   Margaret Eddershaw, "Actors on Brecht." In Thomson and Sacks, *The Cambridge Companion To Brecht*, p. 282.

28   Thomson, "Brecht and actor training. On whose behalf do we act?", pp. 110, 111.

is an unbroken series of successful gestures." Carlos Castenada, the Peruvian-born American writer, said in his book *The Power of Silence*, "The spirit listens only when the speaker speaks in gestures. And gestures do not mean [only] signs or body movements, but acts of true abandon, acts of largesse, of humor." In other words, gestures that emanate from one's heart, that are spontaneous in origin but skillfully expressed in their outward form are an underappreciated way of making meaningful contact and bonding with others. Connectivity, gracefully expressed in natural gestures like a child uses before he is taught how to "properly" act by his parent, is a key aspect of the foundation for living the "good life." Such a way of being and acting is in a sense a lovely emotional "gift" to others, a sign of dignity and love, though not necessarily an obvious one that people can easily understand, assimilate and appreciate. As William Faulkner wrote, "Every man has a different idea of what's beautiful, and it's best to take the gesture, the shadow of the branch, and let the mind create the tree." Thus, finding the right gesture at the right time in the right context requires the good capacity for accurate empathy, a high degree of emotional intelligence, imagination and perhaps most of all, behavioral effectiveness. As Thompson noted, "the measure of Brecht's truth is efficacy: what may be thought or half-thought expressed through what is done."[29]

The significance of gestus for the non-actor is best understood when we briefly consider Brecht's view of emotions, a view that is rather different from how most acting teachers conceptualize emotion in acting and performance. For Brecht, the apt emotion, or cluster of emotions, were mainly developed within the context of rehearsals which had three phases: (1) the actor becomes familiar with his character, how he generally views the world; (2) the actor looks for the contradictions, ambiguities and ambivalences in the role, an empathic immersion, which encourages an affinity with the character; (3) the actor attempts to discern the character from the external point of view, that is, from the perspective of society and social values, especially social injustices involving the less powerful and vulnerable people in society.[30] For Brecht, the expression of the apt emotion was deeply embedded in

---

29   Thompson, "Brecht and actor training. On whose behalf do we act?", p. 102.

30   Ibid., p. 106.

the skillfully chosen gestus such as the example from *Mother Courage* described above. Brecht was against what he described as "the fusion of theatrical elements into one emotional system" meant to suffocate "any genuine interest in understanding the world." Hence, Brecht advocated a non-naturalistic form of realism,[31] perhaps better described as a form of "social realism" (the use of realistic portrayals of life to make social or political points, this is not "socialist realism," which Brecht rejected).[32] While Brecht acknowledged that reason and emotion cannot in theory be completely separated, he did tend to favor an intellectual, rationalizing approach to theater performance, one that would mainly show the social as opposed to the psychological significance of a scene. Brecht had a strong dislike of such Strasbergian techniques that encouraged the actor to plunge into his own psychology to generate the apt emotion of a character (he actually used the word "abhor" in his autobiography). Said Brecht, "the essential point of the epic theatre is perhaps that it appeals less to the feelings than to the spectator's reason."[33] Elsewhere in an interview he makes the point more strongly, if not abrasively: "I don't let my feelings intrude in my dramatic world. It'd give a false view of the world. I aim at an extremely classical, cold, high intellectual style of performance. I'm not writing for the scum who want to have the cockles of their hearts warmed."[34] For Brecht, emotions are less acted as Strasberg would have it, rather they are offered and expressed as types of specific behaviors in particular circumstances (perhaps somewhat similar to Meisner's views).

---

31   John Willet, *Brecht in Context* (London: Methuen, 1984), p. 32. Brecht clarifies what he means by realism, "it needs to be broad and political, free from aesthetic restrictions and independent of convention. Realist means: laying bare society's causal network / showing up the dominant viewpoint as the viewpoint of the dominators / writing from the standpoint of the class which has prepared the broadest solutions for the most pressing problems affecting human society / emphasizing the dynamics of development / concrete and so as to encourage abstraction" (Willett, *Brecht on Theatre*, p. 109). Needless to say, such a view that emphasizes social truth is very different from Stanislavski's psychological realism that stresses internal truth.

32   Willet, drawing from W.H. Auden's definition of social realism, agrees that social realism could be applied to Brecht (Willet, *Brecht on Theatre*, p. 217).

33   Willett, *Brecht on Theatre. The Development of an Aesthetic*, p. 23.

34   Ibid., p. 14.

Brecht did somewhat clarify the role of emotions for the actor and in his theater performances, writing, for instance, that "it is a frequently recurring mistake to suppose that this—epic—kind of production simply does without all emotional effects; actually, emotions are only clarified in it, steering clear of subconscious origins and carrying nobody away." In contrast to Stanislavski, Brecht believes that when it comes to acting it is the conscious level that matters most.[35] Brecht also had a very different view of the role of impulse in acting technique, especially when compared to its central role in the work of Meisner, Grotowski and other world-class acting teachers. Says Brecht, "People's opinions interest me far more than their feelings. Feelings are usually the product of opinions. They follow on. But opinions are decisive....Every act comes from a realization. There's really no such thing as acting on impulse. There again the intellect is lurking in the background."[36] In other words, for Brecht, "if a feeling is to be an effective one, it must be acquired not merely impulsively but through the understanding." Thus, again we see that Brecht was mainly interested in "transforming humanity," to change "the spectator's consciousness,""to teach certain forms of political struggle" and to deal with themes that have "a socially practical significance." The best way to do this was to modify how the audience thought, for in Brecht's view, reason—the ability to think logically and use rational faculties—was a superior human capacity to emotion.[37] While unraveling the relationship between reason and emotion is beyond the scope of this chapter, Brecht never adequately systematically or critically considered his use of these philosophically and psychologically complex and ambiguous terms. This being said, in our view, Brecht was overstating his case about the superiority of so-called reason and the intellect; that is, human beings are driven as much, if not more, by what they feel compared to what they think, certainly when it comes to ultimate issues like love, work, faith and war. Moreover, as Freud has shown, much of what really matters in our personal and social lives is unconscious and unconsciously driven. Brecht, being a certain kind of Marxist in outlook, did not give enough attention to Freud's findings when it came

35   Ibid., pp. 88, 95.
36   Ibid., p. 16.
37   Ibid., pp. 247, 228, 62.

to understanding the relationship between reason and emotion. As Freud showed, reason and emotion co-produce each other; they also potentiate each other, meaning there is no important thought that is not consciously and/or unconsciously animated by strong feeling and there is no strongly felt feeling that doesn't have its associated strongly held conscious and/or unconscious thoughts. Reason and emotion are inextricably dialectically related. How people behave in specific circumstances, the main thrust of Brecht's plays and performance theory, are largely motivated by how this dialectic plays out in real-life.

SOME ASPECTS OF BRECHT'S NOTION OF ACTING TRAINING

In order to best grasp what Brecht was trying to accomplish in his acting training and performances it is useful to compare "dramatic theater" and "epic theater" in Brecht's own words. Brecht provided his readership with a neat little table that clarifies what we earlier said about epic theater, and further indicates what he was trying to change in traditional theater, that is, what he emphasized compared to what was stressed in dramatic theater (the "shift of accent"). The table describes dramatic theater followed by epic theater:

1. plot v. narrative

2. implicates the spectator in a stage situation v. turns the spectator into an observer, but

3. wears down his capacity for action v. arouses his capacity for action

4. provides him with sensations v. forces him to make decisions

5. experience v. picture of the world

6. the spectator is involved in something v. he is made to face something

7. suggestion v. argument

8. instinctive feelings are preserved v. brought to the point of recognition

9. the spectator is in the thick of it, shares the experience v. the spectator stands outside studies

10. the human being is taken for granted v. the human being is the object of the inquiry

11. he is unalterable v. he is alterable and able to alter

12. eyes on the finish v. eyes on the course

13. one scene makes another v. each scene for itself

14. growth v. montage [assembling, overlaying and overlapping many different sources of artistic mediums meant to give the audience critical distance]

15. linear development v. jumps

16. man as a fixed point v. man as a process

17. thought determines being v. social being determines thought

18. feeling v. reason[38]

In light of the above comparative list, Brecht had certain thematics—points of emphasis and focus—that in part emanated from the claims he made about epic theater, claims that informed and shaped his views of acting training. For example, as Thompson pointed out,[39] Brecht required that his actors be educationally worldly, especially in their understanding of history and in particular, the genealogy of certain taken-for-granted concepts in modern social life. In other words, Brechtian actors are politically informed people. This emphasis on the actor as politically engaged was a unique expectation of the aspiring actor and artiste at the time Brecht developed his notion of epic theater.

Brecht, says Thompson, took particular interest in knowing what his actors' first impressions of a play and part were, as he knew that once rehearsal began, some of the sense of astonishment would fade.

---

38   Ibid., p. 37. As Brecht writes, "The emotions always have a quite definite class basis; the form they take at any time is historical restricted and limited in specific ways. The emotions are in no sense universally human and timeless" (Ibid., p. 145). In other words, for Brecht, like thoughts, emotions and how they are expressed are socially constructed, a view that is to some extent disputed by social psychologists and others.

39   We have liberally relied on Thompson's excellent work in summarizing much of Brecht's view of acting training, pp. 102-112 ("Brecht on acting training. On whose behalf do we act?").

Likewise, Brecht was not doctrinaire in how he thought something on the stage should be acted. He recognized that there were many creative ways to portray a character and act in a situation. However, Brecht's focus as a playwright and as an acting teacher was always on how to "disrupt" the audience and the actor so that they could be astonished by the so-called "facts," by what they took to be self-evident about social reality but needed to be radically critiqued and deconstructed. Hence, according to Thompson, Brechtian actors' training commenced with observation of the external world. It was important to fine tune their capacity to look at an ordinary happening and grasp its deep structure, not only "with *what* happened but with why and how."[40] Exactly how this played out in acting training is suggested in Brecht's list of over 20 exercises for acting schools, though his focus is always on cultivating an existential mistrust in the actor and the audience of the obvious, the taken-for-granted "norms" that in part, constitute oppressive social reality[41] (again, Foucault's "dangerous" or "intolerable"). For example, says Thompson, "How can an activity as common as smoking betray the social class of the smoker?" Or, "How do we know, when playing with a cat, that the cat is not playing with us?"[42] The point is for the actor and the audience to embrace a critical and interrogative approach to social reality so as to see for themselves what is wrong and in need of change.

Brecht was well aware that great acting and performance constitute a communal storytelling enterprise and that the particular sociopolitical motivation and mode of performance had to gradually unfold during rehearsals. Interrelatedness, interdependence and group solidarity are what matters most, not self-staging and self-stylization. As Brecht notes, "the smallest social unit is not the single person but two people. In life too we develop one another."[43] Thus, during rehearsals when it came to characterization Brecht encouraged interpenetration—actors spoke with each other about how they felt about their own and the

40   Ibid., p. 104.
41   Willett, *Brecht on Theatre, The Development of an Aesthetic*, p. 129. Said Brecht, "As for the what we want to discover, we must view it, when discovered, with particular mistrust" (Willet, *The Theatre of Brecht*, p. 216).
42   Thompson, "Brecht on acting training. On whose behalf do we act?", p. 105.
43   Ibid., p. 105.

other actor's character within the context of the whole script and the dramaturgy, including sometimes playing a tragic scene as a comedic or the other way around. In this way the actors were more likely to "see" the "unseen" in their part and better coordinate their acting into a compelling ensemble that convincingly revealed the "take home" social message.

For Brecht the actor's goal was nearly always the same, to act as a "double agent," a term first used by the American theater director, playwright and teacher, Joseph Chaikin. The actor is supposed to show what is absent in the literal script of the play but is implied in the questionable or unjust social reality that was the backdrop to the play and the social subtext to the character being played. Actors were thus encouraged to embrace their character and the script in a critical and questioning manner. As Chaikin described a masterful Brechtian-animated actor he saw perform, "I never believe he is the character by name. Nor do I believe that he is 'playing himself.' He performs like a double agent who has infiltrated the two worlds."[44] Thus, for Brecht, the actor's expressed emotion does not have to always correspond with that of the role he is playing; the actor both imparts and closely and carefully examines the behavior of the role and its social and political significance in such a manner as to provoke the audience's criticality and perspective-shifting. Put differently, the actor does not have to try to completely become the character he is playing but rather, sometimes he could bring out emotions in the character and, most importantly, in the audience that were not part of the obvious role he was playing. For example, if a character was "depressed," the audience might perceive "rage" at the situation which prompted the character to feel the way he does.[45] As Thompson notes, Brecht's operating assumption was that "It is circumstance, not human necessity, that governs behavior,

44   Ibid., p. 106. In a related point Brecht said, "We [actors] must be able to lose ourselves in her agony [i.e., in the emotion] and at the same time not to. Our actual emotion will come from recognizing and feeling the double process" (Willet, *The Theatre of Bertolt Brecht*, p. 185). Stanislavski felt similarly, "An actor weeps and laughs on the stage, and all the while he is watching his own tears and smiles. It is this double function, this balance between life and acting that makes his art" [Constantin Stanislavski, *An Actor Prepares* (New York: Routledge, 1964), p. 267].

45   Margaret Eddershaw, "Actors on Brecht." In Thomson and Sacks, *The Cambridge Companion To Brecht*, p. 279.

of always discouraging oneself). By helping us see how we got where we are, the personal and social cost of our current understandings, and that things could possibly be otherwise, Brecht gave us the hope that there is the possibility of new, better interpretations of the self and society. This is Brecht's most enduring and ennobling acting theory value. John Willet, Brecht's preeminent interpreter, came to a similar conclusion and his pithy remarks are an apt coda to our discussion: "For the gist of Brecht's theatre is that it tries to set out the rich (and comic) complications of reality; that it uses intelligible terms and applies all the resources of the stage to furthering the sense; above all that it aims to make us think."[56]

---

56   Willet, *The Theatre of Bertolt Brecht*, pp. 216-217.

CHAPTER SEVEN

CONNECTING THE BODY
TO THE HEAD

TADASHI SUZUKI

"The value of my training can be said to begin and end with the feet."

—Tadashi Suzuki

ADASHI SUZUKI (1939–), ONE OF THE GREATEST
JAPANESE DIRECTORS AND DRAMATIC THEORISTS,
has developed a novel form of acting training called
the "Suzuki Method." Briefly, the method is a powerful physical training discipline drawing from Kabuki
(a highly stylized classical Japanese dance-drama), Noh (a form of
classical and ritualized Japanese musical-drama), Greek theater, martial arts, ballet, and other related disciplines. The main concern of the
training discipline is concisely described in the promotional literature
of one of the well-known Suzuki training workshops:

> The Suzuki Actor Training Method's principal concern is with re-
> storing the wholeness of the human body and voice to the theatrical
> context and uncovering the actor's innate expressive abilities….the
> training seeks to heighten the actor's emotional and physical power
> and commitment to each moment on the stage. Attention is on the

sense of the actor presence.[11] It should be emphasized that Suzuki's method is not just a mainly Eastern-based acting technology that combines classical and modern performance theory, though it is that, but it expresses a different experimental aesthetic, a unique sensibility, a set of attitudes, intentions and values compared to most Western-based performance philosophies.[12] The theater needs to move away from the naturalism and individual psychology that dominates performance theory and practice and reclaim the "spiritual" and "metaphysical" aspects of the theater.[13] What this hybrid Eastern-based acting technique can teach us about the human condition and how to live the "good life" is precisely what we aim to show in this chapter.

THE GRAMMAR OF THE FEET

For Suzuki, the heart of his method is an emphasis on the way the feet relate to the ground: "the way the feet are used is the basis of a stage performance."[14] That is, it is the way the actor makes contact with the ground, how he or she existentially relates to the physical stage, that matters most: "the performer indeed proves with his feet that he *is* an actor;" "The very life of the art [Noh] depends on the fixing and deepening of the relationships of the feet to the stage in order to render the expressiveness of foot movements all the more compelling"(Noh has been described as "the art of walking").[15]

The feet, and the way they relate to the ground, of course, have been viewed throughout history as a great source of information about what a person thinks and feels as well as being a metaphor for being stable or "grounded." The feet have also been a powerful symbol of autonomy. Shakespeare, for example, wrote in the *History of Troilus and Cressida*, "There's language in her eye, her cheek, her lip; Nay, her foot speaks." Kierkegaard wrote that "To dare is to lose one's footing momentarily. Not to dare is to lose oneself." And Sartre noted, "Better to die on one's feet than to live on one's knees." Thus, Suzuki's focus on the feet as a

11   Richard Brestoff, *The Great Acting Teachers and Their Methods* (Lyme, NH: Smith and Krause, 1995), p. 164.
12   James R. Brandon, "A New World: Asian Theatre in the West Today," *The Drama Review* (1989): 33.2: 25.
13   Allain, *The Art of Stillness*, p. 72.
14   Suzuki, *The Way of Acting*, p. 6.
15   Ibid., p. 8

real and metaphoric basis for his acting technique is in sync with the received wisdom about the importance of the feet/ground connection, including for living an authentic life.

STAMPING

For Suzuki, stamping—bringing the foot down forcefully on a surface—the actor is forced to develop "a special consciousness based on striking the ground."[16] Such a changed consciousness, Suzuki claims, is rooted in the assumption that the actor's rudimentary sense of his or her physicality derives from the feet. According to Suzuki,

> In stamping, we come to understand that the body establishes its relation to the ground through the feet, that the ground and the body are not separate entities. We are part of the ground. Our very beings will return to the earth when we die.[17]

It is this "rhythm with the feet" that is essential for the actor to master, says Suzuki, pointing out that the practice on the stage emanates from the powerful foot-stamping used in traditional Japanese and other societies to magically ward off evil. By stamping we are reminded of our "unique foundation and authority."[18]

What does this emphasis on stamping have to do with the ordinary person trying to live his or her everyday life? In part, it puts into sharp focus the need for all of us "to discover a self-consciousness of the interior of the body."[19] By doing so, individuals, and even more so actors in training, are reminded of "the many layers of sensitivity within [our] own bod[ies]."[20] Indeed, Suzuki's claim that the modern actor has become estranged from his or her body and in particular, he or she has become alienated from his or her feet as they make contact with the ground (and "the richness of change in his bodily responses" that occurs), is an important lesson for all of us. While most of us, at least in the Western world, relate to our body as the "thing" that "contains" who we really are, as an instrument of pleasure, or we hyper-focus on our body's every twitter as it is the guarantor of our physical survival,

---

16   Ibid., p. 9.

17   Ibid.

18   Ibid., pp. 11, 15.

19   Ibid., p. 12.

20   Ibid.

Suzuki is calling our attention to the fact that our body, especially our feet, allows for humans to stay connected to our world and to ourselves. To lose sight of this insight is to lose a major source of stability, creativity and even spirituality. Said Henry David Thoreau, "Heaven is under our feet as well as over our head."

Of course, Suzuki is not the first person to emphasize that one's relationship to one's body, including accessing its "animal energy" as Suzuki calls it—our repressed psychophysicality—is vital to well-being. In Buddhist tradition, for example, in Vipassana Meditation (Insight Meditation), the mind and body are viewed as interrelated aspects of our experience. Thus a relaxed body tends to facilitate a relaxed mind. The walking and other psychophysical exercises that Vipassana Meditation uses have some similarity to Suzuki's Method, though the emphasis is more on relaxation rather than the cultivation of action, energy and verbal expression. In Vipassana Meditation and Western acting theory, tension is the great enemy, where for Suzuki, it is the basis for explosive, transgressive energy on the stage. Says Suzuki about Kabuki actors, "the secret of this kind of acting is instantaneous release of suppressed action [a kind of sublimated tension], then suppression (that is nonaction), release again, and so on."[21] Indeed, Suzuki uses the metaphor of "stillness in a performance, or the vision beyond sight"[22] to indicate the importance of the dialectic between action and non-action, the latter being a kind of dynamic immobility (i.e., the body speaks when silent), which facilitates the natural and spontaneous on the stage. Like in Vipassana Meditation, Suzuki's Method stresses repetition of the exercises on the way to mastery as opposed to the Western emphasis on creativity and originality (creativity for its own sake, as an "absolute" is a foreign notion to the Japanese, according to Allain). Allain continues,

> a routine is initially necessary to learn the form but it soon provides the means to examine yourself in relation to a fixed structure, allowing a deepening of the effect of the training on the performer. Repetition also teaches precision and respect for the craft as you understand the complexity contained within the small details.

21   Brandon, "Training at the Waseda Little Theatre: The Suzuki Method," p. 42.
22   Suzuki, *The Way of Acting*, pp. 71-72.

Not simply a set of gymnastic exercises, Suzuki's discipline also requires a degree of "imaginative and emotional involvement"[23] though the emotional realm as the West tends to conceive and work with it, in and out of the theater, is not emphasized (e.g., nowhere are Freud and his followers used by Suzuki in his formulations). Thus, Suzuki's emphasis on mastery as opposed to creativity introduces a different sensibility to the typical Westerner, one that emphasizes expert knowledge and outstanding ability as opposed to using or showing use of the imagination to create new ideas or things. Obviously, both capacities are necessary to be a great actor, and to live the "good life," but the Suzuki's emphasis adds a good counterbalance to the Western near-obsession with individual creativity as the be all and end all.

SACRED SPACE

Like Viola Spolin, the "high priestess" of improv, Suzuki has a broadly defined religious impulse that in part animates his work. Wrote Spolin, "We are working on two levels: the obvious, the story, the scenario, the characters. The other is invisible, the luminous, the spirit-world."[24] Suzuki also was trying to get at something "religious" in his notion of "sacred space," a term that he borrowed from Mircea Eliade, the great Romanian religious historian and phenomenologist of religion. In brief, for Eliade, the religious reflected "the irreducibility of the sacred," that is, such religious moments must be understood on their own terms, not reduced to psychological, social or other non-religious phenomenon. The religious, manifests a universal, essential symbolic structure Eliade called "the dialectic of the sacred and the profane."[25] It was in 1976 that Suzuki was in search of an appropriate environment to set up his new theater, away from Tokyo and other major cities where most Japanese theater had its residence (he advocated a decentralization of theater performance in Japan). He established his theater company in a small, remote mountain village called Toga about 400 miles from Tokyo. Such a place, with its beautiful natural setting, was what Suzuki called a "sacred place."

23   Allain, *The Art of Stillness*, p. 118.

24   Viola Spolin, *Improvisation for the Theater* (Evanston, IL: Northwestern University Press, 1999), p. xiv.

25   Mircea Eliade, http://www.britanica.com/Ebchecked/topic/184589/ Mircea-Eliade, p. 3.

The issue of performance "space" is one of the basic problems for the modern actor. "Any actor who makes light of the fundamental physical relationships within the theatre space will discover that the matter of acting space becomes his fundamental problem. The modern theatre has yet to work a successful plan to deal with this problem."[26] What Suzuki is, in part, getting at is that while in modern theater performance one usually travels to an impersonal, rather alienating concrete building in a metropolis to see a play, there is a strong need for a "fixed, communal performance space as a basis for their creation."[27] Such a fixed, communal playing space is typical to Noh and this requirement is the basis for great performance skills. Indeed, in the West, the emphasis on performance skills is often psychologically based and the performance space is of secondary importance. In Suzuki's conception, performance skills "are indivisible from the place in which they are performed."[28] "Sacred space" as Suzuki uses it, describes "a place where there is a possibility of moving from the territory of one universe or another."[29] In the context of Noh, says Suzuki,

> the bodies of the actors…can remember the indivisibility of the space in which they perform, they…have the ability to make a rent, an opening in that homogeneity. Because of their physical deviations from the movements of everyday life, the actors' bodies…seem equipped with some means to defy those amorphous and sterile perceptions of space that evolved as modern culture has developed.[30]

Obviously, if a theater is lodged in a permanent, beautiful setting that the actors call "home" as it were, their way of relating to the theater space (and the audience) is rather different than the typical Western actor on Broadway who enters a nondescript, anonymous building, the place where his lines are said. In Suzuki's view, his theater space conception tends to generate a communal self-consciousness (e.g., we have all had similar, creative, life-affirming experiences together), much more so compared to a typical Western actor. As Suzuki pointed out, "In its essence, it [the theater] involves the establishment of

26   Suzuki, *The Way of Acting*, p. 36.
27   Ibid., p. 37.
28   Ibid., p. 39.
29   Ibid., p. 40.
30   Ibid., p. 41.

a community of place and time, encompassing both performers and spectators, so that a dialogue may pass between them."[31] Moreover, for Suzuki, the beautiful natural surroundings are not incidental to his vision, "because the environment is so important, a place must be chosen in the middle of nature, where man can feel free."[32] In addition, by the actor and audience identifying with the vital rhythms of nature, the individual participates in the infinity of the universe. His or her life is no longer strictly limited by biology and social context, because he or she is now symbiotically related to the cosmos. This experience of "sacred time" as Eliade calls it, a rupturing of ordinary, everyday time, is a place where one can begin to deeply contemplate life. This context, says Suzuki, is the ideal one for the actor and spectator "to contemplate the human condition" and to begin the perspective-shifting that all great theater tends to facilitate.[33] Such a totality of circumstances is what Suzuki means by the "spiritual"[34] and "sacred space"—"the actor's body and the space reveal a [deep] mutual connection."[35] Playing off Suzuki and Eliade, and quoting from Joseph Campbell, from the point of view of the audience, and perhaps the actor, "your sacred space is where you can find yourself again and again."

The upshot of all of this "space" talk is: In order to live the "good life" one must have a degree of what psychoanalysts like Erik Erikson, Donald Winnicott and Michael Balint called "basic trust"—a sense that one is ontologically secure (ultimately rooted in one's experience of one's reliably loving caregivers). Moreover, a sense of "basic trust" implies the belief that for the most part, the world is essentially a benign and caring place. Most importantly to our discussion, "basic trust" is related in a fundamental way to the interpersonal organization of space and time,[36] and this is where the notion of "basic trust" connects with Suzuki and suggests our "take home" point—that is, the

---

31   Ibid., p. 77.

32   Ibid., p. 81.

33   Ibid., p. 84. Suzuki describes what we call perspective-shifting in terms of the audience examining "themselves from new and unusual angles," and revealing "a new dimension of reality" (*The Way of Acting*, pp. 81, 123).

34   Ibid., p. 90.

35   Ibid., p. 91.

36   Anthony Giddens, *Modernity and Self-Identity. Self and Society in the Late Modern Age* (Stanford: Stanford University Press, 1991), p. 38.

contextual nature of social life and societal institutions as sociologist
Anthony Giddens described it, and the need that we all have to experience great art within a beautiful, if not compelling, context. "Space,"
says Frank Lloyd Wright, "is the breath of art." This is precisely what
art offers: "space, a certain breathing room for the spirit," said John
Updike. Put differently, one must be mindful of the way space (and
time) constitute social life.[37] Through the experience of great art, like
theater, performed in the appropriate transcendent context, we enter into a kind of creative, life affirming, transformative "therapeutic
spacing."[38] Such "therapeutic spacing" is one of the conditions of possibility for experiencing what Suzuki called the "spiritual," a moment of
deep contemplation and inner renewal. "Space," said the French moral-
ist Joseph Joubert, "is the stature of God."

EMOTIONAL EXPRESSIVENESS AS THE
BASIS FOR GREAT ACTING

It is part of the received wisdom of all Western performance theory
that the actor's capacity to generate a truthful emotion in the circumstances in which one finds oneself is in large part what makes the actor believable and impressive. Indeed, the ability to create the right
emotion at the right time and circumstance is what makes for a great
performance. While there are many different ways of accomplishing
the task, depending on what acting theory one follows, the fact is that
Suzuki gives little formal discussion in his writings and interviews to
explain exactly how truthful emotion at the right time and circumstance occurs. For Suzuki, the capacity to create truthful and compelling emotion on the stage emanates from the physical training that
the actor receives and has internalized. The dazzling actress, Shiraishi
Kayoko, for example, electrified the audiences in her performances of
Suzuki-directed Shakespeare, Chekhov and some of the Greek clas-
sics. As one acting theory scholar noted, Suzuki's "actors were capable
of sustaining characterizations of tremendous intensity. The depth of

---

37   Anthony Giddens, *The Constitution of Society. Outline of the Theory of
      Structuration* (Berkeley: University of California Press, 1984), p. 286.
38   Ibid., p. 146.

feeling and range, the combination of expression and control, amazed and moved audiences."[39]

It is rather odd that, in the writings of some of his major explicators (Allain and Carruthers and Takahashi, for example), their indexes do not have an entry for "emotion," "feeling," or "Freud," except incidentally and tangentially in Carruthers and Takahashi's volume. This being said, Suzuki does have some rather vague notion of how the emotions connect with physical disciplines that constitute the Suzuki Method; moreover, we think there is something being said or implied that has a bearing on how to live the "good life." For the capacity to experience a wide range of emotions, strong sentiments about someone or something, and feelings, the part of one's self-awareness characterized by sensation or emotion is an intrinsic part, and we believe, the most important part of living a "good life." Whether on the stage or in real life, one who has mastered one's emotions is most able to love (in the acting context, express emotions) and work effectively (perform well on the stage).

From what we can discern from Suzuki's writings and his commentators, he seems to believe that there is an intimate connection between the body and mind, though he never details this theoretically. Nor does he contextualize his views on the most unrelenting dilemma in the history of philosophy, the mind-body problem. From what we can tell, he has been somewhat influenced by the French phenomenologist, Maurice Merleau-Ponty, whom he sites, who viewed the physical and mental (and what he called the biological) as two of the many conceptual levels to comprehend human behavior. For Merleau-Ponty, the mental assumes the physical and biological, but they are not divisible. Thus, Merleau-Ponty rejected Descartes' mind-body dualism.[40]

So how does the Suzuki-trained actor get from a finely tuned, disciplined body to expressing deep emotions and a wide range of feelings? It can't simply be that a disciplined body, where will and concentration are strong for instance, means that a person is capable of a wide range of emotional expressiveness. I (PM) have seen in psychotherapy many superbly trained athletes, classical ballet dancers and devout Hindus

---

39   Brestoff, *The Great Acting Teachers*, p. 164.
40   W.L. Reese. *Dictionary of Philosophy and Religion. Eastern and Western Thought* (Atlantic Highlands, NJ: Humanities Press, 1980), pp. 350, 360.

who were highly trained in yoga, who were extremely emotionally limited in what they could let themselves experience, and in their capacity
to love in the real world. Obviously, there is more to emotional expressiveness than sensitivity and control of the inner and outer workings
of the physical self, and though that is important, there is a certain
kind of simultaneous psychological consciousness-enhancement that
acting as a "total physical act" requires.

Allain suggests that the "struggle, dedication, repetition and mastery
of technique" that the Suzuki Method demands leads to "emotional
strength."[41] Of course, the same can be said of the Navy Seal training.
In Suzuki's *The Way of Acting*, the only mention of the emotions is in
the context of the actor's relationship to the theater group: "Yet, if the
initial energy involved consists not in the emotion itself but in a belief
in the importance of emotional attachment, then perhaps the individual can indeed come to feel that the emotions of others are genuine as
well."[42] Suzuki is emphasizing the importance of developing a degree
of affection for one's colleagues, what he calls "a mutuality of human
feeling," and a sense of group solidarity, this being the basis for any
group to function adequately.

Perhaps more to our point, Suzuki notes, "All bodies are different
and the emotion one person finds in a discipline will be different from
the emotion another finds." The question is, continues Suzuki, "is the
bodily movement right for the actor's body and for the emotion he
wants to express[?] Most actors haven't sufficient bodily or vocal control to do anything. That's what the disciplines are for, to give him
strength and control he can use as he wants"[43] (Control comes from
the body's center and from mindful breathing, as in most Eastern-
based martial arts.).

For example, according to Goto, one of Suzuki's explicators, *Mie*,
"moving the head in a circular motion and with a sudden snap of the
head, freezes the dramatic tableau. *Mie* halts the action of the play and
functions like a visual exclamation point." Most importantly, "it is the

---

41   Allain, *The Art of Stillness*, p. 189.

42   Ibid., p. 67.

43   Brandon, "Training at the Waseda Little Theatre: the Suzuki Method,"
      pp. 36-37.

culmination of a series of predetermined rhythmic movements and intensifies the essence of an emotion."[44]

Thus, the emphasis in Suzuki's Method is on the external presentation and behavior, rooted in an integrated, controlled, almost primal physicality [from which the actor and the audience have become estranged in real life], which facilitates so-called "natural emotion."[45] By making contact with "the substratum that lies beneath the surface of these diverse styles" of performance, one has tapped the ultimate creative resource.[46] This is starkly different than a training method that stresses the actor's internal world as first principle, such as psychological interpretation (Lee Strasberg) or imaginative construction (Stella Adler). Importantly, Suzuki goes out of his way to point out in an interview that he is not talking about "body language," where "the body unconsciously reveals inner emotion" [though we think it does to some extent], but rather, just the opposite, "the actor deliberately speaks through proportion, line, movement, form of his body. His body creates a picture." This "play of the body," "open, free, creative exploration," is similar to a child's unself-conscious experience of play; in fact, Suzuki regards acting as "serious play."[47]

Now, what does all of this material have to do with the average person who is trying to live the "good life"? What does Suzuki's way of conceptualizing emotion have to do with the typical Westerner influenced more by the Freudian oeuvre and sensibility? Authentic emotion is most authentic if it involves a physical expression, that is, an action, often one that impacts other people, hopefully in a positive way. In other words, emotion as simply a feeling that comes and goes lacks substance and meaning (except to oneself) unless it is translated into action in the real world. For example, love that is just felt is good, but surely not complete. It requires an action to be properly instantiated, such as verbalizing your affection, giving a kiss or hug, and tending to the significant other's needs and wishes before one's own, especially when they are suffering alone. Likewise, anger, if simply felt, is also

---

44   Yukihiro Goto, "Theatrical Fusion of Suzuki Training," *Asian Theatre Journal* (1989): 6.2: 115-116.

45   Ibid., p. 40.

46   Suzuki, *The Way of Acting*, p. 17.

47   Ibid., p. 42.

good, but not complete to get its message across; it requires reasonable verbalization and explanation, perhaps not talking to one's significant other for a while or hitting a pillow. And of course, anxiety and worry almost always have their physiological and behavioral counterparts (e.g., sweaty hands, racing heart, phobic avoidance, etc.). Mastery of anxiety cannot be done only in the head—it requires behavioral interventions. If you are afraid of elevators, ultimately you have to face your fear by going into the elevator. The point is that emotion conceived as simply an internal matter misses the fact that its depth and purpose is best manifested when the controlled behavioral component exists along with the verbal/psychological element. Put differently, emotion, like the physical disciplines can best be expressed through the right form—with proportion, line, balance and movement, or sublimation, as psychoanalysts call it. Most importantly, for Suzuki and for that matter for Freud, so-called "healthy" emotional/body expressiveness requires an ethical thrust to it. It is to this subject that we now turn.

SUZUKI'S ETHICAL SENSIBILITY

Suzuki has made some comments along the way that suggest what his view of the human condition is and what ultimately matters in life. Such beliefs and values, directly and indirectly, consciously and unconsciously, animate and reinforce the physical disciplines of the Suzuki Method of training. While Suzuki has not explicitly detailed his "worldview," there are a few places where one gets a sense of what are some of his core values and which, in our view, inform his training.

As we said earlier, Suzuki was influenced early by the atheistic existentialist Jean Paul Sartre. In fact, Suzuki's view of life is in essence Sartresque, when for example, he writes,

> I have finally been able to see at close range a few people who understand that life is a useless but passionate play, but are driven by the fact that they must continue on, to fight the battle of the defeated. All this has become very important to me.[48]

This is a very particular, though now familiar outlook on life, similar of course, to Shakespeare's famous lines from Macbeth, "Life is but a walking shadow, a poor player, that struts and frets his hour upon the

---

48   Suzuki, *The Way of Acting*, p. 110.

stage and then heard no more; it is a tale told by an idiot, full of sound and fury, signifying nothing."

Suzuki's outlook is embedded in his training, for instance, when he mentions that basic to his method is the idea of struggle, a kind of struggle to survive. As Allain points out, "The essence of Suzuki's acting technique is struggle, but there is a point when obstacles become insurmountable;" "The theatrical matter is the performer's struggle with his or her own physical and mental being..."[49] This requires psychological balance as one confronts problems and assaults, whether coming from the internal or external world. As in the Eastern-based martial arts, stable, regularized and tranquil breathing is the defense against all of this.[50] Suzuki often characterizes acting as a question of difficulty, challenge, problem and combat, these also being fundamental aspects of the human condition and living a "good life." Of course, this is not entirely original, for most acting training theorists assert that great theater depicts the sham, drudgery and broken dreams of life.

However, Suzuki takes the matter further than just an acknowledgment of the well-known truth that part of life is not only struggle but downright painful. He actually advocates a kind of life-affirming dwelling in the misery of life as crucial to fully engaging and appreciating life, and remaining a humane and decent person. Says Suzuki,

> To put this another way, the only way you can achieve anything at all is by constantly confronting yourself with a sense of poverty and wretchedness [Freud would agree with this of course]. I suppose that my initial impetus to enter theater came from a struggle with the problem of how to maintain this sense of human wretchedness.[51]

Suzuki specifically mentions Chekhov's depiction of various characters as expressing extreme alienation, a sub-species of wretchedness: "All of Chekhov's characters are incapable of looking at reality and their lives with any degree of objectivity. They speak constantly of an illusory world that is somewhere other and better than where they

---

49   Allain, *The Art of Stillness*, pp. 181, 122.

50   Ibid., p. 118.

51   Akihiko Senda, "The Wider World for Japanese Theatre: The Art of Tadashi Suzuki," Jordan Sand (Trans.), *Japan Society Newsletter*, June 1991, in the *SCOT* book, pp. 58-59.

are. In the course of conversation, the characters see the state of their misery."[52]

Suzuki takes his emphasis on human wretchedness and goes even further in his evocative notion from his production of *Electra* that "all the world is a hospital and all men and women are inmates." In this production the main character lives in a wordless and lonely world scheming vengeful retribution because her mother deserted her. What Suzuki is getting at in his use of the hospital metaphor is that the radical alienation and sense of powerlessness and depletion that one feels in a hospital is a danger that faces us all in how we live our everyday lives. The antidote to this is signaled in Suzuki's production of *The Tale of Lear* [King Lear], where there are nurses who care for the ill and very troubled patients, some of whom are in wheelchairs.

This brings us to the end of our discussion of Suzuki training, by having pointed out what is his rather dismal view of the human condition. The antidote to experiencing the alienation and the deadening of the self that often follows such estrangement from the world and oneself is to reside in one's personal wretchedness, the wretchedness of the self. By doing this one develops the self-awareness that brings about compassion for oneself and by extension, empathy for others. That is, the capacity to identify with and understand another person's feelings or difficulties ideally emanates from awareness that one is suffering, and by extension others are too. Such self-awareness, implies Suzuki, leads to the necessary "communal self-consciousness" and "communal unity" mentioned earlier, that Suzuki feels is essential for any theater company to flourish, and we would add, for any ordinary person to passionately affiliate with others. Put differently, Suzuki, the humanist, is implicitly advocating an other-directed, other-regarding way of being in the world, on the stage and in real life, as the best antidote to the poverty and wretchedness of performance and real life. Thus, we can say that Suzuki's perhaps most strongly held value, one that is built into his training method and performances, and which has great implication for the average person, is this: Suffering for oneself and more importantly, for the Other, is the mother of all wisdom. It is, ideally, also the royal road to an ethic of responsibility for the Other,

---

52   SCOT: *Suzuki Company of Toga*, no date, no publisher, cited from Allain,
     The Art of Stillness, p. 183.

often before oneself, rooted in radical empathy, or the royal road to Goodness. Such an ethic is the best way to achieve meaning, value and personal truth in one's life.

CHAPTER EIGHT

THE QUEST FOR SELF-TRANSCENDENCE

JERZY GROTOWSKI'S

HOLY ACTOR

"Actors should be like martyrs burnt alive, still signaling to us from their stakes."

—Jerzy Grotowski[1]

POLISH BORN JERZY GROTOWSKI (1933–1999) was one of the most avant-garde theater directors of the twentieth century, and developed unique acting techniques that were strongly based on Stanislavski's ideas about physical actions. As Stanislavski said, "The first fact, is that the elements of the human soul and the particles of a human body are indivisible;" "The method of physical actions is the result of my whole life's work."[2] In other words, for both Stanislavski and Grotowski, one's inner life—one's affects, desires and motivations are expressed mainly through straightforward and effortless external physical actions. What Grotowski did was to take Stanislavski's ideas about physical actions

---

1   Grotowski is quoting from playwright Antonin Artaud. Jerzy Grotowski, *Towards a Poor Theatre* (New York: Simon and Schuster, 1968), p. 125.

2   Sonia Moore, *The Stanislavski System. The Professional Training of an Actor* (New York: Penguin, 1984), pp. 17, 10.

much further as he was disgruntled with both the Master's "realistic approach to acting" and with Bertold Brecht's "eclectic techniques of political theatre."[3] As Thomas Richards points out, while Stanislavski focused on physical actions within the context of the ordinary life of people, that is, individuals in "realistic" everyday situations, "in some social convention," Grotowski looked "for physical actions in a basic stream of life, not in a social and daily-life situation." Moreover, "in such a stream of life the impulses are most important."[4] What Grotowski came up with that differed from Stanislavski and others is a set of formulations and techniques that were meant to teach the actor how to radically "disrupt" himself, a kind of "controlled spontaneity," and thereby rid himself of his social persona, his phoniness, pretense and other forms of inauthenticity, with the hope that if the spectator saw such a truthful display of the actor's inner life it would encourage him to also relinquish his social mask and fraudulence. Exactly how Grotowski accomplished such "truth telling" is the main focus of this chapter.

Grotowski's work is often divided into four interconnected phases: The Theater of Performance (1959–1969), The Theater of Participation (1969–1975), The Theater of Sources (1976–1982) and the last phase, actually two, Objective Drama in California, where Grotowski relocated, and Ritual Arts in Italy (1983–1999), where he completed his career and died.[5] It should be noted that while these phases are interrelated and express the ebb and flow of Grotowski's artistic life, in certain ways they are contradictory developments which therefore make explicating his "final" views about acting theory and performance difficult. As Daniel Gerould describes it, The Theater of Performance focused on eradicating from the stage everything except what was indispensable to the actor audience encounter. Grotowski's training focused on "gymnastics, acrobatics, yoga and pantomime." The Theater of Participation, also known as the "Paratheatrical" phase, attempted to rise above, to bridge the division between the actor and

3   Richard Brestoff, *Great Acting Teachers and Their Methods* (Lyme, NH: Smith and Kraus, 1995), p. 154.

4   Thomas Richards, *At Work with Grotowski on Physical Actions* (London: Routledge, 1995), p. 99.

5   Danile Gerould, in Martin Banham (ed.), *The Cambridge Guide to Theatre* (Cambridge: Cambridge University Press, 1995), pp. 455-456.

audience. Grotowski endeavored to do this through the development of communal rites and interpersonal encounters that were "structured and spontaneous activities in natural surroundings." Sometimes these activities deliberately went on for long periods of time as the aim was to drastically destabilize and defamiliarize the audience's usual way of thinking, feeling and acting (The film *My Dinner with Andre* by Andre Gregory, Grotowski's colleague, is an example of this latter point). The Theater of Sources was a phase of Grotowski's work when he traveled around the world to such places as India, Mexico and Haiti in search of aspects of traditional practices and ritual techniques that strongly impacted the partakers. In Grotowski's final phase, Objective Drama in California and Ritual Arts in Italy, he returned to his interest in ancient traditional cultures, specifically focusing on ritual songs and other evocative performance techniques that decisively emotionally moved participants and spectators. As Gerould concludes, in this final return to the mysteries of ancient traditional cultures, "there is no spectator, actor or theater performance, but only the performer."[6]

These four phases of Grotowski's work had a common thrust to them, at least to some extent, in that in all phases he was trying to revolutionize how theater and performance were understood—theater space, the actor, the audience and the intimate, and at times powerful, interaction between the latter two. Grotowski's impact on theater thus emanated from three basic interrelated ideas: (1) "that the most effective theatre is the 'poor theatre'—one with a minimum of accoutrements beyond the presence of the actors;" (2) "that theatre is intercultural, differentiating and relating performance 'truths' in and from many cultures;" (3) "that powerful acting occurs at a meeting place between the personal and the archetypal—in this he continued and deepened the work of Stanislavski."[7] Perhaps most importantly, as Peter Brook wrote about Grotowski, through his efforts to make contact with the ancient wisdom embedded in the primordial performance practices (the "ancient corporality" Grotowski called it), common to traditional cultures, we get "access," sometimes shockingly so, "to another level of perception" about ourselves and how the world

6   Ibid., p. 456.

7   Richard Schechner, "Jerzy Grotowski, 1933–1999." In *On Grotowski*, Facts. Cine-Notes, 2008, p. 17. This material accompanied the DVD *With Jerzy Grotowski, Nienadowka*, 1980.

hangs together.[8] Thus, says Grotowski, theater should be conceptualized as "a moral and social mission – built on a core of intellectual
values, committed to progress, proposing a new secular and a rational
ethic."[9] Such a view led Grotowski to characterize theater as "a form of
social psychotherapy."

RICH THEATER AND POOR THEATER

In his important essay, "Towards a Poor Theatre," a chapter in the
seminal book of the same name, Grotowski asks the following questions: "What is theatre? What is unique about it? What can it do that
film and television cannot?" His answer is conceptualized in what he
calls "Poor Theatre," as opposed to "Rich Theatre," "and performance
as an act of transgression,"[10] the act or the process of overstepping a
personal and societal limit.

Rich theater, or what Grotowski also calls "synthetic theater," is an
amalgamation of varied creative disciplines such as literature, sculp-
ture, painting, architecture, lighting and acting. It is a form of "artistic kleptomania" that takes from other disciplines, manufacturing
"hybrid-spectacles, conglomerates without backbone or integrity, yet
presented as an organic artwork." In other words, Rich Theatre draws
from many theater styles and systems, using various kinds of atten-
tion-grabbing techniques, like evocative music or lighting, to seduce
and titillate the spectator. Grotowski elaborates his criticism of rich
theater when he distinguishes it from its rivals, film and television,
which he says, "excels in montage and instantaneous change of place"
(so-called "mechanical functions"):

> The Rich Theatre countered with a blatantly compensatory call for
> "total theatre." The integration of borrowed mechanisms (movie
> screens onstage, for example) means a sophisticated technical plant,
> permitting great mobility and dynamism. And if the stage and/or

8   Richard Schechner and Lisa Wolford, *The Grotowski Sourcebook* (London:
    Routledge, 1997), p. 383.
9   Jennifer Kumiega, *The Theatre of Grotowski* (London: Methuen, 1995),
    p. 128.
10 Jerzy Grotowski, *Towards a Poor Theatre* (New York: Simon and
    Schuster, 1968), pp. 18-19.

auditorium were mobile, constantly changing perspective would be possible. This is all nonsense.[11]

What Grotowski is decrying was the tendency, one that is still prevalent, to overly depend on theatrical interventions such as music, light, costume and décor to bring about a sense of spectacle to the audience, that is, to manipulatively foster an impressive, unusual or disturbing impact on what the audience views on the stage. Such an approach has two deleterious consequences; first, it tends to obscure "truth telling," the main function of theater for Grotowski (as with most other great acting teachers): "If you want to create a true masterpiece you must always avoid beautiful lies."[12] Second, Rich Theatre underplays the skillfulness and talent of the actor, how he uses his voice and body to commune with the audience.

Grotowski boldly declared, "If it [the theater] cannot be richer than the cinema, then let it be poor." In contrast to rich theatre, Grotowski puts forth "poverty in theatre," the "Poor Theatre," that is, he knew that theater could never compete with the spectacle and impact of film and television; instead he played to the historical strength of the theater as a truth-telling medium. Thus, he staged plays in the simplest way possible, without the devices and often-used gimmicks of fancy sets, lighting and sound, so that the relationship between the actor and audience had primacy. In this way, the actor and the audience were not distracted and could focus on honestly encountering each other in the service of truth-telling. In Poor Theatre it was the actor-audience relationship, the evoked intellectual, emotional and physical processes between the actor and the audience that mattered most: "We can thus define the theatre as what takes place between spectator and actor. All other things are supplementary..."[13] To the extent that the director can create the "proper spectator-actor relationship for each type of performance and [embody] the decision in physical arrangements" on the stage, authentic communion between the actor and audience is likely to occur unencumbered.[14] Communion, Stanislavski's term, refers to the actor's relationship to the audience, the connection they have to

11   Ibid., p. 19.
12   Ibid., p. 236.
13   Ibid., p. 32.
14   Ibid., p. 20.

each other. Stanislavski and Grotowski also used this term to suggest
the strong connection between actors on the stage. Said Grotowski,
"We must find what it is that hinders him [the actor] in the way of respiration, movement and—most important of all—human contact."[15]

In Grotowski's distinction between Rich and Poor Theatre there
is a deeper point about the art of living the "good life" that is worth
highlighting. Grotowski is emphasizing within the context of stage
productions a simple idea that he simply stated, namely, the virtue of
simplicity. Grotowski noted, for example, that his Laboratory Theatre
Method was never meant to be a doctrinaire and set program; in fact,
as he said, "if something was becoming perfect there was a need either
to surpass it, or return to what was more simple."[16] Indeed, Grotowski's
wish to strip down the theater experience to its bare essentials is in
sync with the received wisdom that suggests that if you want to live
a more contented and creative life, simplification really does matter.
As Lawrence Olivier said, "I take a simple view of living. It is, keep
your eyes open and get on with it;" Leonardo da Vinci indicated that
"simplicity is the ultimate sophistication;" Jazz bassist Charles Mingus
noted, "Making the simple complicated is commonplace; making the
complicated simple, awesomely simple, that's creativity;" And finally,
Walt Whitman wrote, "the art of art, the glory of expression…is simplicity." Many more quotations could be given—our point is simple to
understand though very hard to implement: simplicity is consciously
and unconsciously deeply associated with a sense of beauty and pu-
rity, clarity and truth (e.g., think of Occam's razor) and perhaps most
of all, with goodness (e.g., for St. Thomas Aquinas, God was viewed
as infinitely simple). Living a life in which one can accurately discern
what is essential to survive and flourish from what is a distraction,
what is a self-imposed obstacle and what is futile to pursue, is to have
fashioned a life that implies greater self-knowledge, self-awareness and
freedom. This capacity for "wise attention," as Buddhists call it,[17] allows a person to liberate themselves from the manacles of delusion,

---

15 Jennifer Kumiega, *The Theatre of Grotowski* (London: Methuen, 1985),
    p. 113.

16 Ibid., p. 112.

17 Sharon Salzberg and Joseph Goldstein, *Insight Meditation.
    Correspondence Course Workbook* (Boulder, CO: Sounds True, 1996), pp.
    49, 23.

the inclination to not view things as they are in their radical simplicity. "Discriminating wisdom," on the other hand, leads to better, more sensible judgments about what ultimately matters in life, though this is easier said than done for a variety of reasons. As Einstein aptly said, "Everything should be made as simple as possible, but not simpler"!

THE HOLY ACTOR

Unlike Stanislavski, who attempted to teach his students an explicit, systematic method for acting, one that would produce, at least in theory, a good and repeatable performance result, Grotowski was not offering his students a formalized system or method. Instead, he offered a set of techniques and a worldview, what he called "a way of life and of knowledge." In fact, he disparagingly described those actors who rely on a "bag of tricks," gimmick-like devices meant to give the actor a false sense of security and to superficially captivate the audience. Rather, Grotowski was more interested in process, the series of actions directed toward a particular aim in his view, the process was the result in terms of the actor's creative growth and development. According to Grotowski,

> We do not want to teach the actor a predetermined set of skills or give him a "bag of tricks." Ours is not a deductive method of collecting skills. Here everything is concentrated on "ripening" of the actor which is expressed in tension towards the extreme, by a complete stripping down, by the laying bare of one's own—all of this without the least trace of egotism or self-enjoyment. The actor must make a total gift of himself. This is a technique of the "trance" and of the integration of all of the actor's psychic and bodily powers which emerge from the most intimate layers of his being and his instinct, spring forth in a sort of "translumination"[18] [roughly, having a glowing appearance, as if light were coming through, in other words, being inspired].

Grotowski's objective of educating an actor in his theater, what he tellingly called a "laboratory," was not so much a matter of teaching him something factual, prescriptive and functional. Rather he aimed to eradicate the actor's resistance to this necessary experience of stripping down, unburdening and "untaming," as Grotowski called this process. The goal was to have a "freedom from the time-lapse between inner

18   Grotowski, *Towards a Poor Theatre*, p. 16.

impulse and outer reaction" such that "impulse and action are concurrent." Grotowski describes the result of this joining of impulse and outer reaction for the actor: "the body vanishes, burns, and the spectator sees only a series of visible impulses," impulses that are utterly truthful and compelling to watch.[19]

This notion that acting training is mainly about the dissolving of blockages and undoing inhibitions so that there is a freeing of living impulses Grotowski called "via negativa,"—"not a collection of skills but an eradication of blocks."[20] According to Lisa Wolford, by impulse Grotowski meant, "a seed of a living action born inside the actor's body which extends itself outward to the periphery, making itself visible as physical action."[21] Grotowski says,

> Before a small physical action there is an impulse. Therein lies the secret of something very difficult to grasp, because the impulse is a reaction that begins inside the body and which is visible only when it has already become a small action. The impulse is so complex that one cannot say that it is only of the corporeal domain.[22]

If Grotowski is right that impulses do not only come from the corporeal realm, he must have believed that they emanate from somewhere else. In conventional philosophical nomenclature this leaves either the mind, the center of consciousness that produces thoughts, feelings, ideas and perceptions and stores knowledge and memories, or spirit, that vital force that characterizes a living being as being alive. Of the two options, it is the latter that is by far the more likely option, though Grotowski does make some reference to Carl Jung's archetypes, those "universal thought form[s] (ideas) that [contain] large elements of

---

19   Ibid.

20   Ibid., p. 17.

21   Lisa Wolford, "Grotowski's Vision of the Actor. The Search for Contact." In Alison Hodge (Ed.), *Twentieth Century Actor Training* (London: Routledge, 2000), p. 199. Grotowski wrote about impulses in terms of "signs," "a human reaction, purified of all fragments, of all other details which are not of paramount importance. The sign is the clear impulse, the pure impulse. The actions of the actors are for us the signs." Signs are rooted in the capacity to "perceive" and to "feel" not to "understand," the latter is "a function of the brain" (Grotowski, *Towards a Poor Man's Theatre*, p. 235).

22   Richards, *At Work with Grotowski on Physical Actions*, p. 94.

emotion....structural component[s] of the collective unconscious."[23] For Grotowski, an archetype in the theater context refers "to the basic human situation in the text," roughly analogous to myth.[24] Needless to say, the whole issue of impulse/action and from where it comes is rather unclear in Grotowski's writings, let alone verifiable. For our purposes, impulse is usefully thought of as the subjective experience of an instinctual drive or natural tendency; in psychoanalytic parlance, it is "the psychic awareness that a desire [or wish or drive] towards some action is welling up."[25]

Grotowski tells us how the actor can become more open to, and animated by, impulse, a kind of "elevated spiritual state" as he calls it: "the requisite state of mind is a passive readiness to realize an active role, a state in which one does not 'want to do that' but rather 're-signs from not doing it.'"[26] Such a notion calls to mind the paradoxical techniques meant to help induce calmness of mind that are common to Eastern thought, especially described in Taoism. Specifically, such "internal passivity," as Grotowski calls it, resonates with the Taoist concept of "wu-wei," usually translated as inaction. Wu-wei, according to the pre-eminent Taoist scholar, Burton Watson, "is not a forced quietude, but rather the renunciation of any action that is occasioned by conventional concepts of purpose or achievement, or aimed at the realization of conventional goals."[27] In other words, wu-wei does not mean taking no action, but rather means doing nothing that is not natural or spontaneous. To act otherwise is to come in conflict with the Tao, the primordial source of the universe that motivates everything. Grotowski's vocal and respiratory work, which emphasized discovering the "natural voice" and the "natural respiration," are good examples

---

23   Calvin Hall and Gardner Lindzey, *Theories of Personality*, Third Edition (New York: John Wiley and Sons, 1978), p. 120.

24   James Slowiak and Jairo Cuesta, *Jerzy Grotowski* (London: Routledge, 2007), pp. 58-59.

25   Burness E. Moore and Bernard D. Fine (Eds.), *Psychoanalytic Terms and Concepts* (New Haven: Yale University Press, 1990), p. 94.

26   Grotowski, *Towards a Poor Theatre*, p. 17.

27   Burton Watson, *The Complete Works of Chuang Tzu*. (New York: Columbia University Press, 1968), p. 468.

of his passive readiness, his dissolution of blockages, and his undoing of inhibitions.[28]

All of the above are some of the key elements that Grotowski thought constituted the "holy actor," or what he called a "secular saint" who expressed a kind of "secular holiness."

> If the actor, by setting himself a challenge publicly challenges oth-
> ers, and through excess, profanation and outrageous sacrilege re-
> veals himself by casting off his everyday mask, he makes it possible
> for the spectator to undertake a similar process of self-penetration.
> If he does not exhibit his body, but annihilates it, burns it, frees it
> from everyday resistance to any psychic impulse, then he does not
> sell his body but sacrifices it. He repeats the atonement: he is close
> to holiness.[29]

In contrast to the "courtesan actor," who uses an "arsenal" of "methods, artifices and tricks," the "holy actor" operates from an very different inner space, analogous to the difference between seduction and love:

> The difference between the "courtesan actor" and the "holy actor" is
> the same as the difference between the skill of a courtesan and the
> attitude of giving and receiving which springs from true love: In
> other words, self-sacrifice. The essential thing in this second case is
> to be able to eliminate any disturbing elements in order to be able
> to overstep every conceivable limit. In the first case it is a question
> of the existence of the body; in the other, rather of its non-existence.
> The technique of the "holy actor" is an inductive technique (i.e., a
> technique of elimination), whereas that of the "courtesan actor" is a
> deductive technique (i.e., an accumulation of skills).[30]

What Grotowski is getting at is that for the actor to accomplish this act of "self-penetration" and disarmament requires him to use his "role as a trampoline, an instrument with which to study what is hidden behind our everyday mask—the innermost core of our personality—in order to sacrifice it, expose it." Most importantly, says Grotowski, "If I were to express all of this in one sentence I would say that it is all a question of giving oneself. One must give oneself totally, in one's deepest intimacy, with confidence as when one gives oneself in love. Here lies the key." As in the love relationship at its best, the goal is to give

28   Kumiega, *The Theatre of Grotowski*, p. 123.
29   Ibid., p. 34.
30   Ibid., p. 35.

"oneself fully, humbly and without defense," an act of "self-donation."[31] The "holy actor" is thus a metaphor that describes an individual "who, through his art, climbs upon the stage and performs an act of self-sacrifice,"[32] that is in essence for the Other, perhaps more than it is for oneself. Such comportment on the part of the actor, one that is characterized by jettisoning his social mask, piercing his own personal experience and radically exposing his most inner self, Grotowski calls a "total act." Unlike other acting teachers where issues of character development or acting truthfully under imaginary circumstances is paramount, Grotowski's focus was on "testimony," "provocation" and "transgression."[33]

Grotowski's formulations clearly indicate that self-exploration and self-transformation in order to free oneself from blockages, inhibitions, defenses and other forms of resistances were paramount to becoming a great actor, one where impulse and outer actions were perfectly in sync in the service of truth-telling. In fact, Grotowski spoke of "theatre as therapy" and even noted that there was a "masochistic component" to his conception of a dedicated actor.[34] To accomplish this harmonization of impulse and action in part required working on oneself through a number of psychophysical exercises that the actor modified to his particular needs as he creatively grew and developed (unlike Suzuki where mastery of the set of psychophysical exercises was the main goal). While these exercises were to some extent custom made, Grotowski, following Stanislavski, strongly believed that the actor has to commit himself to daily, rigorous and disciplined training. This was necessary to destroy the bodily resistances to the evocation and channeling of impulse. The main objective of his psychophysical exercises was "not a muscular development or physical perfectionism, but a process of research leading to the annihilation of one's body resistances."[35] Elsewhere Grotowski elaborates the goal of the exercises:

31   Ibid., pp. 37, 38.
32   Ibid., p. 43.
33   Lisa Wolford, "General Introduction," in Schechner and Wolford (Eds.), *The Grotowski Sourcebook*, p. 7.
34   Grotowski, *Towards a Poor Theatre*, pp. 125, 48.
35   Ibid., p. 114.

What do the "holy actor" and the "corporals" and "plastiques" have to do with the non-actor who is struggling to live the "good life"? To answer this question we will discuss some other related thematics in Grotowski's method of acting training and performance, then link these formulations to the question of the art of living the "good life." In particular, we will focus on those thematics that merge Grotowski's psychophysical exercises with what we call his spiritual worldview: organicity, spontaneity/structure and Art as Vehicle. We will conclude by briefly commenting on Grotowski's religious sensibility as it informed his work.

ORGANICITY

The term organicity or organic, at least as Grotowski uses it (remember he was trained as an actor in Stanislavski's Russia), probably emanates from Stanislavski who wrote in *Creating A Role*, "the creative process of living and experiencing a part is an *organic* one, founded on the physical and spiritual laws governing the nature of man, on the truthfulness of his emotions, and natural beauty" (emphasis in original).[45] Jean Benedetti, the author of a biography of Stanislavski, defines "organic actions" as "actions or sequences of actions which have their own logic and must be performed in a specific order whatever the situation."[46]

Organicity, says Slowiak and Cuesta, was "the permanent concern that pervades all of Grotowski's work and research;" it is the bedrock of the "holy actor." They define his version of organicity as "the flow of impulses, coming from inside and moving unhindered toward the accomplishment of a precise action."[47] The "plastiques" that Grotowski developed were meant to evoke "an organic response, *rooted in the body*, and realized in accomplishment through precise details" (emphasis in original).[48]

What Grotowski is getting at that also has bearing on the non-actor is a point that has been made in varying forms in other chapters;

45   Constanatin Stanislavski, *Creating a Role* (New York: Routledge, 1961), p. 44.

46   Jean Benedetti, *Stanislavaski and the Actor* (New York: Routledge, 1998), p. 153.

47   Slowiak and Cuesta, *Jerzy Grotowski*, pp. 56, 65.

48   Kumiega, *The Theatre of Grotowski*, p. 119.

namely, that to the extent to which one can "live in agreement with natural laws...on a primary level" (i.e., Grotowski's organicity), and be more animal-like and child-like by ridding oneself of the normalizing social conditioning of ordinary life, "eliminating the clichés of behavior," one can be more psychophysically in touch with what is most authentic in oneself and others. "Only authenticity is necessary, absolutely obligatory....Aim always for authenticity,"[49] said Grotowski. He further captured the spirit of this point when he wrote that the secret to the "holy actor's" craft is "emotions are independent of the will."[50] To accomplish this kind of spontaneous "naturalness" in behavior, and still effectively operate within society without hurting oneself or others, requires considerable skillfulness (i.e., spontaneity can be positive, negative or neutral, though Grotowski never takes up these distinctions). In particular, it requires blunting the negative side of the "discursive mind," as Richards calls it—that is, depending less on logic and "thinking" and more on intuition and imagination to guide one's behavior. The goal is to be able to go through life with the "blessed" naiveté and excitement for living of a child, but without getting "blown away" by the destructive forces in the world in the process. That is, cultivating a way of being in the world that is straightforward and uncomplicated and refreshingly innocent, without being self-destructive or interpersonally and emotionally dumb. Such comportment reflects an unaffected and trusting view of the world and human nature, rooted in part in one's intuitive access to one's primal, pre-expressive, psychophysical, authentic self.

SPONTANEITY AND STRUCTURE

Spontaneity, doing something without external incitement, and structure, organizing something so that it works as a cohesive whole, are key notions for most acting teachers. While we have discussed the

---

49 Grotowski, *Poor Man's Theatre*, pp. 193, 237. Grotowski also noted, "Better still, he [the actor] must fulfill an authentic act in place of the spectators, an act of extreme yet disciplined sincerity and authenticity" (p. 215). Grotowski never adequately defines authenticity, including taking up such philosophically thorny issues as what constitutes authenticity. How does one make the distinction between acts that are authentic and inauthentic, which are true or false to the self?

50 Richards, *At Work with Grotowski on Physical Actions*, p. 59.

importance of spontaneity, especially in the chapter on the "high priestess" of improvisation, Viola Spolin, what Grotowski has added to the subject is the notion that there is a dialectic between spontaneity, being driven by impulse rather than planning, and structure, the arranging of the impulses into an orderly and aesthetically pleasing whole. Grotowski claimed many times that spontaneity requires structure in acting:

> Spontaneity is impossible without structure. Rigor is necessary to have spontaneity. According to Stanislavski: actions which are absorbed (learned, memorized) completely, only these can become free. [...] Here is the rule: "What to do next?"—is the paralysis. "What to do next?" This is the question that makes all spontaneity impossible.[51]

The point Grotowski is making that has significance for the non-actor is this: creativity requires revealing one's most personal motivations. One must express things one usually conceals. To do this mindfully, skillfully and aesthetically, says Grotowski, requires that one do it in a structured manner, "because an inarticulate confession is no confession at all." What inhibits the person most is the presence of the judgmental others (in the acting context it is fellow actors and the director).[52] Ironically however, it is through the imposed structure that one can be most free, for spontaneity without structure is aesthetically dissonant, disordered and banal. Says Grotowski about the acting score that guides the actor's performance:

> Without a fixed score a work of art cannot exist. That's why a search for discipline and structure is as inevitable as a search for spontaneity. Searching for spontaneity without order always leads to chaos, a lost confession because an inarticulate voice cannot confess. One cannot achieve spontaneity in art without structure of detail. Without this one searches but never finds because total freedom give a lack of freedom. If we lack structured details we are like someone who loves all humanity, and that means he loves no one.[53]

What Grotowski is implying is that there is no contradiction between spontaneity and structure; it is not a problem to be resolved, but rather

51   Ibid., p. 82.
52   Schechner and Wolford, *The Grotowski Sourcebook*, p. 43.
53   Ibid., p. 55.

it is a dialectic not only to live with, but to exploit for creative purposes. In other words, spontaneity and discipline, organicity and precision, potentiate and strengthen each other. Grotowski used the unwieldy term *conjunctio-oppositorum* (conjunction of opposites) to refer to this dynamic. Not only is this dialectic essential for the actor to imaginatively integrate into his craft; it is an inevitable and necessary tension that the ordinary person must learn to gracefully calibrate.[54] In acting training, as in real life, this means that discipline and exactitude, the hallmarks of embracing structure as process, are essential to living a meaningful, sensible and aesthetically pleasing life.

ART AS VEHICLE

Art as Vehicle (coined by Peter Brook to describe Grotowski's work), or Ritual Arts, was Grotowski's last research stage, roughly from 1986 to 1999, before he died. There are two basic ideas that underlay this phase—transmission of his insights to disciples who would carry on his legacy (Thomas Richards was his chosen heir), a form of traditional initiatory practice as Grotowski formulated it; and the objectivity of ritual. As Grotowski conceptualizes it, Art as Vehicle concentrates on "actions related to very ancient songs which traditionally served ritual purposes, and so can have a direct impact on—so to say—the head, the heart and the body of the doers, songs which can allow a passage from a vital energy to a more subtle one."[55]

Grotowski's main concern was with energy transformations, the goal being for the performer to go from "heavy but organic energies (linked to the forces of life, to instincts, to sensuality) [...] to a level of energy more subtle."[56] According to Grotowski, when the performer has achieved this "subtle energy" transformation he has access to his "instinctual body," what Grotowski calls the "objectivity of the ritual."[57] Objectivity of ritual, says Slowiak and Cuesta,

> describes Grotowski's attempt to create a performative structure that functions as a tool for work on oneself. This structure is not

---

54   Kumiega, *The Theatre of Grotowski*, p. 134.
55   Lisa Wolford, "Introduction," in Schechner and Wolford, *The Grotowski Sourcebook*, p. 368.
56   Ibid.
57   Ibid., p. 369.

aimed at a spectator, but is only for the persons doing it. The structure provides a detailed key for energy transformation—to ascend
toward more subtle energy and reach a state of organicity.[58]

What Grotowski was searching for were the structures or techniques
(e.g., spaces, physical movements, vocal sensations and vibrations) that
could have a so-called objective effect on the actor (perhaps he meant
to make contact with an archetype) and most importantly, could potentiate organicity. This is what he meant by the word "ritual." "Ritual
is action and Performer is the doer." Grotowski wanted to "create a ritual for the doer—to lead a rare person toward his/her essence" ("what
you did not receive from others, what did not come from outside, what
is not learned").[59] It was this process of self-discovery of both one's
authentic personal self and a kind of universal self, a common spiritual
substratum, which seems to have been Grotowski's goal. Grotowski
had reached his ultimate objective, delineating the subtle energy transformations that could be evoked within a well-trained performer (e.g.,
via the "corporals" and "plastiques") working with vibratory songs connected to ancient ritual traditions (i.e., African/Caribbean ritual practices), within the context of an exacting and duplicable artistic framework. The "holy actor" was capable of all of this, though it should be
emphasized that the "total act" of self-exposures and self-sacrifice of
the "holy actor" could only come about through an act of "grace,"—
"moments ... in which sources began to activate, deep resources in
a person, when each of their movements becomes as if surrounded
by lightness."[60] That is, says Wolford, "such an act cannot be willed,
cannot be achieved by means of technical skill, but can arrive only
at a moment of grace to one who is in a state of passive readiness."[61]

58   Slowiak and Cuesta, *Jerzy Grotowski*, p. 53.
59   Ibid., pp. 49, 81. Grotowski's foundational notion of essence implies
     that every person has a quality or nature that makes him who he is, a per-
     fect or idealized form of himself, which needs to be actualized. In other
     words, a destiny, a predetermined and inevitable inner purpose to his life
     that needs to be discovered and realized. Many post-modern philosophers
     would regard this view as a questionable one. Grotowski does not system-
     atically discuss this implicit claim about the human condition.
60   Richards, *At Work with Grotowski on Physical Actions*, p. 69.
61   Lisa Wolford, "Grotowski's Vison of the Actor," in Hodge (Ed.),
     Twentieth Century Actor Training, p. 197.

Grotowski's notion of "grace" in part, expressed what we call his religious impulse that to some extent informed his entire oeuvre.

While Grotowski does not adequately define these questionable terms, objectivity (he believed there were objective laws to acting), essence (he seemed to believe that essence precedes existence and not the other way around as Jean-Paul Sartre famously put it) or grace (an esoteric concept usually used by "believers" though Grotowski was not one), at least not in a way that is philosophically rigorous in this post-modern world, he is getting at something that is important for the non-actor. That is, the importance of achieving what Grotowski calls a sense of "totality" and "primitive indivisibility" associated with meaningful ritual that has an integrating and life-affirming impact on the doer.[62] While delineating the function of meaningful ritual (and symbols) is beyond the scope of this chapter, what Grotowski was pointing to was the fact that many of us have become estranged from meaningful, humanistic ritual, especially ritual that involves a lot of physicality and emotional expressiveness. Not only does participating in such collective rituals gratify one's psychological needs, including one's need for social bonds and group identity, but it can have a powerful self-transcendent aspect to it, as religious "believers" often describe it. As Grotowski put it, the goal was "to cross our frontiers, exceed our limitations, fill our emptiness—fulfill ourselves."[63]

CONCLUSION: GROTOWSKI'S RELIGIOUS IMPULSE

Harold Clurman, the great theater director and one of the three original founders of the famous Group Theater in Manhattan, better than anyone else described what we mean by Grotowski's religious impulse:

> Grotowski's art is imbued with strains from Catholic and other litanies and rituals. In *Akropolis* [which is situated in a Nazi death camp], especially, one hears echoes of Roman and Jewish services, as well as Slavic melodies. It is inescapable that while Grotowski is not a "believer," his is a ritualistic, indeed a religious art. (He has said that he wished his productions to be received in strict silence.)

---

62   Kumiega, *The Theatre of Grotowski*, p. 129.
63   Ibid., p. 154.

He seeks purification through the inhuman. We are to be redeemed through hellfire.[64]

Grotowski used religious metaphors throughout his work; for example, "holy actor," "spiritual" and "grace," and his language is saturated with religious themes likes self-sacrifice, suffering, atonement, and redemption. The question is, what was Grotowski trying to get at in his use of such religious metaphors? As Grotowski insinuated, the answer, at least in part, is "the core of the theatre is encounter"—with something outside of ourselves, self-transcendence.[65] Says Grotowski, "For both producer and actor, the author's text is a sort of scalpel enabling us to open ourselves, to transcend ourselves, to find what is hidden within us and to make the act of encountering the others; in other words, to transcend our solitude."[66]

Indeed, Grotowski actually used the term "narcissism" to depict the feeble actor who either "plays to the audience" or "works directly for himself;" both approaches characterized the actor who is not able to "give himself totally" to the Other—his partner,[67] the script, the director, the audience and the Other of the unknown dimension of his personality. Grotowski admits in an interview that there is no "simple answer" to the question of what the actor is acting for if not for the audience or himself, however, "his search must be directed from within himself *to* the outside, but not *for* the outside,"[68] that is, not self-servingly and selfishly *for* the outside approval and praise. Instead, the "holy actor" gives completely of himself through his radical inner exposure and self-sacrifice—*for the Other*. Grotowski equates such giving "for the Other" before oneself as philosopher Emmaneul Levinas calls it, with giving "authentic love, deep love." In other words, what Grotowski is getting at is an "ethical attitude," and this is the point to our conclusion: if one wants to fully embrace a creative and life-affirming ethic

64   Harold Clurman, "Jerzy Grotowski," in Schechner and Wolford, *The Grotowski Sourcebook*, p. 164.

65   Grotowski, *Towards a Poor Man's Theatre*, p. 56.

66   Ibid., pp. 57, 245.

67   Ibid., p. 246. This includes the "secure partner," "this special [imaginary?] being in front of whom he does everything," an impossible to define "human being" that one encounters when one gives himself "absolutely" (ibid., p. 247).

68   Ibid., p. 247.

in one's everyday life, one must be willing to reveal oneself with the fullness of one's whole being: "do not hide that which is basic....our first obligation in art is to express ourselves through our own most personal motives."[69] Put succinctly, whether on the stage or in ordinary life, the working "principle" "is that the actor, in order to fulfill himself must not work for himself. Through penetrating his relationship with others [and more importantly, we believe, for Others]—studying the elements of contact—the actor will discover what is in him."[70] What is in him, and is in part most elemental in man, from which he has become estranged, is his capacity to live more truthfully—what we believe, following Freud, is the royal "vehicle" to increased personal freedom and the capacity to be for the Other in love. As Freud wryly advises, "being entirely honest with oneself is a good exercise" if one is to embrace "humanness," to love and work. Grotowski with his new definition of theater as "a group and a place" aptly makes a similar key point pertaining to truth telling, a fitting coda to our discussion of this brilliant and innovative director:

> And yes, it [theater] can be indispensable to life, if one seeks a space where one does not lie to oneself. Where we do not conceal where we are, what we are, and where that which we do is what it is and we do not pretend it is anything else...And this, in time, will lead us out of the theatre...[71] [toward embracing life without reserve].

---

69   Ibid., p. 244.
70   Ibid., p. 245.
71   Slowiak and Cuesta, *Jerzy Grotowski*, p. 32.

CHAPTER NINE

"THE JESTER IS THE BROTHER TO THE SAGE"

WHAT WE CAN LEARN FROM COMEDIANS, COMIC ACTORS AND CLOWNS

Yelena: "The weather's lovely today, it's not too hot."
Vanya: "Lovely weather for hanging yourself."

Uncle Vanya, Anton Chekhov

"IT'S NICE TO BE KNOWN AS A COMEDIAN ... " said Jimmy Durante, "cause a comedian makes people laugh and that's one of the greatest things anyone can do for his fellow beings ... People laugh they forget their troubles."[1] Indeed, it is part of received wisdom that to survive, let alone flourish in this world, you need a good sense of humor. As Glenn Wilson has pointed out, whether it be satire, farce or burlesque, comedy or, more generally, humor, has many psychological functions: it can be the "airing of social taboos" (e.g., Jackie Mason), a form of "social criticism" (e.g., Lenny Bruce), a "consolidation of group membership" (e.g., Arsenio Hall), "defense against fear and anxiety" (e.g., Woody Allen), or a form of "intellectual play" (e.g., the Marx Brothers).[2] What

1   Larry Wilde, *Great Comedians Talk About Comedy* (Mechanicsburg, PA: Executive Books, 2000), p. 240.
2   Glenn D. Wilson, *Psychology For Performing Artists.* Second Edition (London: Whurr Publishers, 2002), pp. 130-132. All of the listed comedians, of course, perform a wider range of comedy than the kind of humor we have ascribed to them.

underlies all of these functions of humor is the fact that humor has a hugely "protective value," that is, it reduces the negative impact of trauma and other bad happenings, lubricating hard-going or awkward human interactions. It enhances what we communicate to each other, and "it debunks aesthete, de-personalized stiffness by reminding us that all humans, no matter what airs they put on, are made of 'body stuff.'"[3] What great comics do so amazingly, and in a way that we can internalize without our usual defensiveness, is to show us our human flaws—our selfishness, arrogance, meanness and stupidity. This is the moral function of comedy—through understanding how ridiculous we are (e.g., Lucille Ball), that what we take to be accepted behavior or custom is folly, if not completely absurd (e.g., Robin Williams), and that no set of values or beliefs are truer than any others (e.g., Chris Rock)—is to force us to downsize our narcissism, while enlarging and deepening our compassion for others.[4] In a word, and this is our main claim in this chapter, the underappreciated, and we believe transcendent, psychological function of comedy is to bring about in the audience an upsurge of love for the Other, including the otherness in oneself. Exactly how this is accomplished by the great comedian, that is, by his story-telling technique and outlook on life, and what we the audience can appropriate from him into our own lives, constitutes the main body of this chapter. As Paul Ryan, one of Hollywood's top comedy acting coaches, has pointed out, every person has a "comedic core," "your own sense of comedy that arises from your own childhood, family and life experiences, everything that amuses you and that you can bring" to yourself and "to other people to make them laugh." The problem is that often this "comedic core" is repressed, inhibited or in other ways blocked, so that the average person has little access to the lighter side of himself, to his more playful, joyful and creative side.[5] Indeed, from my experience (PM), a successful psychoanalysis is often correlated with an enhancement of the analysand's capacity for good-natured humor, especially light-hearted self-deprecation. As actress

3   Seymour Fisher and Rhoda L. Fisher, *Pretend the World is Funny and Forever: A Psychological Analysis of Comedians, Clowns, and Actors* (Hillsdale, N.J.: Lawrence Erlbaum Associates, Publishers, 1981), p. xi.

4   Ibid.

5   Paul Ryan, *The Art of Comedy: Getting Serious about Being Funny* (New York: Back Stage Books, 2007), p. xviii.

Shirley McClaine aptly noted, "the person who knows how to laugh at himself will never cease to be amused."[6]

More specifically, we will argue that the comedian, at his best, can teach us a rhythm of seeing, a way of comprehending life that makes living much more tolerable, pleasing and, perhaps most importantly, ethically engaging. As Joey Bishop noted, this involves more than simply learning a "comedic attitude," rather, it is "an attitude of life," "how you live your life,"[7] that is the basis for a dazzling comedic result. There are of course straightforward techniques to make others giggle or laugh, like telling a good dirty joke. However, what we are trying to get at is how the great comedian thinks, feels and acts while practicing his craft and art form—his way of "being in the world," and what insights into the human condition and living the "good life" we can derive from him and embrace in our own lives. It should be emphasized at the onset of this study, that we are not mainly dealing with the well-researched question of why a person becomes a comedian or whether he is, in general, a more troubled or pathological person compared to the general population. Nor are we simply re-stating the truism that it is better to have a good sense of humor than not to. Rather, as the great British restoration comedy actor Simon Callow noted, our main focus is on highlighting how the comedian comports himself, especially as he practices his art: "the way in which words may transform [his and] our whole understanding of life … . celebrating aspects of the human condition that are in danger of being lost in the modern world." That is, says Callow, "the theatre's business," and we would add, the comedian's business, is "the giving and restoring of life."[8]

---

6 Patients with serious depression, anxiety and schizophrenia usually have no sense of humor, which of course is diagnostic. There are other patients (and non-patients) who do not suffer from these conditions but are almost completely incapable of being responsive to humor inside and outside of the consultation room, the so called "sticks-in-the-mud." George Saintsbury said that "Nothing is more curious than the almost savage hostility that humor excites in those who lack it." Unpacking Saintsbury's comment is worthy of a book.

7 Wilde, *Great Comedians*, pp. 98, 110.

8 Simon Callow, *Acting in Restoration Comedy* (New York: Applause Theatre Books, 1991), p. 106.

COMEDY IS DEFERRED TRAGEDY

Comedians, and, less obviously, comic actors and clowns, all tend to share consciously or unconsciously, at least one profound moral conviction about life, namely, that the world is deeply flawed and broken, and needs correction and healing via humor. As any Jewish comedian (e.g., Mel Brooks, Myron Cohen, Milton Berle and Neil Simon) from the once thriving "Jewish Alps," the "borscht belt" (the Catskill Mountains),[9] would put it, one of the comedian's main functions in our society is to "kvetch"—to continually grumble and complain about how bad things are. Indeed, in terms of the comedian's actual routines, they are often preoccupied with whether they—and by extension, we—are "good" or "bad." Fischer and Fischer contend that "most of the funny people we have studied are fascinated with the classic struggle between good and the bad. They endlessly debate their own qualifications for entry into Heaven."[10] Whether the comedian is more gently focusing on manifestly moral themes as Charlie Chaplin did in *The Tramp* or *The Great Dictator*, or he is decrying the ills of American social life with the tenacity of a guerilla warrior, like Lenny Bruce, the fact is that the comedian is the archetypical complainer. As stand-up comedian Bill Maher said, "'But for me as a comedian, there's gotta be an element of, 'This is wrong, this is out of place, and I'm gonna shout about it.'"[10] Historically, the court jester and clown, the forerunners of the modern day comedian, though they were entertaining in their silliness and sometimes objects of scorn, were also viewed as the voice of profound truths concerning moral goodness and related themes. In our day, for example, Dick Gregory personifies the comedian as the transmitter of moral truths. As Robert Lipsyte, who collaborated on Dick Gregory's autobiography noted, for Gregory "comedy [was] used in the service of what he felt was righteousness," that is, using civil rights for building the just society.

With all of their concern with both personal and society's "goodness" and "badness," it is not surprising that comedians have often been viewed in the popular imagination as gloomy people beneath their funny surface. While the research on this claim is not at all conclusive,

9   Lawrence Epstein, *The Haunted Smile: The Story of Jewish Comedians in America* (New York: Public Affairs, 2001), pp. 104, 112.
10   Fischer and Fischer, *Pretend the World*, p. 36.

does this by allowing himself to be gracefully "pulled back and forth by his ambivalence."[16] While in some psychological circles, the goal of treatment is to resolve the ambivalence, in the psychoanalytic view, following Freud, a degree of ambivalence, especially in love and work, is inherent in the human condition. According to this view, the best we can do is to keep the presence of opposing ideas, attitudes and emotions, and the feelings of uncertainty that they arouse, in some kind of precarious, though not too unsettling balance. Thus, when the comedian tells jokes that highlight the fact that things are not what they seem to be, that appearance and reality often do not coincide, he is actually affirming a core conviction about the nature of reality, external and internal: reality is most manageable when one gently embraces the ambivalence, when one learns to live humbly with it, as opposed to trying to resolve it once and for all, to do that which is like trying to catch smoke in your hands. As Shultz points out, when it comes to the creation of humor, "the creator of a joke first notices an ambiguity (either linguistic or conceptual) and then creates an incongruity by responding to the hidden rather than the intended meaning of the ambiguity."[17] The result is that we laugh and, for a moment at least, we feel we have hoodwinked ambivalence and mastered life.

What all of this boils down to is this: humor is often connected to the dynamic of hiddenness-revelation, or as Fisher and Fisher called it, a "broad dimension of concealment-openness." It is the ambivalence that underlies this hiddenness-revelation dynamic that one has to make contact with, and make fun of, for in so doing, one can feel a sense of greater control over the everyday harshness of life, as well as over its more traumatic aspects. Most importantly perhaps, this appreciation of the ambivalence-animated, hiddenness-revelation dimension provides the average person with a powerful insight, one that all great comedy provides, that "beneath the surface, we are all members of the same [human] race."[18] That is, despite our superficial

---

16   Ibid., p. 78.

17   Thomas R. Shultz, "A Cognitive-Developmental Analysis of Humour." In Antony Chapman and Hugh C. Foot (Eds.), *Humor and Laughter: Theory, Research, and Applications* (New York: Wiley, 1976), pp. 11-36. Cited from Fisher and Fisher, *Pretend the World*, p. 78.

18   Gerald Mast, *The Comic Mind: Comedy and the Movies* (New York: Bobbs-Merrill Co., 1973). p. 324. Cited from Fisher and Fisher, *Pretend*

differences, we are all engaged in the same struggles and joys that constitute being a sentient human being. When Lucy (Lucille Ball) makes fun of the pretentious and self-important, when Whoopi Goldberg uses humor to undermine social expectations and political correctness, when David Letterman jokes about others' underlying flaws and defects, and when Woody Allen engages in self-effacing humor, we all become acutely aware of our common humanity.[19] Such an awareness is a fertile breeding ground for the growth of greater empathy and compassion for our fellow human travelers, especially the personal suffering that always generates their selfish, arrogant and mean behavior. Such empathy and compassion we have called the upsurge of love for the Other.

MINIATURIZATION

Miniaturization—the mental capacity to make a version of something in a much smaller size or on a greatly reduced scale—is a quality of mind that animates the material of most great comedians and, for that matter, their outlook on life. Through miniaturization, especially when it comes to things that we are afraid of or anxious about, we feel a degree of enhanced control. Indeed, comedians have always been enthralled with size, with the contrast between the big and the small. One only has to think of the clowns of one's childhood to see how size disparities make up much of what they do that makes us laugh (e.g., normal feet are wearing oversized floppy shoes, hugely inflated balloons are suddenly deflated into nothing). Moreover, comedians often mock themselves on the size dimension, Jimmy Durante makes fun of his large snout, Joan Rivers jokes about her petite breasts, while Don Rickles often puts down a man in the audience by insinuating that he has a small penis or can not get, or maintain, a strong erection.[20] There are, of course, many possible psychoanalytic interpretations of the comedian's, and our, fascination with size, such as the sense of bodily insecurity and inadequacy that is rooted in his traumatic childhood.

the World, p. 81.

19   Wilson, *Psychology for Performing Arts*, pp. 141-142.

20   Rickles, like most comedians, though perhaps in a more nuanced fashion, has something of a sadomasochistic way of relating to his audiences. The comedian inflicts pain by skillfully placed insults; some perversely enjoy the derision (Fisher and Fisher, *Pretend the World*, pp. 90-92).

Feelings of smallness and inferiority are common sentiments for most people, at least from time to time. The comedian has figured out a way of dealing with such self-esteem vulnerabilities by a clever reversal strategy, one that can help the average person move beyond that awful feeling of self-deprecation The use of humor can be a way of reducing or denying the fear and anxiety associated with feeling small. As one psychoanalytic author noted, humor allows the comedian to negate the near-lethal self-awareness that feeling small means that he is feeble and vulnerable. By asking, "Am I small?" or declaring, "I am small," especially relative to others who are literally or symbolically "big," by making fun of the fact that one may be small in say height, or small in wealth or status, the comedian actually assumes a courageous, self-affirming stance in relation to his sense of inferiority. For by making us laugh at his manifest reduced self-esteem and status, by facing it head on, as it were, he paradoxically gains great respect in our eyes (think of the lovable loser routine of Rodney Dangerfield, "I can't get no respect"). Theodore Reik called this dynamic, victory through defeat. Through brutally honest self-presentation and self-criticism of one's inadequacies, including of one's fears and anxieties, one can actually assume a degree of moral grandeur—greater self-respect for one's integrity and emotional fortitude. Finally, in part, through the use of miniaturization and other types of size-related imagery within the context of this "victory through defeat" metaphor, the comedian magnificently enacts his moral function for the audience. He makes us feel genuinely guilty. That is, we in the audience feel a degree of culpability for our superficial and harsh judgment of people who are "small" and feel inferior. We gain, by means of the comedian's use of size-related imagery and the like, a greater sense of responsibility for the Other and compassion for the otherness of the devalued and weak of the world. Such use of humor is also an effective way to undo those same or similar feelings of self-doubt and self-diminution that so demoralize most of us.

MARGINALITY

Marginality, the ability to creatively exist or operate on the fringes of a group or movement, is a way of being in the world that characterizes nearly every great comedian. While some comedians have been

associated with the so-called mainstream of society and have comfortably hobnobbed with the powerful and rich, Bob Hope, for example,
for the most part the comedian is the quintessential "marginal man,"
a concept first coined by the American sociologist, Robert E. Park,
who in 1937 wrote, "The marginal man ... is one whom fate has con-
demned to live in two societies and in two, not merely different but
antagonistic cultures. ... his mind is the crucible in which two different and refractory cultures may be said to melt and, either wholly or
in part, fuse." Though Park originally formulated his concept of "marginal man" in relation to his discussion of the causes and consequences
of human migrations, there is an aspect of this description that aptly
characterizes the comedian's way of being in the world that is instruc-
tive to all of us about how to better manage life's fears and anxieties.

The comedian's historical and to some extent contemporary social
location is to be both in, but not of, the society he is humorously cri-
tiquing. Think of the court jester who was both engaged in the daily
life of the court but was also on its fringes as something of a social
outcast, though a truth-telling one. Likewise, on the one hand, the
comedian shares intimately in the life of the mainstream community,
but, on the other, he is often the consummate outsider. There, in part,
lies the basis for his unique insights into the human condition. One
only has to remember the rebel comedians of the 1950s and 1960s,
such as Mort Saul, Lenny Bruce and Dick Gregory, [21] to be convinced
that the proper social location of the comedian is the borderland, the
narrow ridge between the mainstream and the fringe, between the in-
sider and the outsider. In other words, when one is in a certain sense
marginal, one can better see and understand, for example, those social
taboos, usually around sex and aggression, that tend to over-regulate
individual autonomy and cause considerable unhappiness. Moreover,
not only is the creatively marginal comedian able to identify those
ludicrous taboos that make us miserable, but by satirizing them he
opens up space for us to think differently about them. Through his
wit, especially his irony, sarcasm and ridicule, he attacks the vices and
follies of society and individual behavior that condemn us to live truncated, if not absurd lives. Such humorous deconstruction that derides
our repressive social and political institutions, including our submis-

---

21   Nachman, *Seriously Funny*, p. 5.

sion to their oppressive norms, provides the psychological context for constructive, life-affirming change. Only when you live close to the edge, as do so many comedians, do you comprehend the limits and bountifulness of life. It is within his marginal context that the comedian assumes the role as the purveyor of transgressive ethical values that go beyond his own self-aggrandizement. These values that expose our selfishness, meanness and stupidity, are meant to be curative, healing and restorative to both society and the individual. They express in the broadest sense his wish to rescue us from ourselves. They are a form of love conceived as responsibility for, and to, the Other.

HUMOR AS AN EXPRESSION OF HOSTILITY

Hostility, that feeling or attitude of hatred, enmity, antagonism, or anger toward somebody or something, is often part of a comedian's routine in one form or another. Whether it is Alan King's sense of righteous indignation at exploitive banks, unfair insurance companies or unreasonable airlines,[22] or the angry violent outcries of other comedians on a variety of subjects, we in the audience identify with the comedian's angry protest and his wish for vengeance. Humor, as Freud pointed out, is a way of expressing and sharing what is usually repressed, in this case, hostile feelings, often in a non-straightforward and indirect manner. Many professional comedians have recognized this intimate connection between hostility and comedy: "I think a lot of people in comedy are sitting on a lot of anger, and comedy is a way, obviously to relieve that" (Richard Belzer); "I'm lucky that my art allows me to express this anger and dismay" (George Carlin); "There is a close alliance between anger and humor" (Bill Maher).[23] As Janus quotes from one of the humorists in his important study of the personalities of fifty-five great comedians, "The comedian must practice his comedy in order to avoid destroying himself." This is not an altogether surprising observation considering that Janus describes his sample as "brilliant, angry, suspicious, and depressed."[24] For, as is

---

22   Samuel S. Janus, "The Great Comedians: Personality and Other Factors." *The American Journal of Psychoanalysis* (1975): 35: 173.

23   Ajaye, *Comic Insights*, pp. 64, 85, 158.

24   Janus, "The Great Comedians," pp. 169, 173.

well-known, psychodynamically speaking, depression is often aggression turned against the self.

In addition to the conventional claim that humor is, in part, a socially acceptable expression of hostility, there is an often unrecognized or at least underappreciated insight about hostility and humor that has bearing not only on how we understand the comedian's story-telling technique and outlook on life, but, more importantly, on what we in the audience can take from him to use in our own lives. That is, in the average person there is a certain bizarre ecstasy in expressing hostility, especially the raw kind, and especially at people and institutions we do not like. As Jerzy Grotowski pointed out in a different context, the comedian's hostile expression touches the audience deeply and powerfully. Such a moment liberates us all from the hold of our own hostile wishes. By our watching the comedian's humorous way of enacting our hostile wishes, we are cleansed of them. Through creating this intensified reality and enacting the taboo wish in a humorous manner, he thus jolts us into a new mode of awareness about the "badness" of the external and internal worlds we have created. By sharing this shameful and guilt-inducing awareness that our hostile wishes often ideally engender, we are joined together and we are all purged and prompted to make things better.[25] What we are saying is more than that hostile humor reduces tension and is a social safety valve, though it is, but that hostile humor that is enacted with truthfulness and artfulness breaks down some barriers and provides the context for internal change, especially for ethical deepening. Such hostile humor makes us laugh for a few seconds, but think for a lot longer about what is objectionable in the world we live in and about the way we live in the world. Moreover, great hostile humor does this by releasing other psychic capacities, especially reparative impulses that can be applied to the work of changing the external and internal worlds for the better. Norman Cousins has perceptively commented on this point: "What was significant about the laughter ... was not just the fact that it provides internal exercises for a person ... [a] form of jogging for the innards, but that it creates a mood in which the other positive emotions can be put to work, too." In this sense, there is a place for hostile humor in everyday life, though

---

25   Richard Brestoff, *The Great Acting Teachers and Their Methods* (Lyme: NH, Smith and Kraus, 1992), p. 159.

it must be done very skillfully to be effective and helpful; otherwise it is just hurtful, mean and gratuitously violent. Well-executed hostile humor actually is a sub-species of love, what has been called "tough love" in the worlds of drug rehabilitation and wayward teens—harsh, severe and aggressive treatment that is rooted in the clinician's sense of responsibility and affection for the troubled person that is ultimately helpful to him. In our case it is the audience that is the comedian's ethical concern, as he, perhaps unknowingly, summons it to greater responsibility. As St. Augustine said, "sometimes the stick is a form of love too."

CONCLUSION

Peter Ustinov correctly said that "comedy is simply a funny way of being serious." This is not at all surprising when we consider the profound self-described personal motivations of some professional comedians and comic actors: "exhibitionism and narcissism" and "the need to form relationships and be accepted" (Woody Allen), the inordinate need to feel special and loved (Jack Benny), and unsatisfied needs for attention and affirmation stemming from childhood (Dustin Hoffman).[26] While in many cases, a degree of personal hardship or suffering may propel someone to want to become a professional comedian, his way of being and seeing when he is performing reflects his personality and strengths: "tenacity, self-confidence, and an acute understanding of human nature ... talent, creativity, perseverance, mastery of the craft," and, of course, that "extra intangible something."[27] Thus, it is not surprising that the comedian, and his forerunners, the court jester, clowns and the like, though they are simultaneously looked down on and respected, have some important practical insights to teach us non-comedians about the art of living the "good life."

We want to conclude this chapter by emphasizing that the main underappreciated, if not unrecognized, function of comedy and perhaps other forms of humor, is to facilitate in the audience an upsurge of love for the Other, including the otherness in oneself. What the comedian's way of comporting himself teaches us is that his humor is most effective when it transcends his inordinate narcissistic and exhibitionistic

---

26   Wilson, *Psychology For Performing Artists*, p.143.
27   Wilde, *Comedians*, pp. 4, 5.

needs. According to Jerry Seinfield, "you have to love those people out
there for some unexplainable reason, and be willing to take a chance
on perhaps embarrassing yourself so that they have a good time."[28]
Richard Belzer, another well-known comedian, similarly noted, "The
idea of making a bunch of strangers laugh and share the same thing at
the same moment is a very profound metaphysical and physical force.
To be able to do that can be taken for granted or it can be thought of
as a responsibility. Let's put it this way—it's my religion."[29] Finally, former comedian Jamie Masada, who opened the famous Laugh Factory
said, "My goal came from something my father told me when I was a
kid, which was [that] the greatest mitzvah or greatest good deed you
could do for people was to make them laugh."[30] Many more quotations
could be provided, but our point is clear: humor at its best, when it
is most effective, if not therapeutic, emanates from a loving impulse,
that is, it is other-directed and other-regarding. For the average person
to develop his "comedic core," as we described it earlier, requires an
analogous loving impulse. Jimmy Durante famously said, when he was
asked what is the greatest quality a comedian can have—"Heart. He's
gotta have heart. Other-wise he's nuthin."[31] Only then can he refine his
ability to take what he hears, sees and suffers in his life, and transform
it into one of those beautiful moments of humor that we are privileged
and so grateful to experience.

28   Wilde, *Great Comedians*, p. 347.
29   Ajaye, *Comic Insights*, p. 67.
30   Ibid., p. 267.
31   Wilde, *Great Comedians*, p. 243.

CHAPTER TEN

"DENY NOTHING, INVENT NOTHING, ACCEPT EVERYTHING AND GET ON WITH IT"

DAVID MAMET'S PRACTICAL AESTHETICS

"The actor is, primarily, a philosopher. A philosopher of acting. And the audience understands him as such....Your task is to tell the truth."

—David Mamet

YOU CAN'T HELP BUT BE A LITTLE BIT TAKEN BACK, BEWILDERED, AND/OR STRANGELY AMUSED by David Mamet's *chutzbah* (audacity) for what he said about Lawrence Olivier, an actor who many believe was the greatest actor of our time. For the gadfly Mamet, Olivier exemplified the type of "Great Acting" he did not trust or like ("polite and predictable"),[1] a performer who was "stiff, self-conscious, grudging,

1   David Mamet, *True and False: Heresy and Common Sense for the Actor* (New York: Pantheon Books, 1997), p. 56 (hereafter, *True and False*). The great actor Anthony Hopkins praised Mamet's book for its ability to "[demolish] the myths and the psychobabble-gobbledygook that pass for theory with regard to acting." *True and False* was "a revealing book of

coy and ungenerous."[2] To be fair to Mamet, he was not the first acting teacher to make such an outrageously judgmental comment. Sanford Meisner, one of Mamet's mentors and theoretical forerunners of his development of Practical Aesthetics, also trashed poor Olivier, saying, "See, I maintain, and will continue to maintain, that Laurence Olivier is not a great actor."[3] What is noteworthy about Mamet's rather provocative views on acting (and on theater in general) is not so much any original insights into acting theory and technique, for Practical Aesthetics is mainly a useful amalgamation, adaptation and simplification of some of the best ideas of Stanislavski and secondarily of Meisner. Mamet and his co-originator of Practical Aesthetics, actor William H. Macy, have done the acting community a service by putting into sharp focus, and recasting a little bit differently, at least three key acting principles made by Stanislavski 70 years ago, principles that have been creatively appropriated by Practical Aesthetics:[4] (1) the actor must show a "simplicity of action;" (2) "the removal of emotion" as "the focal point of the actors work to" view it as "the by-product of physical action;" and (3) "the pursuit of an objective ["What do I want?"] with passion and excitement."[5] This being said, what is mainly of interest in this chapter is to suggest what is the "broader aesthetic consciousness"[6] that Mamet is putting forth in his Practical Aesthetics. Mamet claims that more than technique, it is "Philosophy, Morality and Aesthetics" that is most worth transmitting to the next

---

the highest order." (http://www.instantcast.com/LearnAbout/Articles/ become_an_actor, p. 2).

2   Christopher Collard, "Living Truthfully: David Mamet's Practical Aesthetics," *New Theater Quarterly*, 26:4 (November 2010), p. 331. Collard is quoting from C.W.E. Bigsby, "David Mamet" in Bigsby (Ed.), *The Cambridge Companion to David Mamet* (Cambridge: Cambridge University Press, 2004), p. 6.

3   Sanford Meisner and Dennis Longwell, *Sanford Meisner on Acting* (New York: Vintage, 1987), p. 121.

4   Collard, who is rather critical of Mamet's views, does not describe Mamet's amalgamation of Stanislavski as creative, but rather calls it "crudely amalgamating." "Living Truthfully: David Mamet's Practical Aesthetics," p. 330.

5   Bella Merlin, "Mamet's Heresy and Common Sense: What's True and False in 'True and False.'" *New Theatre Quarterly*, 16 (2000), p. 254.

6   Collard, "Living Truthfully: David Mamet's Practical Aesthetics," p. 331.

generation of actors and actresses.[7] Put differently, this chapter will mainly concern itself with describing some of the important valuative attachments that are the basis for effective, if not great, acting and by extension, great living, as conceived by Practical Aesthetics. As Mamet said, "A life in the theater need not be an analogue to 'life.' It *is* life."[8] Also, "the ethical laws of life on the stage are no different than those on the street."[9] Perhaps, more than most acting teachers we have discussed in this book, though similar to Stanislavski, Mamet is mindful of the crucial connection between what "core" life and identity-defining values and beliefs the actor embraces in his everyday life and his capacity to give an effective acting performance. Such ethical terms like "sacrifice," "sense of truth," "discipline and simplicity," and "courage" permeate Mamet's writings on theater. Most importantly in terms of the animating thesis of our book, the actor should be guided in his performance by "generosity," "the need to love rather than our need to have," and "his goodness."[10]

By way of organizing this chapter, we will first describe the working "Philosophy" of Practical Aesthetics, followed by its "Aesthetics," and lastly, we will discuss what we feel is perhaps most compelling about its theory and technique, its deep commitment to an ethical outlook both on and off the stage (what Mamet loosely calls "Morality"). While it is tempting to focus only on Mamet's views of acting, especially as contained in his irreverent and polemical book, *True and False: Heresy and Common Sense for the Actor* (1997), and some of his other essays, we will resist the temptation to make this chapter mainly about Mamet, especially Mamet the playwright. In addition to drawing from Mamet, we will liberally draw from Bruder et al.'s (henceforth, "Bruder") *A Practical Handbook for the Actor* (1986), the "bible" of Practical Aesthetics as taught at its main conservatory, Atlantic Theater Acting School in New York City.

---

7 David Mamet, *Writing In Restaurants* (New York: Penguin, 1986), p. 20.
8 Ibid., p. 106.
9 Ibid., p. 28.
10 David Mamet, "Introduction," in Melissa Bruder et al. (Eds.), *A Practical Handbook For the Actor* (New York: Vintage House, 1986), pp. x, xi (henceforth, *Practical Handbook*); Mamet, *Writing in Restaurants*, pp. 127, 128.

PHILOSOPHY

Mamet is firstly a great playwright; he is also an essayist, a screenwriter and film director. He is not, however, a systematic philosopher, let alone one who uses terms in a rigorously philosophical manner. In fact he prides himself in using "a little common sense"[11] in developing his pragmatic views on acting. Of course, "common sense" is itself a radically philosophical term because it is a term whose meaning is highly debatable if not up for grabs. This being said, like all of the acting teachers discussed in our book, we have to search for the "philosophy," and especially the "philosophy of life" that is embedded in his various writings, the outlook that tends to animate his acting theory and technique and which is suggestive of what constitutes living a "good life."

As Mark Westbrook, a Scottish professional acting coach, noted in his overview, Practical Aesthetics is best conceived less as a system, and more as "a set of pragmatic principles on the craft of acting" (a "noble art," says Mamet), one that can be straightforwardly taught and learned by just about anyone if only they are committed to doing so. Paraphrasing Mamet, Westbrook notes, "To be an actor, does not require the mysterious impalpable thing called talent, or the ability to 'become' the character [an illusory goal for Mamet], none of these things are within our control."[12] Mamet argues that the effective actor must simply have the courage and discipline needed to generate a clear, specific objective (i.e., establishing what the character "wants"), to stay focused on that objective, and to act simply to realize that objective in doable physical action.[13] He does this, in part, as a revolt against the overbearing, expressively muting aspects of the introspective, self-concerning, interpretive approach of Stanislavski, especially its "extreme" American version as articulated by Lee Strasberg, such as in his notions of "emotional preparation" and "affective memory." As Mamet noted, "The actor is on stage to communicate the play to the audience" (to tell a compelling story). "That is the beginning and the end of his

---

11   Mamet, *True and False*, p. 4.

12   Mark Westbrook, http://EnzineArticles.com/?expert=Mark_Westbrook, p. 3.

13   Annette J. Saddik, http://mamet.eserver.org/review/1998/saddik.html, p. 1.

and her job."[14] "Wisdom lies in doing *your* job and getting on with it."[15] Moreover, to accomplish this, the actor needs "a strong voice, superb diction, a supple, well-proportioned body, and a rudimentary understanding of the play."[16] The latter attributes are part of any competent actor's learned skill-set if only he decides to put the time and effort into perfecting these skills.

There are mainly three works in philosophy that loosely underlay Practical Aesthetics, the *Enchiridion* by the Stoic philosopher Epictetus, William James's *Principles of Psychology* and Aristotle's *Poetics*. While there are thousands of scholarly books written on these three masterpieces, we only want to suggest how Practical Aesthetics has "cherry picked" from these sources and applied them to its acting theory and practice, especially from the insights of the Stoics and from James's notion of habit.[17]

The key Stoic notions that underlay Practical Aesthetics are clearly stated in its *Practical Handbook* in Mamet's introduction:

> The technical suggestions [to be a great actor], finally, are reducible to a simple stoic philosophy: be what you wish to seem. Stanislavski once wrote that you should "play well or badly, but play truly." It is not up to you whether your performances will be brilliant—all that

14 Mamet, *True and False*, p. 9. And again, "To serve the real theater, one needs to be able to please the audience and the audience only" (p. 42).

15 Ibid., p. 57. It is worth noting that in Greek tradition, *sophia*, wisdom or knowledge, is not so much a "purely theoretical wisdom than know-how, or knowing-how-to-live" (Pierre Hadot, *What Is Ancient Philosophy*. Trans. Michael Chase. Cambridge, MA: Harvard University Press, 2002, p. 44).

16 Ibid., p. 42.

17 According to Westbrook, *The Poetics* is the basis for the simple three-step script analysis technique of Practical Aesthetics. When analyzing a scene the actor should ask himself: (1) "What is the character literally doing? (2) What is the essential action of what the character is doing in the scene? (3) What is that action like to me? *It's as if...*" Incidentally, the "as-if" is "a simple fantasy that makes specific for" the actor "the action you have chose in step 2 of the analysis," it is a kind of "mnemonic device to bring the action to life in you." The "as-if," of course, has a conscious emotional component to it in that it is that "which you remind yourself of what the action means to you in personal terms," in other words, a good "as-if" "get[s] your motor going" (Bruder, *Practical Aesthetics*, pp. 19, 87, 28, 30). Some believe that the "as-if" has a degree of "family resemblance" to "emotional memory" and "substitution."

is under your control is your intention. It is not under your control
whether your career will be brilliant—all that is under your control
is your intention.[18]

In the context of acting, what this boils down to is that by concentrating on those aspects of the performance that the actor has some
control over, the actor is more likely to be successful in creating an
effective performance. Actors have many things that they do not have
much or any control over, for example, the audiences' reactions, the
critics' reviews, the directors' commands, the script, and the way his
partner performs in a scene. Likewise, and most importantly perhaps,
according to Pragmatic Aesthetics, you do not have the capacity to
feel things "on demand"; that is, the actor does not have reliable control over producing and sustaining the appropriate emotion to "fit" the
character he is playing and the circumstances of the scene. To think
otherwise, says Bruder, is to be victim to "the emotional trap." Bruder
further notes, "Once you accept that there is no such thing as a correct
emotion for a given scene, you will have divested yourself of the bur-
den of becoming emotional....There is one simple guideline to follow
concerning emotional life onstage: it is beyond your control, so don't
worry about it. Ever."[19] Similar to Meisner's formulations, for example,
Bruder says that the apt emotions "are the natural and inescapable by-
product of your commitment to your action" as you truthfully and
spontaneously "play off" your fellow actors. What an actor needs to
learn is how to skillfully "work through" the upsurges of emotion "rag-
ing through you" during a performance.[20] That is, how to seamlessly
"channel" or "direct," not "create," the felt emotion into the action, a kind
of sublimation in psychoanalytic terms. "Once you've learned to commit fully to a physical action, your only task concerning emotions will
be…to let them exist as they will, for they are beyond your control and
will come to you quite unbidden."[21]

As discussed in our Meisner chapter, there is something sensible
about suggesting to the actor (and non-actor) that focusing on his actions, on his behavior, and not on his emotional state, is most likely

---

18   Mamet, "Introduction," in *Practical Handbook*, p. xi.
19   Bruder et al., *Practical Handbook*, p. 71.
20   Ibid., p. 73.
21   Ibid.

to bring about an effective performance on and off the stage. First, in a way it is true, as Bruder points out, that if an actor pushes or forces himself into an emotional state he will create an "attitude" that will then likely obligate him to perform according to that "attitude" for the rest of a scene. The downside of this is that the "the truth of the moment will be completely lost because your attention will fall on yourself." Most importantly, the actor will lose touch with his all-important "impulses," including the "impulses" and "offerings" of his fellow actor, thus the performance of the scene will be boring. Second, Bruder claims that "you can't execute a physical action while trying to maintain an emotional state," that is, the specificity of action that is rooted in a skillful scene analysis will no longer be operative and you will be acting "in general," mainly because your action will be lost in the emotional quagmire you have worked yourself into. Third, says Bruder, a technique lodged in emotion is frequently unreliable, mainly because you cannot predictably control what you feel, and therefore "emotions can desert you at any time." Rather, says Bruder, "a technique based on physical actions calls upon the *will* and can be used at any time and in any situation, regardless of how you are feeling."[22] Mamet, always the provocateur, makes this point rather unforgettably, "'Emotional memory,' 'sense memory,' and the tenets of the Method back to and including Stanislavski's trilogy are a lot of hogwash. This 'method' does not work; it cannot be practiced." Also, "The Stanislavski 'Method' and the techniques of the schools derived from it [which is probably every major acting technique], is nonsense."[23]

One of the conceptual problems with the way Practical Aesthetics formulates its emphasis on physical action "versus" emotion is that it assumes that they are somehow two distinct realms, two modes of

22   Ibid., pp. 71-73.
23   Mamet, *True and False*, pp. 12, 6. To be fair to Mamet, there are passages in his writings where he shows appreciation for the insights of Stanislavski. In *Some Freaks*, he notes, "Stanislavski's ideas were and are very useful." (New York: Penguin, 1989 p. 76). As Wilmeth noted, "Mamet is, by his own admission, contradictory and inconsistent" in his views on theater. It is hard to believe that Mamet "really" believes that Stanislavski is a "dilettante" as he calls him, as somebody who is interested in acting and theater but has only a superficial understanding of it. Don B. Wilmeth, "Mamet and the actor," in Bigsby, *The Cambridge Companion to David Mamet* (Cambridge, MA: Cambridge University Press, 2004), p. 140.

experience that are in actuality separate realms. Even more troubling is the assumption that emotions and actions can "willfully" be separated, as if human experience isn't an organic, integrated unity of mind, body, and some believe, spirit. While the mind-body problem, such as whether mental and physical process are the same or not, is one of the most intractable problems in the history of philosophy, the fact is that the "received wisdom" on the matter is that the mind and body work together as an interrelated, integrated, organic whole. Psychosomatic medicine personifies this assumption but so does "common sense," to use one of Mamet's favorite tropes of persuasion. There is never an action that does not have its correlated conscious and/or unconscious emotion(s), nor an emotion that does not have its physiological correlate(s). When an actor feels anxiety before a stage performance, his heart rate goes up, he sweats and he may begin to tremble or feel other forms of bodily tension; when he does a fight scene, a love scene or comical scene, he feels energized, aroused, and more alive. As is well known among psychoanalysts and others, every psychic event has its physical counterpart broadly described, even if they are organized in different ways and conceptualized from different standpoints, such as being conscious and/or unconscious. The upshot of our point is this: by Practical Aesthetics focusing solely on the actor's doable action, and jettisoning *any* conscious focus by the actor on his emotions and "inner world" (the actor is "free of the necessity of 'feeling'"; "The skill of acting is finally a physical skill; it is not a mental exercise"),[24] he is making an assumption that not only is probably impossible to implement, but it is not in sync with current views of how the human being resides in the world, as a "being-in-the-world," to paraphrase Martin Heidegger and others. Human comportment is best comprehended without any binaries, dualities or clear divisions, no subject/object, mind/body, or emotions/actions, but rather as a holistic "person-in-the-world." (Strasberg, in his ultra-focus on "emotional preparation" and "affective memory," makes a similar mistake as Mamet and company do, but from the other side of the binary.) The most reasonable "solution" to this conceptual and practical problem is to develop an acting theory that more adequately formulates the relationship between mind/emotions and body/actions and then develop a technique that better takes

---

24   Mamet, *True and False*, pp. 9, 19.

into consideration the integrated, organic nature of human experience as it is currently viewed by most sophisticated thinkers on the subject.

According to Bruder, the actor should never concern himself with the question of "talent," that so-called natural ability to do something well. As Mamet noted, "I don't know what talent is, and, frankly, I don't care."[25] Bruder explains,

> Talent, if it exists at all, is completely out of your control. Whatever talent may be, you either have it or you don't, so why waste energy worrying about it? The only talent you need to act is a talent for working—in other words, the ability to apply yourself in learning skills that make up the craft of acting. To put it simply, anyone can act if he has the will to do so, and anyone who says he wants to but doesn't have the knack for it suffers from the lack of will, not a lack of talent.[26]

As Mamet further noted, instead of dwelling on the question of whether an actor has or does not have "talent," he should think about the qualities of mind and heart that he has some control over: "I do not think it is the actor's job to be interesting. I think that's the job of the script." Rather, "it is the actor's job to be truthful and brave—both qualities which can be developed and exercised through the will."[27]

Thus, the only thing, says Mamet, that the actor has control over, is creating the right action for the scene and going after that goal as if it were the most important objective in the world. By doing this, the audience will feel that they have seen an effective performance because the actor has passionately advanced the overarching goal of a play—to tell a compelling story. To help accomplish this, the actor should concentrate on what he can control before he is on the stage, "on developing measurable skills," such as a stronger and clearer voice, "to analyze a script correctly," to better concentrate and to strengthen and make more supple one's body.[28] It is hard to argue with aspects of this "common sense" approach to acting, as Mamet and company describe it, though sometimes Mamet, in his more rhetorically magnified moments, throws the baby out with the bath water, "For acting

---

25 Ibid., p. 98.
26 Ibid., p. 5.
27 Ibid., p. 98.
28 Ibid.

has nothing whatever to do with the ability to concentrate....[For
Mamet, a forced and uncontrollable activity that reflects self-occu-
pation.] Elect something to do which is physical and fun to do, and
concentration ceases to be an issue."[29] To be fair to Mamet, we doubt
he is against all forms of concentration, simply defined as the direction
of all thought or effort toward one particular task, idea, or subject.
Rather what Mamet is troubled by are the ways that concentration,
like "trying" to be interesting, or "trying" to feel an emotion, become
a form of self-absorption and prevent the actor from focusing on the
actions of the play. To do them [the actions] is more interesting than
to concentrate on them .... Choose something legitimately interesting
to do and concentration is not a problem. Choose something less than
interesting and concentration is impossible." Similar to his analysis of
emotion, Mamet believes that "the ability to concentrate flows naturally from the ability to choose something interesting."[30]

What Mamet and his cohort are getting at as it relates to acting is, to
some extent, applicable to the art of living a "good life." That is, following Epictetus and other Stoics,[31] the art of living a "good life" entails
the capacity to distinguish that which one could control by human
means (e.g., beliefs, judgments, desires and attitudes) and to accept
with dignified resignation, without complaint and fear, that which is
beyond our control (e.g., things external to us such as the actions and
opinion of others, our partners, children, money, jobs, world power,
death, etc.). For Epictetus, this distinction was based on the Stoic belief that the whole universe was a living, organic, intelligent entity animated by the Logos which was roughly equivalent to such entities as
God, Zeus, reason, creative fire, nature, providence, destiny, order. All
people were under the dominion of the ruling Logos. Since the Logos
permeated everything, whatever happened in the universes was controlled by the universal law of nature or providence. All human beings
were interrelated parts of this universal, living, intelligent entity. Thus,
since everything that happens to individuals was determined, the only
way in which individuals could control their fate was to control how

29   Ibid., pp. 93, 96.
30   Ibid., p. 95.
31   Mamet for example, draws from Epictetus and Stoic philosophy
      in *Writing in Restaurants* and *True and False*, as does Bruder et al. in *A
      Practical Handbook*.

they reacted to external events. In other words, human freedom was manifested in attitudinal freedom and, given the Stoic cosmology, this was the only way the Stoic could triumph over providence. (The Stoics never provided an adequate rationalization for the fact that if providence controls everything, does it not also control our attitudes?) As Epictetus famously said, "What troubles people is not things, but their judgment about things." Interestingly, Practical Aesthetics has not only quoted these wise words in its *Practical Handbook*, but it has claimed that if you keep "the four virtues" always in mind you will be a productive actor, one who will avoid creativity-draining, petty conflict with others and not be angered by other people's views—(1) "humility," so that when someone criticizes and/or corrects you, you will not be affronted or hurt; (2) "generosity,"[32] so that when someone makes a mistake, you do not judge and/or condemn them, but show compassion and forgiveness; (3) "consideration," so that when someone strongly believes something, you do not deprecate or condemn his belief; and (4) "tact," so that when you passionately believe something, you are mindful of the appropriate place, manner, and time to put forth that belief. And perhaps the fifth "virtue" is, always arrive prepared to rehearsal and performance.[33]

One of the obvious problems with Stoicism as it applies to acting is that the actor has the sole responsibility to choose the "right"[34] (the most apt) action that he believes best "fits" the scenic circumstances, just as it is his responsibility to interpret the script "correctly," as Bruder put it. However, given that the capacity to choose such a "right" action is a judgment that the actor has to make, and like any judgments, they are greatly affected by personal, and yes, emotional considerations, conscious and unconscious ones as well as other contextual factors, the actor is still caught in the same, or at least a similar "emotional trap" that Practical Aesthetics decries other acting theories mistakenly fall into. For any choices about objectives and physical actions are governed by the subjectivity of the actor and this means that to some extent, he must be self-concerned (e.g., he must concentrate, look "in-

32   Says Mamet, "the organic actor must have generosity and courage..." (*Writing in Restaurants*, p. 127).

33   Bruder et al., *Practical Handbook*, p. 76.

34   There is no one "right" action for a specific scene literally speaking, that is, there are "any number of actions that can be correct" (ibid., p. 14).

wards"), at least enough to sense whether his choices are the "best" ones that he can make, the most truthful, and not the choices that are easiest to make, in that they are not in one's comfort zone. Similarly, there is no way of knowing in advance whether one has chosen the "right" action or whether there could have necessarily been a better choice made, just as there is no "correct" way of interpreting a script, only better or worse ways as judged by a particular actor, teacher, critic or audience. In short, Practical Aesthetics assumes that the actor is more in control of what he does, not to mention the consequences of his actions, than he may actually be. This is not surprising since following Stanislavski, Mamet points out that acting at its best is an attempt to bring to the stage "the life of the human soul," and as Freud has so vividly described, the human soul is characterized by marked ambiguity and ambivalence, contradiction and conflict. To expect the actor (or the audience) to somehow "pin down" or have a transparent, easily thematizeable "God's-eye" view of the "human soul," in acting terms, to reduce the "human soul" to a few simple acting principles (e.g., the "right" physical action), is to not give enough credence to the complex and mysterious nature of human experience and the creation of Beauty, Truth and Goodness, the main "higher" goals of great acting and living. As Judy Dench recently said, "You can't really award prizes [such as Oscars] for acting anyway. Acting is such a personal, imperfect kind of art."[35]

Stoic philosophy has also infiltrated Practical Aesthetics, and for that matter, all acting theories, in its devotion to "living in the present." In acting jargon, this is termed, for example, "being in the moment" and "being present." Most importantly, as Bruder points out, it means learning "to recognize and act upon the *truth of the moment*, or that which is actually happening in the scene as you are playing it."[36] Marcus Aurelius, for example, had a particular notion of time that he kept reminding himself of in his magisterial *Meditations*. "Letting go all else, cling to the following truths. Remember that man lives only in the present, in this fleeting instant; all the rest of his life is either

---

35   *New York Times*, February 15, 2011, p. C5.
36   Bruder et al., *Practical Handbook*, p. 40.

past and gone, or not yet revealed."[37] What Aurelius was getting at is that the "good life," the skillfully lived life is geared to living in the present and experiencing the moment. There is a danger of becoming too lodged in a retrospective consciousness as a point of reference with all the well-known detrimental ramifications. Perhaps this is the mistake that Strasberg made in his insistence, against Stanislavski, that "affective memory," using one's personal past to act in the present, is the key to great acting. Likewise, worrying about the future makes you less emotionally receptive, responsive and responsible to your fellow actor, to the scene and to the audience.

In contrast, Practical Aesthetics, like with Meisner's theory, emphasizes that while an actor can make up his mind about precisely how a scene will be played,

> This is not the purpose of text analysis, nor is it desirable in terms of execution. *The difficulty of executing an action lies in dealing with that which is actually happening in the other person* [your fellow actor]. You can't execute your action in general; you must stay in tune with the responses you are receiving. This requires a great deal of bravery and will due to the fact that you can never know exactly what is going to happen next. You must learn to embrace each moment and act on it according to the dictates of your action. As Sanford Mesiner says, "That which hinders your task *is* your task."[38]

As ancient Greek scholar Pierre Hadot notes, the Stoics insisted on concentrating on the present moment for a number of reasons: "it allows us both to grasp the incomparable value of the present instant, and to diminish the intensity of pain, as we become conscious of the fact that we only feel and live pain within the present moment."[39] The point that Aurelius and Hadot are making is that only the present is within our influence, because it is the only thing that we can live. Becoming more mindful of the present, as the Buddhists say, implies becoming more mindful of our agency, and this increases the sphere of our freedom of thought and action. In other words, by encouraging ac-

---

37   Marcus Aurelius, *Meditations*, Maxwell Stanforth (Trans.) (Middlesex, England: Penguin Books, 1964), 7:59, p. 115.

38   Bruder et al., *Practical Handbook*, p. 40.

39   Pierre Hadot, *The Inner Citadel: The Meditations of Marcus Aurelius*, Michael Chase (Trans.) (Cambridge, MA.: Harvard University Press, 1998), p. 107.

tors and non-actors to live in the present, we increase their awareness of the precious and transient nature of their lives and their freedom and responsibility to act and to live well.

The American philosopher and psychologist William James wrote a famous chapter on habit in his *Principles of Psychology*. The basic idea was that any functional psychology worth its salt should view habit, simply defined as an action or behavior pattern that is regular, repetitive, and often unconscious, as a fundamental building block of human behavior, including one's way of thinking. Habit, said James, is thus an underappreciated aspect of personal development. In Practical Aesthetics the important role of habit is expressed in its emphasis on "rote memorization of lines that leaves inflections to be driven by the pursuit of an action in the truth of the moment."[40] This permits the specific line to serve any likely tactic without fixing a line reading. Mamet takes the human disposition to behave in a certain way and looks for what is positive in this observation, namely, that it is to the actor's advantage to "*habitually* perform the task of our craft in the same way." What Mamet has in mind is very practical, "Know your lines cold. Choose a good, fun, physical objective. Bring to rehearsal and to performance those things you will need and leave the rest behind—the concerns of the street," of normal life.[41]

Mamet also has some easy to understand, though deceptively hard to implement, "habits," or practical moral wisdom for the actor that calls to mind the values and literary genre of the great Stoics. This wisdom has obvious applicability to the non-actor trying to create a "good life":

> Put things in their proper place. Rehearsal is the time for work. Home is the time for reflection....Be generous to others..... Cultivate the habit of only having aversion for those things you can avoid (those things in yourself) and only desiring those things you can give yourself. Improve yourself. Cultivate the habit of pride in your accomplishments, large and small....Cultivate a love of skill. Learn theatrical skills.....Cultivate the habit of mutuality..... Cultivate the habit of truth in yourself....Be your own best friend and the ally of your peers...

40   Westbrook, http;//EnzineArticles.com/?expert=Mark_Westbrook, p. 3.
41   Mamet, *True and False*, p. 101.

The goal of all of these sensible, though ethically demanding "habits," is well worth the effort, as Mamet concludes, "If you do these things, you will begin to cultivate the habit of humility, which means peace."[42] Mamet is emphasizing that the very tools for being an effective actor on the stage are the same tools and forms of attunement that are most useful for living skillfully and wisely off the stage.

There are two aspects of Mamet's emphasis on "habit" that we want to put into sharp focus as it relates to the actor and the non-actor in quest of a "good life." First, habit has a broader significance in that without what sociologist Anthony Giddens calls "routine" we feel chaotic agitation in our life. Routines, or routinization, are "the habitual, taken-for-granted character of the vast bulk of one's day-to-day social life."[43] Routines, says Giddens, are "vital to the psychological mechanisms whereby a sense of trust or ontological security [feeling safe and grounded] is sustained in the daily activities of social life." Moreover, they are "integral to the continuity of the personality of the agent, as he or she moves along the paths of daily activities."[44] In other words, routines foster a sense of autonomy, integration and safety in that it is through them that the person experiences the world as a place that can be controlled and understood and most importantly, effective decisions and interventions can be made. People are also deeply emotionally invested in their routines because routines organize and sublimate our deeper desires. Thus, without routines life is nearly impossible to successfully negotiate, let alone enjoy.

The problem with all of this is that sometimes too much routine is inhibiting, if not deadening; it sucks the life out of you. Mamet and Practical Aesthetics seem to be aware that for the actor there has to be a balance between the "hard won habits"[45] acquired through training and experience and the fact that the actor has to be receptive, responsive and responsible to the truth of the moment as it spontaneously plays out with one's fellow performers during a particular scene. As Bruder points out, "acting can...be looked at as improvising within

---

42 Ibid., pp. 101-103.

43 Anthony Giddens, *The Constitution of Society* (Berkeley: University of California Press, 1984), p. 376.

44 Ibid., p. 60.

45 Mamet, *Writing in Restaurants*, p. 105.

this framework of given circumstances." That is, "the improvisation is
the act of impulsively choosing from moment to moment how to do
that action and these choices are based on what is going on in the
other actors in the scene at that instant."[46] This is not as easy as it
sounds. For example, to identify a strong, playable action for a scene,
to accurately empathize such that one knows what is going on in one's
fellow actor, and then to act on these observations impulsively, is a tall
order, to put it mildly.[47] This being said, what is true on the stage is
also true off the stage: a "good life" requires the capacity to skillfully
navigate amidst the dialectical interplay of routine (habit) and spontaneity, and most importantly, to do so in a way that is properly attuned
to both the context-dependent and setting-specific nature of social life
while also being mainly other-directed and other-regarding.

AESTHETICS

Aesthetics is a term in philosophy that refers to the domain of "beauty." It is concerned with such questions as what is the nature of the
beautiful in art and the natural world. Bruder's *Practical Handbook*
and Mamet's *True and False* do not contain a systematic rendering of
the aesthetic theory underlying Practical Aesthetics, if indeed there
is one that could clearly be articulated. Nor is this chapter, given its
scope, the place to try and distill such a theory (and we certainly are
not qualified to do so). Rather what we want to do is to suggest what
Mamet and his colleagues seem to have in mind when they speak about
the perfection of the craft of acting—when an actor gives a "beautiful"
performance—and how the technique of Practical Aesthetics can be
a fertile breeding ground for the development of this acting potential.
As Bruder's *Practical Handbook* admirably lays out the nuts and bolts
of the technique of Practical Aesthetics, we will focus only on a few aspects of the technique that are particularly noteworthy and pertinent
to the main thrust of this chapter, the "broader aesthetic consciousness," the valuative attachments that animate Practical Aesthetics.

---

46   Bruder, *Practical Handbook*, p. 9. Mamet was exposed to Spolin's work
     when he worked backstage at Chicago's Hull House settlement where he
     also attended workshops by Spolin (Collard, "Living Truthfully: David
     Mamet's Practical Aesthetics," p. 329).
47   Ibid.

By technique we mean the procedure, skill and art used by actors. Perhaps more profoundly, technique, says Mamet, is "a knowledge of how to translate inchoate desire into clean action—into action capable of communicating itself to the audience." Such technique cannot be mastered intellectually, but must be learned from someone with first-hand knowledge of the skills of the theater, such as a seasoned actor. Mamet describes technique as being infused with "philosophy," that is, "this care, this love of precision, of cleanliness, this love of the theater is the best way, for it is love of the *audience*—of that which *unites* the actor and the house: a desire to share something which they know to be true." An effective actor has the skills "to respond truthfully, fully and lovingly to whatever he or she wishes to express." [48]

According to Mamet, "Stanislavski and, more notably Vakhtangov, suggested that—that to which the artist must be *true* is the aesthetic integrity of the play." Elsewhere Mamet notes, "For much of the beauty of the theatre, and much of the happiness, is a communion with the audience." And finally, Mamet declares, "The theater is a beautiful life but a harsh business."[49]

In these quotations Mamet is pointing to what are three of the most important aspects of what the actor needs to be able to do to create a "beautiful" performance. He needs to always honor the playwright's words and intentions, at least as much as he is capable of from a detailed study of the play; he needs to remember that the actor's only job is to tell a good story to his audience such that the audience feels emotionally included, moved, made to think differently, and maybe even transformed by the story; and lastly, the actor must not allow his challenging lifestyle to undermine his confidence and dedication to the theater he lovingly serves. A few elaborating comments on these three points are in order.

Being "true to the aesthetic integrity of the play" is Mamet's way of saying that the actor has the awesome responsibility "to care for the *scenic truth*." What this means, following Stanislavski, is "a conscious devotion to the *Idea* of a play," that is, "the truth in *this particular scene*."[50] Mamet gives a crystal clear example of what is meant by scenic truth:

---

48   Mamet, *Writing in Restaurants*, pp. 20-21.
49   Mamet, *True and False*, p. 45; *Writing in Restaurants*, pp. 130, 101.
50   Mamet, *Writing in Restaurants*, pp. 130-131.

So what if the play is set in a cafeteria? A cafeteria has no objective
reality, as far as we artists are concerned. Our question is *why* is the
play set in a cafeteria, what does it mean that the play is set in a
cafeteria, and what aspect of the cafeteria is important *to the meaning of the play*. Being demonstrated that, we may discard immediately all other aspects of the cafeteria and concentrate *only* on that
which puts forward the meaning of the play. E.g.: in our particular
play the cafeteria means a place where the hero is always open to
surveillance, the designer can build a set which reflects this idea:
inability to hide. If the meaning of the cafeteria is a place where
reflection and rest are possible, the designer's work can reflect these
ideas. In neither case is the designer's first question: "What does a
cafeteria look like?" His first question is; "What does it mean in this
instance?" This is a concern for scenic truth.[51]

According to Mamet, the goal is not "this performance," but rather "to
put forward the action" in the service of "the *meaning* of the play," in a
way that is most in sync with how the actor believes the author wrote
the character and scene.[52] Such judgments mainly require the actor to
make good "choices" in terms of doable physical actions. This mainly
involves always being mindful of the "through-action" and "super-objective." Following Stanislavski, according to Bruder, a "through-action"
is "the single overriding action that encompasses all the actions an actor pursues from scene to scene, from the beginning of a play to the
end,"[53] in other words, the idea of the play. A "super-objective" is the
fact that "the purpose of the play is to bring to the stage the life of the
soul," the animating concern by which all acting, and for that matter
the entire production, should be guided.[54] With this focus, according
to Practical Aesthetics, the actor will be able to fully give himself up to
the play and by doing so there will be a felt immediacy and aliveness to
his performance that comes from telling the story simply.[55]

Mamet and his colleagues repeatedly insist that the only function
of the actor is to tell the author's story in a simple, honest and direct manner: "The actor is on stage to communicate the play to the

---

51   Ibid., pp. 131-132.
52   Ibid., p. 132.
53   Bruder et al., *Practical Handbook*, p. 88.
54   Mamet, *Writing in Restaurants*, p. vii.
55   Mamet, *True and False*, pp. 3, 32, 109.

audience. That is the beginning and the end of his and her job"; "Acting is bringing the play to the audience."[56] As Collard notes, following Spolin, Practical Aesthetics views acting as mainly "an act of reciprocal, outward-directed creation rather than internalized reproduction." The actor is "a communicative vessel mediating between the text, the stage and the audience."[57] What Mamet is saying, which to some extent goes against many of the other more "introspective" and "self-absorbed" acting theories that he criticizes, is that "the very purpose of the theater… is communication and communion" with the audience. This requires, perhaps above all else, "respect for the audience,"[58] or an openness to their openness to engage the actors (including paying for tickets and traveling to the theater), as they simply, honestly, directly and perhaps most importantly, lovingly tell the story of the play. Communion, that feeling of emotional and spiritual closeness that ideally exists between the actors and the audience, should not be a secondary or tertiary concern of the actor, or as some acting teachers suggest, of no concern to the actor as he does his craft on the stage. Rather, Mamet, similar to Brecht, who "influenced [him] a great deal," insists that it is precisely the actor's sacred responsibility to "connect" with the audience in a way that profoundly touches their hearts and minds, soul to soul as it were. Perhaps this is the basis of Mamet's criticism of Lawrence Olivier's acting when he wrote, "I'm hungry for lunch, and all he's serving is an illustrated menu." In other words, Mamet "wants actors who act, not 'act,'"[59] and who willingly, courageously and lovingly subjugate themselves to serving the "other," the play, his fellow actors and most of all, the audience. Says Mamet, "A life in the theater is a life spent giving things away." It is "an act of selfless spirit."[60]

Finally, Mamet tells us that which is common knowledge among the acting community—that "the theater is a beautiful life but a harsh

---

56   Ibid., pp. 9, 53.

57   Collard, "Living Truthfully: David Mamet's Practical Aesthetics," p. 329.

58   Mamet, *True and False*, pp. 58, 30.

59   Christopher Bigsby, "David Mamet," in *The Cambridge Companion to David Mamet*, p. 7. For Mamet, Olivier personifies the actor that draws the audience to focus on his acting technique rather than the telling of the story. As Mamet says, "Technique is the occupation of a second-rate mind. Act as you would in your fantasy" (*True and False*, p. 120).

60   Mamet, *Writing in a Restaurant*, p. 104; *True and False*, p. 24.

business." Indeed, much of Mamet's *True and False* is a devastating critique of the business side of the entertainment industry of which commercial theater and film are a part (as is non-commercial theater/film, though less so, for they too have to keep a close eye on the "bottom line"). Mamet's disdain for what he calls "the industrial model" that assumes the actor is "one of the myriad of interchangeable pieces" that can be exploited by the gatekeepers of the entertainment industry is palpable: "Show business is and has always been a depraved carnival."[61] And again, "Hollywood people are very, very cruel and also very, very cunning."[62] Indeed, these observations are well known in the industry. Sir Anthony Hopkins, now age 73, from a somewhat different perspective has made a related point about Hollywood and commercial theater. Citing a recent sojourn to a cinema complex in suburban Memphis, he noted, there were "[e]leven cinemas. They were just about to start the matinee and I looked inside. All these people waddling around with their popcorn and their hot dogs…I thought. 'That's it'? This is the movie industry I've invested my life in?'" The stage, says Hopkins, is hardly much better. "I did some Shakespeare. Jesus Christ, never again. You always have an illusion about yourself that nobody can wait to see your next big Shakespeare performance, but I've been onstage and seen people in the front row fast asleep."[63]

Most actors and actresses are not commercially successful, that is, they can't make a living, let alone a decent one, off their craft. Moreover, being a working actor requires putting yourself out there to be judged day in and day out by the gatekeepers of the industry during auditions, in most ways a brutal and dehumanizing experience. In fact, Mamet notes that "the audition process is an abomination."[64] It has been estimated that the average actor gets a part in a play or movie about once every 40 or so auditions, which means that about 97.5% of the auditions are a waste of time in terms of employment. Even when one does get a part, one is at the mercy of the critics who often

61   Mamet, *True and False*, pp. 51, 50.

62   Mamet quoted in David Savran, *In Their Own Words. Contemporary American Playwrights* (New York: Theater Communications Group, 1998), p. 142.

63   *The Week*, February 18, 2011, p. 12.

64   Mamet quoted in Karen Kohlhaas, *The Monologue Audition. A Practical Guide for Actors* (Pompton Plains, NJ: Limelight Editions, 2000), p. xi.

delight in tearing actors down when they themselves couldn't perform well in an elementary school production of *Cinderella*, let alone write a play or screenplay that was good enough to get produced. Mamet also has his criticisms of the acting training schools and conservatories, which he despairingly calls "the academic-bureaucratic model of the theatre," the one that he believes is "put forward by the school and by the critics." Such an approach is overly "intellectual," even hyper-intellectual and rejects "the innovative, the personal, the simple, and the unresearched,"[65] this being the basis of fashioning an effective actor.

It was psychoanalyst Bruno Bettelheim and Catholic philosopher Gabriel Marcel, among others,[66] who have superbly described the difficulties of maintaining one's autonomy, personal integration and humanity amidst the "mass society," of which the entertainment industry is an integral part. Indeed, as Bettelheim points out, the actor, just like the non-actor, must reckon with the "impersonal bureaucracy [e.g., "Hollywood" and "Broadway"], impersonal taste makers [e.g., the critics, homogenizing acting schools] and impersonal sources of information" [aspects of the internet and computers] that make up our organized industrial society.[67] The actor has to contend with the de-individuating bureaucracy (e.g., the acting school—the "Schools of the Anointed," the audition), the trend-setting mass media (e.g., the marketers, casting and other agents, and others who decide what is in vogue, governed mainly by the "bottom line"), and forms of surveillance (e.g., the critics who discourage creativity and individuality and maintain the so-called "standards," the "status quo" of what is "acceptable" theater and film).

All of these and other indignities are frankly brutalizing to the spirit and humanity of the actor, as they are to the non-actor who has to negotiate, if not resist the profoundly negative side of the "mass society." Over time, an actor who resides in the "industry" can begin to feel intense anxiety that he is losing individual identity. Such a corruption of

---

65   Mamet, *True and False*, p. 111.

66   Paul Marcus, *Autonomy in the Extreme Situation. Bruno Bettelheim, the Nazi Concentration Camps and the Mass Society* (Westport, CT: Praeger Publishers, 1988); *In Search of the Spiritual. Gabriel Marcel, Psychoanalysis and the Sacred* (in press).

67   Bruno Bettelheim, *The Informed Heart. Autonomy in a Mass Age* (Glencoe, IL: Free Press, 1960), p. 99.

his self-concept and erosion of his self-esteem has a deleterious impact on his ability to practice his noble craft with any kind of creativity and passion. Similar in spirit to Bettelheim and Marcel, Mamet believes that the actor must resist the dehumanizing aspects of the profession-al acting world mainly by developing a counter-narrative that allows him to maintain his sense of dignity and self-respect. From what we can determine from our interviews with many actors and actresses, it is the loss of personal dignity and self-respect, even more than finan-cial and other lifestyle considerations, that leads aspiring performers to get so estranged, if not frustrated and depressed, that they throw in the towel and completely give up on their childhood passion and dream. Needless to say, a person pays a hefty personal price in terms of happiness by not following their calling, at least in some form that does not feel like they are "selling out."

So what is an actor supposed to do to maintain a modicum of per-sonal dignity and self-respect so that he can continue to do that which he loves to do—to act, to be a "truth-teller" to the audience that he ide-ally, graciously and generously serves? What can the non-actor learn from the struggling actor (and for that matter, all actors, for none of them are ever really secure in their careers), about living a "good life"? While adequately answering this question would require a book,[68] actually many books, we want to conclude this chapter by mention-ing a few of the suggestions that Mamet and Practical Aesthetics have put forth that are good "food for thought" about this most impor-tant problem of how to keep the "dream" alive. For as Mamet noted, "the theater is an expression of our dream life—of our unconscious aspirations."[69] Even more pertinent to everyday life are the wise words of Henry David Thoreau, who wrote, "If one advances confidently in the direction of one's dreams, and endeavors to live the life which one has imagined, one will meet with a success unexpected in common hours."

68   See Marcus, *Autonomy in the Extreme Situation. Bruno Bettelheim, the Nazi Concentration Camps and the Mass Society.*

69   Mamet, *Writing in Restaurants*, p. 19. Elsewhere Mamet notes, "We are drawn to the play because it speaks to our subconscious—which is what a play should do" (ibid., p. 125).

MORALITY

Maria Schneider, who recently died, was the vulnerable, young, sexy and largely unknown actress who tangoed with Marlon Brando in the 1972 film, *Last Tango in Paris* (directed by Bernardo Bertolucci). The film is about a widower and a young woman whose serendipitous meeting in an empty Paris apartment escalates into a lustful affair. In the most striking scene, Brandon sodomizes Schneider on the floor of the apartment, a scene that evoked public outrage such that some European countries refused to show the film. Schneider herself was relentlessly hounded by intrusive reporters and photographers. "The whole scandal and aftermath of the film turned me a little crazy and I had a breakdown." According to Schneider, the film made her feel "humiliated" and "a little raped" by both Brando and Bertolucci (in fact she never spoke to Bertolucci again, though she maintained a friendship with Brando). Later in her career when she was asked to do nude scenes in Tinto Brass's sexually unambiguous sword-and-sandals epic, *Caligula* and Luis Bunuel's *That Obscure Object of Desire*, she refused and resigned from the films halfway into production. Said Schneider to her fellow actresses, "Never take your clothes off for middle-aged men who claim that it's art." [70]

Indeed, while the above example of exploitation of young actresses is admittedly an extreme one, Schneider is putting her finger on a key aspect of what an actress has to do in order to preserve her dignity and self-respect in an industry that cares little for her humanity, despite giving lip service to the contrary. As Mamet noted, "theater people are prepared to *espouse* a moral act, but not to *commit* it." [71] Mamet's suggestions to actors are of interest because they put into sharp focus the lynchpin of how to maintain a modicum of personal dignity, namely, autonomy of thought, especially in relation to how one judges oneself. Below are some of Mamet's suggestions given to the young actor on how to maintain her sense of dignified personhood in the "harsh business," the depersonalizing atmosphere of so much of the actor's everyday world. Needless to say, all of these practical suggestions have direct applicability to the non-actor trying to live a "good life" in the "mass society." We will only list a few of Mamet's suggestions, without

70 *The Week*, February 18, 2011, p. 37.

71 Mamet, *Writing in Restaurants*, p. 26.

much elaboration and not in order of importance. We include those
suggestions that strike us as most emblematic of what Mamet believes
are especially important to the actor's development of a humanizing
counter-narrative to the "harsh business."

1. "The artist must avow humanity in him- or herself, and also in the
   audience" (*Writing in Restaurants*, p. 29).
2. "We must support each other *concretely* in the quest for artistic
   knowledge, into the struggle to create" (ibid., p. 22).
3. "The theater affords an opportunity uniquely suited for communicating and inspiring ethical behavior" (ibid., p. 26).
4. "In a morally bankrupt time we can help to change the habit of
   coercive and frightened action and substitute for it the habit of
   trust, self-reliance, and cooperation" (ibid., p. 27).
5. "A life in the theater is a life with attention directed outward, and
   memory and substantiation of others is very important" (ibid.,
   p. 105).
6. "Tolstoy wrote that the only time human beings treat each other
   without pity is when they have banded into institutions" (ibid.,
   p. 109).
7. "The first task of the actor, the first lesson, and one of the hardest,
   is to learn to take criticism—to learn to view self-consciousness
   as a tool for *bettering* the self, rather than as a tool for *protect-
   ing* the self....without this self-critique there is no improvement
   and there is no happiness" (ibid., p. 138).
8. "The rational individual will, when the bell rings, go out there
   anyway to do the job she said she was going to do. This is called
   courage" (*True and False*, p. 59).
9. "Be a man; be a woman. Look at the world around you; onstage
   and off. Do not forsake your reason. Do not paternalize yourself. Your creative powers [the "royal road" to remaining human]
   lie in your imagination, which is eternally fertile, but cannot be
   forced, and your *will*, i.e., our true character, which can be developed through exercise" (ibid., pp. 65-66).
10. "And in the Golden Age we would judge an actor's 'character' on
    stage the exact same way we judge it off stage: not by his protes-
    tations and assurances but by his determination, his constancy

of purpose, his generosity—in effect, his "goodness" (*Writing in Restaurants*, p. 128).

And finally, never forget to be grateful, for as Mamet says, "It is a gift from God to be able to act...it takes an extraordinary, very, very rare gift to be able to do it surpassingly."[72]

CONCLUSION

Practical Aesthetics is a creative and useful re-working and refining of Stanislavski and Meisner's ideas about acting theory and technique, and to a lesser extent, the appropriation of Spolin's insight that skillful improvisation is the basis of all effective acting.[73] As Mamet noted, "the magic moments, the beautiful moments in the theater always come from a desire on the part of the artist *and* audience to live in the moment—to *commit* themselves to time."[74] Indeed, Practical Aesthetics has produced some good actors and actresses, like William H. Macy, Felicity Huffman, Christopher Carley, Jessica Alba, Clark Gregg and Eddie Cahill. This being said, what is most interesting and important about Practical Aesthetics, especially as put forth so effectively by Mamet, is a broadly defined aesthetic consciousness, an array of valuative attachments that the actor can internalize and use to both bring out his creativity, his skillfulness and most importantly, his humanity as an actor on and off the stage. Mamet and company have argued for a way of thinking, feeling and acting that is meant to help the actor and, by analogy, the non-actor to maintain a modicum of autonomy, integration and humanity amidst the challenges and difficulties of life on and off the stage; for in a certain sense, everyone is an actor. Probably more than any other acting theory or technique, Practical Aesthetics, especially as described by Mamet and Bruder, has put forth a powerful set of arguments, actually, more of an "ethos," for the actor to embrace without reserve if he wants to lovingly and

---

72   Wilmeth, "Mamet the Actor," p. 150.

73   According to Wilmeth, Meisner's influence on Mamet was, for example, "focusing on others rather than yourself; demanding truthful, moment to moment responses to other actors; and even a down-playing of Stanislavski's 'emotional' memory" (ibid., p. 140). It should be remembered that both Meisner and Spolin were greatly influenced by Stanislavski, who therefore indirectly influenced Mamet.

74   Mamet, *Writing in Restaurants*, p. 30.

effectively serve his "noble art." Moreover, as we have suggested, it is precisely embracing these values and beliefs that are also useful to the non-actor who is struggling amidst the "harsh business" of living, to create a "good life." Advises Mamet, "Treat the theater," and we would add, oneself and especially everyday life with others, "with love."[75]

---

75   Mamet, *Writing in Restaurants*, p. 140.

CHAPTER ELEVEN

LOVE ART IN YOURSELVES, NOT YOURSELVES IN ART

CONSTANTIN STANISLAVSKI

"The fundamental aim of our art is the creation of this inner life of a human spirit, and its expression in an artistic form."

—Constantin Stanislavski

"IMMORTAL SIRE" is the phrase that Ernest Jones, Freud's biographer, used in his dedication to the founder of psychoanalysis and his daughter Anna. Indeed, "immortal sire" is also the fitting term to describe Stanislavski's role in the history of acting theory and the craft of acting. As will become clear as the reader works his way through this book, Stanislavski and his so-called "System" has been the major influence on nearly all of the great acting teachers, whether as disciples of one sort or another (e.g., Lee Strasberg and Stella Adler) or as mavericks who reacted against some of Stanislavski's ideas (e.g., Bertolt Brecht and Jerzy Grotowski). Like Freud, Stanislavski's thinking evolved; he was self-critical and not afraid of changing his mind as experience taught him otherwise: "I have lived a variegated life during the course

of which I have been forced more than once to change my most fundamental ideas"[1]; "Create your own method, Don't depend slavishly on
mine. Make up something that will work for you. But keep breaking
traditions. I beg you."[2] His "final" views culminated in what has been
called "the method of physical actions" (or more precisely, the "Method
of Analysis through Physical Action") which Stanislavski characterized as "the result of my whole life's work."[3] As Jean Benedetti noted,
Stanislavski felt that while he was engaged for many years understanding and dissecting the creative process, breaking it down into its con-
stituent elements, "now there was a need to re-emphasize its organic
unity," its "integrity," as actors and directors were cherry picking aspects
of his System that they liked and either overlooked or disregarded the
rest.[4] In this chapter we will review some of the key, ground-breaking
insights that Stanislavski made, mainly through understanding some
of the important elements of an action—roughly defined as doing
something with a conscious purpose—such as the "magic if," given
circumstances, imagination, concentration of attention, truth and belief, communion, adaptation, tempo rhythm and emotion memory.[5]
Unquestionably, for Stanislavski, the leitmotif of his work, "the key" to
great acting was "to apply your inner life to the circumstances of the
character. In this way, you do not just play yourself, you *use* your self
in the service of the part."[6] More specifically, the questions that occu-
pied Stanislavski during his entire career were "how does one combine

---

1   Constantin Stanislavski, *My Life in Art* (New York: Routledge, 1952),
     p. 3.
2   Sonia Moore, *The Stanislavski System. The Professional Training of An
     Actor* (New York: Penguin Books, 1984), p. xvi (Joshua Logan's foreword).
     British actress Judy Dench has a similar view: "I don't think anybody can
     be told how to act. I think you can give advice. But you have to find your
     own way through it."
3   Ibid., p. 10.
4   Jean Benedetti, *Stanislavski. An Introduction* (New York: Routledge,
     2000), p. 85.
5   We have, in part, used Sonia Moore's categories to organize this chap-
     ter as described in her very good primer, *The Stanislavski System. The
     Professional Training of an Actor*, p. v.
6   Richard Brestoff, *The Great Acting Teachers and Their Methods* (Lyme,
     NH: Smith and Kraus, 1995), p. 38.

the need to pretend, with the need to express something true?"[7] How does one inhabit another person, the role, and yet also remain oneself? Unpacking what these two interrelated quotations mean will be the main thrust of this chapter. Moreover, we hope that the reader gets a sense of what strands of Stanislavski's System have been "picked up," developed and further elaborated by particular acting teachers discussed in this book.

THE METHOD OF PHYSICAL ACTIONS

Stanislavski was a great observer of everyday life; in fact he mainly based his System on his detailed understanding of everyday behavior of the ordinary individual. This being said, Stanislavski had some underlying guiding assumptions about the human condition and the nature of creativity that need to be briefly mentioned, for they animate his method of physical actions and, for that matter, his whole System.

As Sharon Carnicke points out, perhaps the most basic assumption that Stanislavski maintained was the "holistic belief that mind and body represent a psychophysical continuum."[8] This view is now part of the received wisdom of how the mind and body are connected, but at the time Stanislavski articulated his view, he was taking a position that was not so readily accepted: "In every physical action there is something psychological, and in the psychological, something physical"; "One must give actors various paths. One of these is the path of [physical] action. But there is also another path: you can move from feeling to action, arousing feeling first."[9] Indeed, as Freud has shown, the psychological experience of, say, anxiety has its physiological manifestations such as sweating, heart palpitations and the like. Mind and body always work together, though not in ways that are always easily discernible. In light of this mind/body assumption, Stanislavski claimed that the enemy of great acting is physical tension, the mental worry or emotional strain that makes natural, relaxed behavior impossible. Physical tension impedes the easy flow and loveliness of

---

7   Ibid., p. 20.

8   Sharon Marie Carnicke, "Stanislavski's System. Pathways for the Actor," in Alison Hodge (Ed.), *Twentieth Century Actor Training* (New York: Routledge, 2000), p. 16.

9   Ibid., pp. 16-17.

expression of the body just as it hampers the mind's capacity to focus and imagine.[10]

The second assumption that underpins Stanislavski's System is "that successful acting places the creative act in the laps of the audience. By insisting on the immediacy of performance and the presence of the actor, Stanislavski argues against nineteenth-century traditions which taught actors to represent characters from the stage through carefully crafted intonations and gestures."[11] In other words, a Stanislavski-trained actor is "dynamic and improvisatory during performance;" Stanislavski's emphasis was on getting the actor to maximally "experience" what he was communicating to the audience, or "living the role" as Carnicke terms it.

Lastly, Stanislavski developed his whole System to invoke the kind of "experiencing" that was believable and truthful on the stage, and most importantly, in sync with what he believed were the "natural laws of the actors' organic creativeness."[12] That is, Stanislavski believed that he had discerned some of the governing axioms of human creativity. His specific acting techniques were meant to assist the actor to foster a receptive mind and supple body so that he fully "experienced" the role in the here and now. As Carnicke notes, "Stanislavski believes that the 'sense of self' (as he calls it) provides the 'soil' from which the role can grow"[13] such that the actor can passionately impact how the audience feels and thinks:

> My task is to elevate the family of artists from the ignorant, the half-educated, and the profiteers, and to convey to the younger generation that an actor is the priest of beauty and truth....The theater infects the audience with its noble ecstasy....The most important thing is to build the life of the human spirit.[14]

---

10   Ibid., p. 17.

11   Ibid.

12   Ibid., p. 18.

13   Ibid.

14   Moore, *The Stanislavski System. The Professional Training of an Actor*, pp. 3, 4. 8.

THE "MAGIC IF"

Stanislavski understood that an actor could not actually believe in the truth and reality of his role or what was occurring on the stage, for it was "make believe" from beginning to end. However, as Moore pointed out, the "actor can believe in the possibility of events." The actor must be able to answer this question: What would I think, feel and, most importantly, do if I were in the same circumstances as Macbeth? Without coming up with a plausible answer to this question, an actor can't adequately generate the reality of a dramatic situation. In a nutshell, the "magic if" changes "the character's aim into the actor's," it is a powerful motivation for internal and physical actions.[15] Stanislavski was thus advocating a strange state of mind, a double reality that the actor must master. On one hand, he must believe in the truth of what he is doing on the stage, and yet on the other he knows it is all "made up." He called this creative experience when the boundaries between the actor and the role he is playing are fuzzy and unclear, "I am being." According to Stanislavski,

> The actor above all must believe in everything going on around him, and most of all he must believe in what *he* is doing. And he can only believe what is true. And so he must genuinely feel the truth, look for it and for that he must develop his artistic awareness of truth.[16]

What Stanislavski means by the word truth is important to understand, for it is central to his System and for that matter, to all acting theories. Truth, as conventionally defined, is that which corresponds to fact and reality. Stanislavski had something else in mind:

> But I am talking about another kind of truth, the truth of my feelings and sensations, the truth of the inner creative urge that is desperate to find expression. I don't need the truth out there, I need the truth in here, the truth of my relationship to the happenings on stage, the props, the set, the actors playing other roles and to their thoughts and feelings.[17]

The "magic if'" is one kind of imaginative process that allows the actor to fervently believe in his created truth similar to how he believes in

---

15   Ibid., p. 25.
16   Benedetti, *Stanislavski, An Introduction*, p. 48.
17   Ibid., p. 49.

real truth, only with more exigency. "It is," says Stanislavski, "like a child
believing in a doll, its inner life and circumstance....once he [the actor]
believes in that [imagined] life, he can begin to be creative."[18] Thus, the
mindset of the actor involves both embracing the truth and reality of
the script and being able to enter into the imaginary playground of
the child via the character he is playing. It is interesting to note that
Stanislavski developed the "magic if" based on the thoroughly enjoyable "what if" games that he played with his six-year-old niece.[19]

GIVEN CIRCUMSTANCES

Circumstance, or living in a particular state or set of conditions, is
a key concept in Stanislavski's System. As Stanislavski said, "the
whole basis of the success of this method lay in the magic *if* and given
circumstances"[20]:

> During every moment we are on the stage, during every moment of
> the development of the action of the play, we must be aware either
> of the external circumstances which surround us (the whole mate-
> rial setting of the production), or of an inner chain of circumstances
> which we ourselves have imagined in order to illustrate our parts.[21]

Thus, the "given circumstances" are the situations in which the actor
finds himself during a play. This includes everything that the actor
comes upon while he creates his character (e.g., "the plot, the epoch,
the time and place of the actions, the conditions of life, the director's
and the actor's interpretation, the setting, the properties, lighting and
effects," etc.).[22] Only once the actor is thoroughly immersed in the circumstances of the play, that is, only after he has made it part of himself, will he be able to choose the apt actions that convey in a believable
and truthful manner the psychological experiences of the character.

---

18   Ibid.
19   Carnicke, "Stanislavski's System, Pathways for the Actor," p. 21.
20   Constantin Stanislavski, *An Actor Prepares* (New York: Routledge,
     1989), p. 146.
21   Ibid., pp. 63-64.
22   Moore, *The Stanislavski System. The Professional Training of an Actor*, p.
     26.

To do this precisely and effectively, and to be able to repeat it at will, requires considerable training and rehearsal.[23]

IMAGINATION

"The aim of the actor," said Stanislavski, "should be to use his technique to turn the play into a theatrical reality. In this process imagination plays by far the greatest part."[24] What does Stanislavski mean by the imagination, what we previously defined as that capacity to form images and ideas in the mind, especially things never seen or never experienced directly? While Stanislavski does not spell it out in a systematic, psychologically or philosophically rigorous manner, he does make some interesting observations about the phenomenology of the imaginative process in the acting context.

First, he says that imagination is different than fantasy: "Imagination creates things that can be or can happen, whereas fantasy invents things that are not in existence, which never have been or will be." Always pushing the limits of his thinking, Stanislavski adds, "And yet, who knows, perhaps they will come to be."[25] Second, Stanislavski indicates that imagination cannot be "forced"; rather it requires "coaxing." Imagination without an "interesting subject" to the actor is also lethal for the imagination. Finally, he notes, your thoughts must not be "passive." That is, "activity in imagination is of utmost importance. First comes internal, and afterwards external action."[26] When these psychological processes or "moments," as Stanislavski calls them, are properly fashioned and integrated, "an unbroken series of images, something like a moving picture" emerges in the mind of the actor. "As long as we are acting creatively, this film will unroll and be thrown on the screen of our inner vision, making vivid the circumstances among which we are moving." Most importantly perhaps, "these inner images create a corresponding mood, and arouse emotions, while holding us within the limits of the play."[27] This requires that the actor "find some single

23   Margaret Eddershaw, "Acting Methods: Brecht and Stanislavski," in Graham Bartram and Anthony Waine (Eds.), *Brecht in Perspective* (London: Longman, 1982), p. 131.

24   Stanislavski, *An Actor Prepares*, p. 54.

25   Ibid., p. 55.

26   Ibid., p. 58.

27   Ibid., p. 64.

new circumstance that will move you emotionally and incite you to action." It is mainly based, says Stanislavski, on one's self-knowledge and
self-awareness, "when you know the inclinations of your own nature
it is not difficult to adapt them to imaginary circumstance." He suggests to the actor to identify and "name some one trait, quality, interest,
which is typical of you," which is likely to create the "inner images, for
your role."[28]

Stanislavski was well aware that a vivid and exacting imagination
was not something that usually comes to an actor in a moment of
easy inspiration; it requires a lot of internal and external preparation. "Every invention of the actor's imagination must be thoroughly
worked out and solidly built on a basis of facts. It must be able to
answer all the questions (when, where, why, how) when he is driving
his inventive faculties on to make a more and more definite picture of a
make-believe existence." Imagination must also be specific and precise,
"To imagine 'in general,' without a well-defined and thoroughly founded theme is a sterile occupation." This being said, Stanislavski was frequently dialectical in his self-understanding of his acting technique.
He adds, "On the other hand, a conscious, reasoned approach to the
imagination often produces a bloodless, counterfeit presentment of
life. That will not do for the theatre."[29] What Stanislavski demanded
from the actor was a total commitment to the artistic process:

> Our art demands that an actor's whole nature be actively involved,
> that he give himself up, both mind and body, to his part. *He must
> feel the challenge to action physically as well as intellectually* because the
> imagination, which has no substance or body, can reflexively affect
> our physical nature and make it act. This faculty is of the greatest
> importance in our emotion-technique. Therefore: *Every movement
> you make on the stage, every word you speak, is the result of the right life
> of your imagination* (emphasis in original, as in all other quotations
> in this chapter).[30]

Stanislavski's discussion of the "magic if," "given circumstances," "truth"
and the "imagination" attempts to describe the psychological processes
that an actor needs to perfect in order to be able to creatively transform

28   Ibid., p. 69.
29   British actress Emma Thompson has a similar view: "I don't have a tech-
      nique because I never learnt any."
30   Ibid., pp. 70-71.

a script into a believable, truthful and beautiful scenic reality. Perhaps the main underlying idea that connects all of these concepts that is also relevant to the non-actor and actor in search of the "good life," is that without a cultivated imagination one is not able to have the sensibility to adequately appreciate that which is beautiful and pleasing in the world (like theater, art, music and most importantly, the pleasant or-dinariness of people and things), and to live at a "high level" as a func-tioning social being. Indeed, the negative impacts on one's everyday life of having a "disordered imagination," as it has been called by Gregory Currie—being unable to properly visualize and generate imagery, in-cluding mentally stimulating a purposeful action, in a context-sensitive manner, such as occurs in autism and schizophrenia—are well known. While focusing on the centrality of the imaginative faculty as it relates to acting technique, Stanislavski was in effect arguing for what can be called an "aesthetic attitude," a specific way of experiencing or focusing on objects and people, one that is characterized by a heightened recep-tiveness, a sharpened reactivity to what is going on inside and outside of oneself. Without this developed capacity to imagine, a non-actor and actor are destined to live emotionally blunted and muted lives, for it is the imagination that gives a person the ability to be inspired, to get in touch with his deepest desires, and to empathically and inven-tively relate to people and things. While the study of the imagination is a huge subject in psychology and philosophy, one thing is clear, that Stanislavski was "spot on" in his theorizing. He says that it is essential to be conversant with one's unconscious in order to have the capac-ity to imagine, visualize, mentally stimulate action, have easy thought flow, fantasize, engage in counterfactual thinking, stimulate the past—to create alternative states and selves and the like.[31] As Stanislavski noted, "the fundamental objective of our psycho-technique is to put us in a creative state in which our subconscious will function naturally"; "All of these things come out of the subconscious. They are like shoot-ing stars"; "This precipitated my search for some method of *inner tech-nique*, ways leading from the conscious to the subconscious, that realm

---

31   Keith D. Markman, William M.P. Klein and Julie A. Suhr (Eds.), *Handbook of Imagination and Mental Stimulation* (New York: Psychology Press, 2008).

where nine-tenths of any genuine creative process takes place."[32] Thus, the royal road toward healthy, creative, "higher" psychological functioning travels through the unconscious. In this view, acting training is a form of imagination training via accessing unconscious processes, just as is psychoanalysis. The goal, in part, is to give free rein to fantasy and then to use these imaginative constructions to generate a "narrative imagination," a holistic and dynamic way of "telling" one's life that is not simply creating and articulating visual pictures, but involves a way of vividly and precisely describing and making intelligible the "subtext"—the underlying meaning and message of one's present, past and, as the Jungians believe, even the future.[33] As Stanislavski said, "Spectators come to the theater to hear the subtext. They can read the text at home." Likewise, the capacity to live the "good life" requires the ability to go beyond surface meanings and to imaginatively intuit the unconscious meaning of things.

CONCENTRATION OF ATTENTION

Stanislavski realized that the actor is typically overly anxious about the audience's judgment of his performance, which creates inhibiting tension; therefore he needs to concentrate elsewhere: "In order to get away from the audience you must be interested in something on the stage….*an actor must have a point of attention, and this point of attention should not be in the auditorium.*" He advocated learning how to fix one's attention freshly on literal things on the stage, "*and to see them.*"[34] Stanislavski elaborated his insistence that the actor restrict his attention to specific domains of the stage, such as objects, through his concepts of "circle of attention" and "public solitude." Circle of at-

32 Ibid., pp. 281, 236; Constantin Stanislavski, *Stanislavski's Legacy*, Elizabeth Reynolds Hapgood (Ed.) (New York: Theatre Arts Books, 1989), p. 184.

33 Athinodoros Chronis and Ronald D. Hampton, "Living in Another World: The Role of Narrative Imagination in the Production of Fantasy Enclaves," *Advances in Consumer Research*, 31 (2004): 193-195. The subtext also has a more technical meaning for Stanislavski. According to Benedetti, it refers to both "the thoughts that go through our [the actors] mind, the inner monologue" and "the pictures we see in our mind, our mental images," those which are "the sum of our mental activity during the dialogue" (Benedetti, *Stanislavski and the Actor*, pp. 57-58, 153).

34 Stanislavski, *An Actor Prepares*, p. 75.

tention, says Stanislavski, consists "of a whole section, large or small in dimension, and will include a series of independent points of objects. The eye may pass from one to another of these points, but it must not go beyond the indicated limit of the circle of attention."[35] The "circle of attention," the domain on the stage to which the actor's concentration is attending, is a skill that an actor needs to master. Actors must have the capacity to completely focus on what they are doing in the here and now as well as quickly change focus to respond to the next moment, otherwise they are not emotionally present, they are wandering, which is disastrous for a performance, and the audience instantly knows this.

As Benedetti notes, for Stanislavski, the "circle of attention" or the art of focusing, has four interrelated stages, "focusing in the real world, focusing in the imaginary world, multi-level focus [or 'split-focus'], and focusing as a means of developing new aspects of a role."[36] Moreover, "circles of attention" can be small, medium or large. A small circle of attention is a small domain that incorporates the actor and, say, a nearby sofa with a few items on it. The actor is the focal point of such a small domain and can with little effort have his attention engrossed by the items inside it; the medium circle of attention is a domain that may comprise numerous persons and assemblages of furniture. An actor should ideally look at this slowly but surely, not attempting to absorb it all in one go; the large circle of attention is everything an actor is able to view on the stage. The larger the circle, the more problematic it is to keep the attention from fading or disappearing.[37]

The point of the "circle of attention," and the exercises that Stanislavski developed to train better concentration, was to highlight the need for the actor "to look at and see things on the stage" in a different way—more heightened, with greater precision and sharper than one looks at things in everyday life. The purpose for perfecting this different way of seeing is that being in front of people on a stage is an enormous emotional and cognitive strain. Learning how to focus intensely in the here and now on the details of what is happening is the antidote to inhibiting and debilitating self-consciousness and

35   Ibid., pp. 81-82.
36   Benedetti, *Stanislavski and the Actor*, pp. 32-33.
37   Moore, *The Stanislavski System, The Professional Training of an Actor*, p. 31.

distractibility. When the actor is able to perform his role without self-consciousness, when he is able to forget all his personal worries and troubles, when all the things that undermine his complete attention to what he is doing, including his imaginative constructions that animate his physical actions, then he is said, by Stanislavski, to have accomplished "public solitude." Public solitude means that the actor has forgotten about the audience's judgment, has forgotten about the auditorium he is performing in, and he delivers his lines with the ease and comfort of a person speaking in his kitchen—acting private in public, as if no one were observing him.

What Stanislavski is putting into sharp focus is the need for the actor and non-actor to mindfully pay attention to what he is doing in the here and now ("here, today, now" he called it), an obvious point, though a very difficult one to implement on the stage and in real life. Indeed, what Stanislavski is getting at is strikingly similar to what Buddhists call "bare attention," defined as "awareness of the present moment," a key element in achieving "enlightenment."[38] It is also a crucial skill in the art of living the "good life." What Stanislavski and the Buddhists are stressing is that one needs to have the ability "to cut through the mental patterns," the various internal resistances, that distance us from our direct and immediate experience. As Buddhists Sharon Salzberg and Joseph Goldstein further note, through learning to sustain awareness in movement, the actor and non-actor can slowly bring bare attention to all actions that he performs on the stage and in real life. What Stanislavski was putting forth in the context of his acting theory, but with applicability for all of us, was the need to become more present and open to our everyday experience, including our thinking, feeling and acting. By doing so, one can enlarge and enhance one's field of awareness, a vital aspect of living the "good life." As Stanislavski wrote, "An actor should be observant not only on the stage, but also in real life. He should concentrate with all his being on whatever attracts his attention. He should look at an object, not as any absent-minded passer-by, but with penetration. Otherwise his whole creative method will prove lopsided and bear no relation to life."[39]

38   Sharon Salzberg and Joseph Goldstein, *Insight Meditation. Correspondence Course Workbook* (Boulder: Sounds True, 1996), p. 21.

39   Stanislavski, *An Actor Prepares*, p. 91. It should be noted that Stanislavski had some familiarity with Hindu ideas, especially yoga, which he to some

TRUTH AND BELIEF

"An actor is a teacher of beauty and truth," Stanislavski wrote in a letter to a young student. Indeed, there is probably no precept in the literature of acting theory that is more important to learning the craft than how to live truthfully and completely in the imaginary circumstances of the script. This valuative attachment has been strongly articulated by every major acting teacher, though it was Stanislavski who made it a most central aspect of acting theory and technique. As Russian actor I. Sudakov said in his essay, "The Creative Process," "an actor who loses his sense of truth is like a blind man."[40]

While we have briefly commented on Stanislavski's notion of truth, we want to further elaborate this all-important concept. For Stanislavski, there are two kinds of truth and sense of belief in what an actor is doing: "*First, there is the one that is created automatically and on the plane of actual fact…*and second, there is the *scenic type, which is equally truthful but which originates on the plane of imaginative and artistic fiction.*"[41] Moreover, says Stanislavski, "*in ordinary life, truth is what really exists, what a person really knows. Whereas on the stage it consists of something that is not actually in existence which could happen.*"[42]

For Stanislavski there is a major difference between the truth on the stage and the truth in real life: "Of significance to us is: *the reality of the inner life of a human spirit in a part and a belief in that reality. We are not concerned with the actual naturalistic existence of what surrounds us on the stage, the reality of the material world.* This is of use to us only in so far as it supplies a general background for our feelings."[43]

Thus, what Stanislavski means by truth on the stage "is the scenic truth which an actor must make use of in his moments of creativeness." Put succinctly, he further says, "*Truth on the stage is whatever we can believe in with sincerity, whether in ourselves or in our colleagues.*"[44] In order to create a "truthful" persuasive performance, this being the main

---

extent integrated into his acting exercises and theoretical formulations.

40   Toby Cole (ed.), *Acting. A Handbook of the Stanislavski Method* (New York: Three Rivers Press, 1983), p. 98.

41   Stanislavski, *An Actor Prepares*, p. 128.

42   Ibid.

43   Stanislavski, *An Actor Prepares*, p. 129.

44   Ibid.

goal of Stanislavski's System, the actor has to construct the illusion of reality on stage, he has to persuade the audience that he is depicting a real person, that his thoughts, feelings and actions are precisely those of the character he embodies. Embodiment, the act or process by which something is made tangible and visible, is the main thrust of Stanislavski's specific style and method of acting.[45]

There is one other point that Stanislavski made about truth and belief that has bearing on the non-actor and actor in search of the "good life," that "truth cannot be separated from *belief*, nor *belief* from truth....without both of them it is impossible to live your part, or create anything."[46] The deeper point that grows out of Stanislavski's observation that is also applicable to real life is this: when one believes strongly in what one takes to be true, one has created the conditions of possibility to have faith and trust in oneself, in what one is doing. "Faith in what you are doing," says Stanislavski "keeps you on the right track." Elsewhere he says that a "fully justified physical action...is what an artist can place his whole organic faith in."[47] Not only does a strong belief in the truth of what one believes give a person greater self-confidence, trust and a viable praxis ("keeps you on the right track"), it does much more. In real life, deep inner convictions rooted in what one believes to be true are the basis for greater autonomy and personality integration, and perhaps most importantly, they provide something of a protective shield against the assaulting aspects of life. As I (PM) have shown, for example, in the extreme environment of the Nazi concentration camps, it was those inmates with strong beliefs and transcendent values (e.g., Jehovah Witnesses, Orthodox Jews, Catholic priests, Marxists), especially the belief in the truth of their moral values, who were most likely to maintain their autonomy, integration and humanity.[48] Thus, not only do strong beliefs in the truth of what one is doing make for a great performance on the stage, especially if one views oneself as "a teacher of beauty and truth" as Stanislavski advocates, but

45   Eddershaw, "Acting Methods: Brecht and Stanislavski," in Bartram and Waine (Eds.), *Brecht in Perspective*, p. 130.

46   Stanislavski, *An Actor Prepares*, p. 129.

47   Ibid., pp. 148, 135.

48   Paul Marcus, *Autonomy in the Extreme Situation. Bruno Bettelheim, the Nazi Concentration Camps and the Mass Society* (Westport, CT: Prager, 1999), pp. 87-116.

it also gives one the inner resources to endure what Freud called the "harshness" of life, to "hang tough," even flourish when life bears down on you.

COMMUNION

Communion, generally defined as a feeling of emotional or spiritual closeness, a sense of fellowship, was an important valuative attachment for Stanislavski, as well as a human capacity that the actor needed to deepen and expand. Communion, a sub-species of attention, refers to the effect that actors have on each other, "the living exchange between the characters in a scene," the potentiating "chemistry" between actors.[49] Stanislavski describes communion in his comments on "The Art of the Actor and the Art of the Creator":

> It is only then that action on the stage reaches its proper expressiveness; between the characters in the play a living bond is formed [communion], such as is necessary in order to convey the drama to the fullest extent while always observing the right rhythm and tempo for the overall performance.

The essential feature of communion, says Stanislavski, is "wholly receiving and wholly giving himself up" to the other, whether a person or object.[50] In contrast to directly addressing the audience, straightforwardly making the audience one's main focus, which Stanislavski felt was an empty acting style of reporting, the Stanislavskian goal of becoming a believable, truthful, embodied character, was best accomplished through sincere, candid, continuous communion between actors. This way of indirectly making contact with the audience was the most honest and effective way to captivate them.

Stanislavski's discussion of communion begins with the idea of communing with an ordinary object. He says to one of his students after an exercise:

> You were trying to find out *how* and *of what* that object was made. You absorbed its form, its general aspects, and all sorts of details about it. You accepted these impressions, entered them in your memory, and proceeded to think about them. That means that you

---

49   Brestoff, *The Great Acting Teachers and Their Methods*, pp. 53, 54.
50   Stanislavski, *Stanislavski's Legacy*, p. 186.

drew something from your object, and we actors look upon that as necessary.

Stanislavski then extends his discussion to communing with other actors:

> Yet without absorbing from others or giving of yourself to others there can be no intercourse on the stage. To give or to receive from an object something, even briefly, constitutes a moment of spiritual intercourse.[51]

If an actor is to enthrall an audience he must engage his fellow actor both as a character in the play and as a real person, a fellow actor, with an "uninterrupted exchange of feelings, thoughts and actions among themselves."[52] Sounding like the preeminent philosopher of dialogue, Martin Buber, Stanislavski notes that to effectively and wholeheartedly communicate with another performer the actor must firstly "seek out his soul, his inner world. Now try to find my living soul: the real, live me."[53] It is this "contact" with the other actor's "living spirit" that matters most for a "natural, mutual exchange" to occur between actors.[54] Such dialogue is a form of mutual self-creation between actors.

Stanislavski expanded his discussion of communing to include self-communion, a form of talking to ourselves. Self-communion was not formally part of Stanislavski's System but it involved Stanislavski making his brain and solar plexus communicate, or "talk" to each other. The brain and solar plexus in certain Hindu conceptions were viewed as the two main energic, "radiating" centers of our nerves' life and the psychological centers of our self. It was if he initiated a kind of "splitting" of his self that facilitated a continuous dialogue between the two parts of himself, analogous to two actors talking to each other.[55]

Finally, Stanislavski described the necessity of the actor to be able to commune with an "imaginary, unreal, non-existent object" such as with a ghost in a Shakespeare play. What the experienced actor understands is that it is not the ghost itself that ultimately matters, but the

---

51   Ibid., p. 195.

52   Ibid., p. 197.

53   Ibid., p. 199.

54   Ibid., p. 200.

55   Moore, *The Stanislavski System. The Professional Training of an Actor*, p. 36; Stanislavski, *An Actor Prepares*, p. 198.

actor's internal relation to it. In other words, the actor does not try to convince himself that he really sees the ghost, but rather he attempts to provide a candid and sincere answer to the question: "what should I do if a ghost appeared before me?"[56] The "magic if" is important here.

Communion, while being a technical concept for Stanislavski, has a profound implication for living the "good life." What Stanislavski was suggesting is true, compelling and essential on the stage is also true, compelling and essential in real life, namely, the capacity to engage the "Other," a person, object or even an object of one's imagination, with the fullness of one's whole being, in a "relation of mutuality," as Stanislavski says. Stanislavski's description greatly resonates with the work of the Jewish philosopher, Martin Buber. As Buber saw it, there were two main ways of relating to the Other, whether a man, animal, object or God, the "I-Thou" or the "I-It." Briefly, in the "I-Thou" relationship one relates to the Other in a way that is mutually and utterly self-revealing, in the here and now, and completely respectful of the Other's otherness and freedom. Thus, the "I-Thou" relation is characterized by genuineness, responsiveness and presentness. In the "I-It" relationship the other is treated more as an "it," an object, a thing to be used for objective and instrumental purposes and it is tied to the past, not the present like the "I-Thou." As Stanislavski noted, to be in authentic communion with one's fellow actor while performing requires that one be mindful of the other's existence, to make certain that you and she are communicating clearly, intelligibly and mutually, either in words or actions. The point we are making is that whether on the stage or in real life, the capacity for open, responsive and mutual engagement with animate and inanimate others, in the here and now, is not only a prerequisite for effective and genuine communication, it is a prerequisite for responsible acting, living and perhaps most importantly, for loving. Buber wrote—and we would add, following Stanislavski—love in real life, toward one's fellow actor on the stage, "is responsibility of an I for a Thou." Stanislavski insinuates a similar insight when he writes that "Collective creativeness, on which our art is based, necessarily demands ensemble ['the logical, truthful, purposeful mutual behavior of all the characters' the actors are playing]. Those

---

56   Stanislavski, *An Actor Prepares*, p. 202.

who violate it commit a crime…against the art [and other actors and audience] which they serve."[57]

ADAPTATION

Adaptation refers to the kinds of adjustments that actors need to make with each other while performing a scene. Exactly what adjustments are necessary depends on what a fellow actor is doing as well as other obstacles that emerge during a performance.

Adaptation, says Stanislavski, is "both the *inner and outer human means that people use in adjusting themselves to one another in a variety of relationships and also as an aid in effecting an object.*"[58] What Stanislavski is highlighting is the interdependence of actors as they play a scene and work together during rehearsals. For example, if an actor has to speak with a woman during a scene who has just been raped, his approach, his actions, objectives and adjustments will be different than if he were speaking with a woman who just had her first baby. The point is that the actor must be able to make his behavior psychologically and behaviorally "fit" the context, especially the emotional context, in which the other character is situated and behaving. Moreover, adaptations are not just to other characters during a scene, but also to the general circumstances of the scene, such as the literal place of the action (e.g., a kitchen or a train station), time (e.g., sunrise or sunset) and historical context (e.g., Middle Ages or the year 2009). Good adjustments, says Stanislavski, have the following qualities: "vividness, colorfulness, boldness, delicacy, shading, exquisiteness, taste."[59]

Stanislavski summarizes what he means by the actor "adjusting or conforming oneself to a problem." In a certain sense, adaptation is a form of deceit, a kind of "trick" to solve a problem. But it is much more than this. Adaptation

> is a vivid expression of inner feelings or thoughts…it can call the attention to you of the person with whom you wish to be in contact…
> it can prepare your partner by putting him in a mood to respond to you…it can transmit certain invisible messages, which can only be
> felt and not put into words. And I could mention any number of

57   Moore, *The Stanislavski System. The Professional Training of an Actor*, p. 14.

58   Stanislavski, *The Actor Prepares*, p. 224.

59   Ibid., p. 227.

other possible functions [of adaptation], for their variety and scope is infinite.[60]

Adaptation, the process or state of changing to fit new circumstances or conditions, or the resulting change, involves modifying one's behavior for a conscious purpose. To accomplish this effectively on and off the stage, the latter during social interaction, requires a highly skilled form of empathy, the ability to identify and understand another person's feeling or difficulties. Having to speak to a person in high position from whom one needs a favor but whom one does not know, requires the ability to make oneself stand out from the other people who are also trying to get assistance from the person in a high position, says Stanislavski in his scenic example. Stanislavski's empathic immersion in the other is evident when he asks himself the following questions:

> I must rivet your attention on me and control it. How can I strengthen and make the most of the slight contact between us? How can I influence you to take a favorable attitude toward me? How can I reach your mind, your feelings, your attention, your imagination? How can I touch the very soul of such an influential person?[61]

Adjustments, which are always based on empathic immersion in the world of the other, are "made consciously and unconsciously," says Stanislavski. They often rely on intuition and are "created naturally, spontaneously…at the very moment when emotions are at their height."[62] Stanislavski's observations and formulations are in sync with contemporary psychological understandings of how empathy works. "The great gift of human beings is that we have the power of empathy," says Meryl Streep. As psychoanalyst Charles Rycroft notes, sounding similar to Stanislavski, accurate empathy "implies that one is both feeling oneself into an object [another person] and remaining aware of one's own identity as another person."[63] Empathy, according to psychoanalytic theory, and the adjustments that one needs to make in order to effectively access the other and give and receive from the other, "is developmentally related to preverbal mother-infant interac-

---

60   Ibid., p. 224.

61   Ibid., p. 225.

62   Ibid., p. 233.

63   Charles Rycroft, *A Critical Dictionary of Psychoanalysis* (London: Penguin, 1995), p. 47.

tion in which there is a concordance of wish, need and response."[64]
Stanislavski probably had something like this in mind when he wrote,
"When we are communing with one another [on the stage] words do
not suffice. If we want to put life into them, we must produce feelings.
They fill out the blanks left by words, they finish what has been left
unsaid."[65] The larger point we are making that has bearing on living
the "good life" is this: As for the actor on the stage, the capacity to
accurately empathize with the other's needs and wishes is critical to
properly and creatively relate to another person. Moreover, empathy
is essentially the capacity to temporarily imagine oneself "as if" one
were the other, thus empathy is a very skilled imaginative activity. For
example, individuals who are on the autistic spectrum who have a reduced capacity to empathize and imaginatively take the other person's
perspective have a hard time having relationships with other so-called
"normal" people. As Stanislavski further suggests in his discussion
of adaptation, and psychologist William Ickes has strongly argued,
empathy is a complicated type of psychological inference involving
such ego functions as observation, memory, knowledge, and reasoning which are joined together to harvest insights into the inner world,
the momentary psychological condition of another person.[66] Perhaps
most importantly, suggests Stanislavski, effective adaptation and adjustments, always based on accurate and intense empathy, allow one
to serve the Other (though this is not always true—a psychopath can
empathize with the other but feel no compassion for him). "Your first
duty," says Stanislavski, "is to adapt yourself to your partner."[67] What
Stanislavski is suggesting and social psychologists have demonstrated
is that there is often a strong link between empathy and altruism, and
for the person in search of the "good life" this capacity for "being for the
Other" is crucial to having satisfying relationships.

---

64   Burness E. Moore and Bernard D. Fine (Eds.), *Psychoanalytic Terms and
      Concepts* (New Haven: Yale University Press, 1990), p. 67.

65   Stanislavski, *An Actor Prepares*, p. 225.

66   William Ickes, *Everyday Mind Reading: Understanding What Other
      People Think and Feel* (Amherst, NY: Prometheus Press, 2003).

67   Stanislavski, *An Actor Prepares*, p. 232.

TEMPO-RHYTHM

Tempo, the pace or rate of something, and rhythm, the regular pattern of movement of something, which, combined, Stanislavski calls
"tempo-rhythm," is "the basic pace of a scene and the rhythm of the
individual actions within the pulse."[68] For example, there is an emotional difference between acting a role that takes place in a disco versus
at a Catholic Mass. Tempo-rhythm has many functions. It facilitates
"concreteness and truthfulness" in the doing of physical actions, it in-
duces "concentration," it helps the actor grasp "the logic and consecu-
tiveness of actions," it encourages "communion and ensemble work,"
and by making an action truthful, it acts as a catalyst for the "actor's
emotions."[69] Tempo-rhythm is both inner and outer, conscious and
unconscious, and, says Stanislavski, getting it right is crucial to playing a character properly in a set of circumstances. "*Apparently tempo-
rhythm has the power to suggest not only images but also whole scenes!*";
"*Tempo-rhythm of movement can not only intuitively, directly, immediately suggest what one is doing but also it helps stir one's creative faculty.*"[70]
While tempo-rhythm is an enormously complicated topic, the details
of which are beyond the scope of this chapter, the main point we want
to emphasize, the one that has bearing on living the "good life," is that
tempo signifies "the speed of action or feeling—fast, slow, medium,"
while "rhythm, internally, indicates the intensity with which an emotion is experienced." Moreover, continues Benedetti, "externally," it suggests the "pattern of gestures, moves, and actions which express the
emotion." To accomplish "organic unity," Stanislavski's overarching goal
of any performance requires "rhythmic coherence both in the parts
and in the organization of the whole."[71] A good illustrative instance
of tempo-rhythm comes from a film with Jack Nicholson, *As Good
As It Gets*. As J. Gorman describes it, Nicholson superbly plays an ob-
sessive-compulsive character, and when preparing for playing his role,
he had to rationalize and make logical his character's bizarre behavior.

---

68   Benedetti, *Stanislavski and the Actor*, p. 153.
69   Moore, *The Stanislavski System. The Professional Training of an Actor*,
      pp. 40-41.
70   Constantin Stanislavski, *Building a Character* (New York: Routledge,
      1977), pp. 203, 202.
71   Benedetti, *Stanislavski. An Introduction*, p. 68.

For example, he had to ask himself, "How many times did he need to switch the light from on to off and back again? How many times did he need to lock and double lock the door? What action would his character perform?"[72]

For the non-actor and actor in search of the "good life," mastering tempo-rhythm is essential, for without it one cannot harmonize and synchronize one's general comportment with the needs and wishes of the Other. Being able to pace one's way of being, both internally, such as with one's energy level, and externally in terms of one's actual behavior, is vital to properly and inventively interact with others. A skillful, perceptive tempo-rhythm requires empathic immersion, while also being in sync with the context, the given circumstances in which one is situated. Mastering tempo-rhythm thus requires good self-regulation and social intelligence. It facilitates the appropriate and effective expression of emotion, attitudes and one's personality, and also helps one successfully manage interactions, all of which is axiomatic for living a life of meaningful dialogue, a core component of the "good life."

EMOTION MEMORY

"An artist," says Stanislavski, "must have full use of his own spiritual, human material [i.e., his emotional life] because that is the only stuff from which he can fashion a living soul for his part."[73] Emotion memory was a concept that Stanislavski developed from French experimental psychologist Théodule-Armand Ribot's notion of "affective memory." Ribot (1839–1916) was studying the relationship between memory and progressive brain disease. To Stanislavski, emotion memory was a key mode of access into the actor's "spiritual material." Emotion memory is "the conscious use of the recall of experiences, either physical or mental, from one's own life, which match the experiences of the character as described by the author."[74] For many years, emotion memory was viewed by Stanislavski as the all-important technique for the actor to make contact with his deepest and most sincere emotions in playing a character; however, later in his career emotion

72   J. Gorman, "What Makes a Good Actor: Tempo-Rhythm," *Arts and Entertainment*, http://www.associated content.com/article/138434/ what_makes_a_good_actor-temporhythm.html

73   Stanislavski, *An Actor Prepares*, p. 304.

74   Benedetti, *Stanislavski and the Actor*, p. 152.

memory was devalued and for the most part, replaced by an emphasis on physical actions. According to Stanislavski, "Carrying out the logic of physical actions will bring you to the logic of emotions, and this is everything for an actor."[75] Emotion memory had its down side, said Stanislavski. It was an unreliable, at times extremely tiring, anxiety-filled and a contrived technique. How could an actor instantaneously and repeatedly, night after night of performances, truthfully feel such consecutive emotions as "delight, apprehension, fear, hope, doubt and finally panic?"[76] Emotions could not be "forced" to flow on conscious demand whether at rehearsal or during a performance. There are also formidable internal resistances, "defenses," against retrieving painful and other emotions as psychoanalysis has taught us. Rather, truthful and believable feelings, rooted in the unconscious where Stanislavski thought creativity mainly comes from, must be coaxed, "enticed," not coerced to appear at will ("you cannot assault the subconscious," it cannot be activated by will power). "The unexpected is often a most effective lever in creative work," said Stanislavski.[77]

Stanislavski was aware that experiencing truthful and believable emotion on the stage was not the same as experiencing emotion in real life, in real time. Thus, his goal of emotional arousal was for-mulated somewhat differently: "Time is a splendid filter for our re-membered feelings—besides it is a great artist. It not only purifies, it also transmutes even painfully realistic memories into poetry."[78] By "poeticized" emotions, Stanislavski meant graceful, rhythmic, sincere and imaginative expressiveness. Poeticized emotions are elevating and uplifting and convey profound insights about the human condition, Stanislavski's overarching goal of all great theater performance and, for that matter, art in general.

There are many technical aspects of emotion memory that Stanislavski discusses, a subject beyond the focus of this introductory chapter to his System. These include, for example, exercises meant to improve one's sensory memory (the five senses), memory of past

---

75   Moore, *The Stanislavski System. The Professional Training of an Actor*, p. 45.

76   Stanislavski, *An Actor Prepares*, p. 166.

77   Ibid., p. 165.

78   Ibid., p. 173.

happenings and ways to activate the memory without willfully "forc-
ing" strong feelings to emerge.[79] Suffice it to say, Stanislavski's goal was
to generate emotional arousal, a heightened sensibility in the service
of playing a character. A brief word on Stanislavski's view of emotions
is necessary.

For Stanislavski truthful and believable emotions that are in sync
with the circumstances of the scene are byproducts of well-chosen and
detailed physical actions. Says Stanislavski,

> On the stage there cannot be, under any circumstances, action which is
> directed immediately at the arousing of a feeling for its own sake. To ig-
> nore this rule results only in the most disgusting artificiality. When
> you are choosing some bit of action leave feeling and spiritual content
> [inner intensity] alone. Never seek to be jealous, or make love or to
> suffer, for its own sake. All such feelings are the result of something that
> has gone before. Of the thing that goes before you should think as hard
> as you can. As for the result, it will produce itself.[80]

In other words, for Stanislavski apt emotions must "grow out of your
living them," of choosing the fitting action that will adequately express
the feeling of the character. "The more delicate the feeling, the more it
requires precision, clarity and plastic quality in its physical expression."
While the authentic feeling will occur "spontaneously"—"an emotion,
if it is sincere is involuntary," said Mark Twain—the best the actor
can do is "prepare the ground" via well-chosen and elaborated physical
actions for the upsurge of truthful feeling to take place. Such a psychological scenario, Stanislavski says, is an important condition of possibility for the experience of "inspiration." Inspiration, what every actor
and non-actor dreams of, is "when an actor is completely absorbed by
some profoundly moving objective, so that he throws his whole being passionately into its execution."[81] Thus, "one cannot play or represent feelings, and one cannot call forth feelings point blank." Rather they
emerge when the actor willfully does the right physical action which
"prods" his conscious and unconscious "creative fantasy," which then

---

79   Benedetti, *Stanislavski and the Actor*, p. 63.

80   Stanislavski, *An Actor Appears*, pp. 40-41.

81   Ibid., pp. 41, 107, 189, 280, 310. Said Stanislavski, "Inspiration is born
      of hard work. It is not the other way around." (*Stanislavski's Legacy*, p. 48).

"stirs up" emotion memory, which has the "echo" of appropriate feelings to the circumstances of the scene.[82]

An important "take home" point from our discussion of emotion memory, one that has bearing for living the "good life," is that rather than try to feel this way or that way, to conjure up pleasurable or other feelings, one should focus on one's behavior, especially toward others, animate or inanimate. That is, skillfully implemented, context-sensitive, truthful, other-directed and other-regarding behavior will spontaneously evoke the appropriate satisfying emotion in the doer. For example, doing good for someone feels good. Being responsible for the Other before oneself, say with one's child, one's elderly parents, a friend or for that matter, a theater audience, will tend to evoke a feeling of ethical height, of having done the right thing. Focusing on giving sexual pleasure to one's significant other before oneself leads to heightened pleasure for the doer as it "fires up" one's partner and evokes her thankfulness. Tending to one's life-sustaining cornfield produces sweet-tasting corn which sells better and leads to both a feeling of self-efficacy and gratitude to Mother Earth. There are many more examples that could be given, but the point is clear: real living, that is, authentic feeling and being, emanate from doing, especially doing for the Other.

CONCLUSION:
STANISLAVSKI'S ARTISTIC SENSIBILITY

In this chapter we have tried to give the reader a sense of the dazzling brilliance of Stanislavski's System, an incredibly detailed, integrated, whole and once revolutionary tradition of acting theory/technique and theater performance, that has influenced knowingly or unknowingly, nearly every major acting teacher, actor and director. While we have covered a lot of ground in our discussion, there is a lot we have left out as space does not permit a review of, for example, Stanislavski's innovative reflections on character building, creating a role, the actor's physical apparatus, the subtext of behavior, and the super-objective and the through line of actions, among other important subjects. This being said, we want to conclude this chapter with a few comments on

---

82   Stanislavski, *Stanislavski's Legacy*, p. 87.

Stanislavski's views on a variety of features of an actor's art and life,
what we are calling his "artistic sensibility."

   "Learn how to love art in yourselves, not yourselves in art…that
should be your guiding thread," Stanislavski told to a group of op-
era and acting students. From this quote we get a deep sense of
Stanislavski's worldview as it related to his beloved art. The art of acting "requires sacrifice," "the service to art consists in the ability to make
selfless sacrifice to it." Moreover, he warns, "if you undertake to exploit
art it will betray you; art is very vindictive." If you serve your craft,
"There is no higher satisfaction than working in the field of art." [83]
Stanislavski thus felt that an actor has to deserve to perform in front
of an audience, that is it is a privilege to make "people think, suffer, be
joyful along with him," to reveal the "human condition." To serve the
audience and the public, is a great "responsibility," thus the actor must
have a strong personal and social justification for performing: "what
gives us the right to come out on the stage?" he asks his students.[84] For
Stanislavski, acting, like any form of art, is firstly a sacred act of service to the Other—the audience, one's fellow actors and director and
the text of the play with its enduring insights into the human condition. "Unless the theater can ennoble you, make you a better person,
you should flee from it;" furthermore, the emotional and intellectual
"donation" that the actor makes should be perspective-altering to the
audience: "When a spectator leaves the theatre he should be able to
look at life and his times with deeper perception than when he came
into the theatre."[85]

   Stanislavski described his work as a form of "spiritual naturalism,"
a term which implies a certain kind of desirable internal life that the
actor needs to have. "The value of any art is determined by its spiritual
content"; "The essence of art is not its external form but its spiritual
content." While he uses the word "spiritual" many times in his writings
he never properly defines it. It seems to be related to the actor's inner
emotional intensity and his capacity to deeply connect with, and serve,
his fellow actors, the text and the audience with the goal of being a

83   Ibid., pp. 28, 33.
84   Ibid., pp. 36, 37.
85   Ibid.

"teacher of beauty and truth."[86] "You must work all your life to develop
your mind and perfect your inner self...you must love your art with
all your strength and love it unselfishly." Only then will the theater be
able to fulfill its main objective as an art, creating "the life of a human
spirit...clothed...in a beautiful physical form"; "To be able to transform one's self physically and spiritually is the first and principle object
of acting arts." More generally, the spiritual ideal of the actor should
always "be to strive for what is *eternal* in art, that which will never die,
which will always remain young and close to human hearts."[87]

Thus, Stanislavski was arguing for a particular way of being in the
world as an artist, one that has bearing on the non-actor as well. Says
Stanislavski, "Our type of creativeness is the conception and birth of
a new being—the person in the part. It is a natural act similar to the
birth of a human being."[88] Stanislavski's lifelong search as he described
it was to achieve "a method of work for actors which will enable them
to create the image of a character, breathe into it the life of a human
spirit and, by natural means, embody it on the stage in a beautiful
artistic form."[89] Such artistic attainments as these last two quotations
suggest reflect Stanislavski's belief that to be an actor at its best is to
embrace "a whole way of life."[90] Perhaps the underpinning of this creative "whole way of life" is related to the capacity to love deeply and
widely. Indeed, says Stanislavski,

> Whereas the first period of work on a role was only one of prepara-
> tion, this second period is one of creation. If the first period could
> be compared to the early courtship between two lovers, the second
> represents the consummation of their love, the conception and the
> formation of the fruit of their union.[91]

Elsewhere, Stanislavski clarifies the centrality of love in being a great
actor,

86   Ibid., pp. 77, 27, 69.
87   Ibid., pp. 128, 129, 19,171; Stanislavski, *An Actor Prepares*, pp. 37, 192.
88   Stanislavski, *The Actor Prepares*, p. 312.
89   Stanislavski, *Stanislavski's Legacy*, p. 128.
90   Stanislavski, *Building a Character* (New York: Routledge, 1977), p. 290.
91   Constantin Stanislavski, *Creating a Role* (New York: Routledge, 1989),
     p. 44.

> If you will carry out in your imagination—with the right basis of
> detailed circumstances, proper thinking, sincerity of feeling—each
> step in the series of actions, you will find that first externally and
> then internally you will reach the condition of a person in love.
> With such preparations you find it easier to take on a role and a
> play in which this passion figures.[92]

What Stanislavski is suggesting to the actor and, by extension, to the
non-actor in his emphasis on "selfless sacrifice," "responsibility," the
"spiritual," "loving [your art] unselfishly," striving for what is "eternal"
and what is "beautiful in artistic form" calls to mind two deep and
abiding ethical values which Stanislavski suggests should animate the
actor's being. These are the necessity to lodge one's identity in the powerfully transformative experiences of love, conceived as responsibility
for the Other, the Other in the broadest sense as described above, and
the self-ennobling and creativity that comes from disciplined work:
"inspiration is born of hard work. It is not the other way around."
Stanislavski has thus provided generations of actors with a set of artistic, ethically-infused valuative attachments that have made it possible
for those in and outside the acting profession to feel worthy of being
the teachers of "beauty and truth."

---

92   Stanislavski, *Building a Character*, p. 280.

CHAPTER TWELVE

THE ART OF LIVING
THE "GOOD LIFE"

THOUGHTS AND MUSINGS FROM THE
ACTOR'S PERSPECTIVE

"The stage is not merely the meeting place of the arts, but is also the return of art to life."

—Oscar Wilde

THE "GOOD LIFE," dictionary-defined as a life of carefree comfort and luxury, is an evocative term meant to connote much more than its literal meaning. It centrally includes what an individual believes ultimately matters in life, especially in everyday living. What constitutes the "good life" is often equated with one's view of happiness, that enduring feeling of pleasure, contentment or joy that most people episodically experience though they spend a lifetime striving for it. Historically, the "good life" is another way of describing one's deeply held beliefs and values, what one takes to be the highest good. For example, the highest good for the Greeks was formulated in a number of different ways; for Aristotle the highest good was happiness, for Epicurus it was pleasure, for Marcus Aurelius it was resignation without despair, and for Plato it was the quasi-mystical apprehension of the forms—that is, knowledge. Finally, for ethical philosopher Emmanuel Levinas, who along with Freud is one of the key thinkers who has underpinned our study, the only "absolute value" is "Goodness," being for the Other before oneself. For Freud, following Aristotle, the highest good was happiness, equated with "high-level" and well-sublimated functioning such as is exemplified in "mature" love and creative work.

What then is the actor's view of the "good life"? As we have seen there are many different acting theories and techniques meant to cultivate the internal sensibility and external skills necessary to create a great actor. For the most part, each acting teacher has tended to develop different parts of Stanislavski's System, often in ingenious and unimaginable ways, so it is very difficult to generalize about anything let alone the "worldview" that is common to all actors. While not diminishing the conceptual and technical differences between the various acting theory perspectives, there does seem to be an underlying, common set of beliefs and values about what ultimately matters to the actor if he is to "perform" brilliantly on the stage, and we would add, "perform" brilliantly in real life. Many of these valuative attachments and techniques have already been discussed throughout this book. Stanislavski, however, put his finger on three of the deepest and most abiding, transcendent values underlying all acting theory at its best in the advice he gave to young actors:

> Do not try to push your way through to the front ranks of your profession; do not run after distinctions and reward, but do your utmost to find an entry into the world of beauty.[1]

> Young actors, fear your admirers! Learn in time, from your first steps to hear, understand and love the cruel truth about yourselves. Find out who can tell the truth and talk of your art only with those who can tell you the truth.[2]

As we have discussed in the Stanislavski chapter, Stanislavski's main goal was to communicate to the next generation of actors, "the actor is a teacher of beauty and truth." Perhaps most importantly, Stanislavski emphasized that an actor must be capable of "Goodness," whose luminous core is love, instantiated, as he said, by "selfless sacrifice" and "responsibility" for the Other—to his craft, his fellow actors, the director,

---

1   http://thinkexist.com/quotes/konstantin_stanislavsky/, p. 2.

2   http://www.giga-usa.com/quotes/authors/konstantin_stanislavsky_a001.htm, p. 1.

the script and the audience, his "spiritual acoustics" that he fervently and reverently "serves." "Love art in yourselves, not yourselves in art," Stanislavski famously said. Thus, Stanislavski noted, "success is transient, evanescent. The real passion lies in the poignant acquisition of knowledge about all the shading and subtleties of the creative secrets." In closing this book, we want to briefly explore what these "creative secrets" are that Stanislavski, and those acting teachers who have followed him, felt were correlated with the so-called "eternally unchanging laws,"[3] the "natural laws"[4] that underlie the field of creativeness, which "creates the life of a human soul"—in other words, the psychology of the creative artist.[5] Our assumption is that most people have become estranged from, if they have not repressed, their fundamental capacity to be bearers of Beauty and Truth and the consecrators of Goodness, the enmeshed ideals of great acting and living the "good life." As Stanislavski pithily opined, "How do we introduce yeast into our creative state?", a "poetic essence, its integrity and harmony of proportion,"[6] whether on the stage or in real life.

While the subjects of Beauty, Truth and Goodness are regarded by philosophers and theologians as important human values "belonging to aesthetic, epistemological and ethical categories respectively" (the qualities of desirability, meaningfulness and worthiness), what philosopher Rudolf Steiner called "the great transcendents of the classical tradition," "the three great ideals...representing the sublime nature and

3   Constantin Stanislavski, *Stanislavski's Legacy*. Elizabeth Reynolds Hapgood (Ed. & Trans.) (New York: Theater Arts Books, 1968), p. 198.

4   Constantin Stanislavski, *Building a Character* (New York: Routledge, 1989), p. 288.

5   Stanislavski and many of the great acting teachers that followed him, most notably Jerzy Grotowski, believed that they were discerning and describing the objective laws of the actor's art. Whether there are such things as objective laws is of course debatable, especially to those who believe that objectivity is a flawed notion particularly in the arts. In this philosophical view there is no such thing as "mind-independent" facts that are always true under all conditions irrespective of human cognition and affect, so-called discovered truths rather than created ones.

6   Constantin Stanislavski, *The Actor Prepares* (New York: Routledge, 1989), pp. 303, 183.

lofty goal of all human endeavors,"[7] they are enormously complicated notions and therefore not easy to define, distinguish or explicate in a few pages.[8] This being said, as with the actor at his best, we want to suggest, at least in a rudimentary way, that to the extent that one can consciously and unconsciously embrace and live the ennobling values of Beauty, Truth and Goodness in one's everyday life, one is more likely to experience the "good life": the capacity to love deeply and widely and to engage in productive and effective work, guided by reason, in a manner that is aesthetically pleasing and radiates an habitual inner beauty,[9] what Shelley called "virtuous goodness." As Stanislavski noted, "That is why I propose for actors a complete inner and external metamorphosis."[10] Stella Adler further elaborated that an "individual actor's total personality was supposed to be dealt with" to properly practice his craft.[11]

THE CALL OF BEAUTY

Beauty, most simply defined, is the combination of qualities that make something pleasing and impressive to listen to or touch, or especially to look at. While this definition is a serviceable one, it does not connote what the engagement with beauty, and its internalization in terms of one's feeling, thinking, and acting, actually means for one's general comportment, one's way of being in the world. As Stanislavski advised to singers who were training as actors, "learn to see, hear, love

---

7   Chung-hsuan Tung, "Beauty is Goodness, Goodness in Beauty": Sheely's 'Awful Shadow' and 'Ethical Sublime.'" http://benz.nchu.edu.tw/-intergrams/082-091/082-091-tung.pdf, p. 1.

8   Luc Ferry, *What Is the Good Life*. Lydia G. Cochrane (Trans.) (Chicago: University of Chicago Press, 2005).

9   The authors of course realize that this definition is radically philosophical, that is, that each term in our definition is highly perspectival and open to a range of meanings. This being said, we have only tried to briefly suggest the way of being in the world for someone who has deeply internalized beauty, truth and goodness as his or her working life principles.

10   Stanislavski, *Stanislavski's Legacy*, p. 18.

11   Toby Cole and Helen Chinoy (Eds.), *Actors on Acting* (New York: Crown Publishers, 1954), p. 537.

life—carry this over into art, use it to fill out the image you create for yourself of a character you are to play."[12]

According to Catholic philosopher and poet John O'Donohue, beauty is a kind of "invisible" and "eternal embrace," a tender but pressing call to awaken to the world of the Spirit, that vital force that characterizes a living being as being alive at his best.[13] As Stanislavski said, "Our ideal should always be to strive for what is *eternal* in art, that which will never die, which will always remain young and close to human hearts."[14] For O'Donohue, like Stanislavski, beauty is not so much a thing "out there" that we experience through our senses, though it is that too, as the person maintains the sense of a distinction between "what is in me and what is before me."[15] However, more importantly, as Adler described acting, the capacity to perceive, feel and create beauty is a different, more refined way of "imaginatively....seeing and describing" the world and one's experience of it. As O'Donohue noted, "Beauty inhabits the cutting edge of creativity—mediating between the known and unknown, light and darkness, masculine and feminine, visible and invisible, chaos and meaning, sound and silence, self and others."[16] In this context, beauty can be adequately defined for the actor and non-actor as "human subjectivity expressed in ideal form"; in other words, "it is an aspect of experience of idealization in which an object(s), sound(s), or concept(s) is (or are) believed to possess qualities of formal perfection." In most instances, the experience of beauty is enjoyable and can evoke a gamut of emotional states, "from a gentle sense of disinterested pleasure to awe and excited fascination" (e.g., like watching a tsunami on TV). Moreover, while the observer usually believes that the beautiful object is inherently beautiful, it is the appropriate and skillful subjective involvement in the object of beauty that is crucial to experience its beauty.[17]

12   Stanislavski, *Stanislavski's Legacy*, p. 31.

13   John O'Donohue, *Beauty. The Invisible Embrace* (New York: Perennial, 2004), p. 13.

14   Stanislavski, *An Actor Prepares*, p. 192.

15   Brian Treanor, "Gabriel Marcel," *Stanford Encyclopedia of Philosophy*, http://plato.stanford.edu/entries/marcel/#13, p. 7.

16   O'Donohue. *Beauty. The Invisible Embrace*, p. 40.

17   George Hagman, *Aesthetic Experience. Beauty, Creativity, and the Search for the Ideal* (Amsterdam: Rodopi, 2005), p. 87.

The capacity to experience and most importantly, create beauty is thus a huge subjective accomplishment that implies a "high level" mode of psychological functioning. Indeed, psychoanalysis and other psychological perspectives have elaborated in thousands of books and professional articles the psychology of creativity. For our purposes, we want to simply suggest some of the internal conditions of possibility for a person to experience and create the beautiful whether in the performing arts or in the art of living the "good life."

George Hagman, a psychoanalyst, has aptly summarized much of the psychoanalytic literature on the sense of beauty. He notes that the main contribution of psychoanalysis has been carefully explicating "the nature, sources, and functions of the subjective experience of beauty."[18] His integrated findings are worth thinking about as they relate to acting and living the "good life," though not surprisingly, as with Stanislavski, much of what has been written by psychoanalysts on creativity has to do with unconscious processes. Stanislavski asked, "How can we come closer to this nature of creation? This has been the principle concern of my whole life." His answer: "Through the conscious to the unconscious, that is the motto of our art and technique."[19] Mainly drawing from Hagman, this brief review of some of the most interesting psychoanalytic formulations about the sense of beauty are provided mainly to give the reader a "feel" for the internal accomplishments that experiencing and creating beauty seem to entail.

SUBLIMATION

For Freud, beauty was understood as a sublimation of sexual and aggressive wishes. Sublimation can be simply defined as a "developmental process by which instinctual energies [i.e., sex and aggression] are discharged in non-instinctual forms of behavior."[20] Put differently, for the actor as with any creative "artsy" person, or for that matter anyone, sublimation is "a resolution of intraspychic conflict [conflict between two parts of the psyche] by changing the sexual and aggressive aim of

---

18   Ibid., p. 94.
19   Stanislavski, *Building a Character*, p. 9.
20   Charles Rycroft, *Dictionary of Psychoanalysis* (London: Penguin, 1995), p. 176.

an urge and finding a substitute gratification."[21] Sublimation by definition involves a socially approved result that is gratifying, supple and
judged to be personally and socially beneficial. For example, an actor
may have had a childhood in which he was rarely genuinely listened
to, appreciated and otherwise validated by his parents; his need to be
heard and admired gets sublimated in his choice of an acting career, of
playing to an adoring audience. In authentic sublimation, the original
strong desire always comes through in the substitute activity. Meryl
Streep and Marlon Brando have superbly described sublimation, the
former with a pinch of humor, the latter acerbically: "Let's face it, we
were all once 3-year-olds who stood in the middle of the living room
and everybody thought we were so adorable. Only some of us grow
up and get paid for it"; "Acting is the expression of a neurotic impulse.
It is a bum's life. The principal benefit acting has afforded me is the
money to pay for my psychoanalysis." Paul Newman and Al Pacino,
respectively, have also regarded their acting careers as a kind of sublimation: "To be an actor you have to be a child"; "My first language
was shy. It's only by having been thrust into the limelight that I have
learned to cope." And finally, Stanislavski perceptively noted in his autobiography, "Actors often use the stage to receive what they cannot
get in real life."[22]

IDEALIZATION

The experience and creation of beauty always involves the capacity
to idealize. Idealization, a life-long process, especially observed when
one is in love, is an unrealistic overstatement of a person's qualities.
It involves the capacity for illusion; the other person or activity, like
acting on a stage, is regarded as living perfection and magnificence.
Idealization can be defensive in nature, that is, it can be a defense
against ambivalence ("I love and hate my wife," "I love and hate the

---

21   Ethel S. Person, Arnold M. Cooper and Glen O. Gabbard (Eds.),
     Textbook of Psychoanalysis (Washington, DC: American Psychiatric
     Publishing, 2005), p. 560.

22   Ian McKellan illustrates this point rather well, as does Betty Davis, re-
     spectively: "When you were on stage, you could be absolutely open about
     your emotions and indulge them and express yourself in a way that—in
     real life—I wasn't doing"; "People often become actresses because of some-
     thing they dislike about themselves. They pretend they are someone else."

profession of acting"), it is a way of warding off disenchantment, sadness, guilt and other negative emotions. However, idealization in the
context of beauty can represent a "healthy need" to be connected to
someone or something that is experienced as perfect or ideal. This being said, idealization of the other, whether a beautiful person, thing or
activity is a delicate and fleeting enterprise. Hagman states,

> the yearning that we experience before beauty is for an experience
> that is ultimately unattainable, which is already lost, perhaps forev-
> er. This is what makes beauty at times unbearable: the simultaneous
> sense of the ideal as both recovered and lost.[23]

Thus, the experience and creation of beauty is at times a painful and
subjectively wounding process, something of which Stanislavski was
acutely aware:

> Life [and the creative process] is an unremitting *struggle*, one over-
> comes or one is defeated. Likewise on the stage, side-by-side, with
> the through action there will be a series of *counter-through actions*
> on the part of other characters, other circumstances. The collision
> and conflict of these two opposing through actions constitute the
> dramatic situation[24] [emphasis in original].

ACTIVE ENGAGEMENT

To experience and create beauty is not a passive undertaking; it requires marked involvement, energy and action. Only in this way, when
the doer merges with the beautiful animate or inanimate other, is he
liberated from his limited, subdued if not truncated sense of himself.
The experience of beauty and its creation involve an intellectual, emotional and spiritual engagement, an "interactive and intersubjective"
process,[25] one that tends to foster a sense of self-transcendence. Perfect
self and perfect world, creator and observer, loss/disappointment and

---

23   Hagman, *Aesthetic Experience. Beauty, Creativity, and the Search for the
     Idea*, pp. 95, 96.

24   Stanislavski, *Creating a Role*, p. 80. "Through-action/Counter-through-
     action" is "the logic of the sequence of actions, which bind together all the
     single actions and enables the character to reach his goal." (Jean Benedetti,
     Stanislavski and the Actor (New York: Routledge, 1998), p. 154.)

25   Hagman, *Aesthetic Experience. Beauty, Creativity, and the Search for the
     Idea*, p. 96.

abundance/satisfaction constitute, in part, the psychological landscape of the sense of beauty. In a way, as Donald Winnicott pointed out, the experience of beauty, and for that matter all forms of art, takes place between these above mentioned dualities and polarities, in the overlapping "half way" space between subjective and objective, the psychic and the external worlds. The result of residing in this "betweenness" psychic space is a wide range of emotions such as "awe, joy, excitement, optimism and contentment" as well as "anger, sexual excitement and fear," as this range of emotions are embedded within the "formal structure" of the experience of beauty.[26]

GIVING WAY TO THE HEALING AND SELF-ENHANCING EXPERIENCE OF BEAUTY

In order to yield to the self-transcendent, transformative experience of beauty and its creation, one must be able to "let go," to hurl oneself into the invisible embrace. This "letting go" can be done in many different ways and intensities depending on the context, from passionately surrendering to the allure of a beautiful person or to the felt presence of God through prayer, to quietly admiring a lovely sunset or the elegance of a mathematical equation. As Hagman noted, following Emmanuel Ghent, "Through this experience of surrender that we break out of the confines of our false selves and allow ourselves to be known, found, penetrated, and recognized—it is a vital, natural force toward psychological and spiritual growth."[27] This capacity to be open and responsive sounds easier than it actually is. As the great Roman lyric poet Horace wrote, "If you want to move me, you had first better move yourself."[28] There are many people who are twisted up like pretzels, too inhibited, defended and in other ways internally

26   Ibid., p. 97
27   Ibid., p. 98.
28   Acting, said Stanislavski, can be a "painful process," it "requires enormous self-mastery," "physical endurance" and "awareness" among other personal qualities difficult to cultivate (Stanislavski, *Stanislavski's Legacy*, pp. 9, 70). Stella Adler also advocated that actors have to push themselves out of their comfort zone which can cause anxiety: "You're here to learn to stretch yourself in life, and in so doing on stage as well" (Stella Adler, *The Art of Acting*, Howard Kissel (Ed.) (New York: Applause, 2000), p. 207). All of this being said, "Acting is happy agony," said Sartre.

restricted that they cannot appreciate beauty nor creatively imagine and produce something beautiful. For them, life lacks the "presence and possibility" of a "real" encounter with the mysteriously beautiful which is also always a striking self-encounter. O'Donohue states, "Yet ultimately beauty is a profound illumination of presence, a stirring of the invisible in visible form and in order to receive this, we need to cultivate a new style of approaching the world."[29] Thus, when beauty and its creation touch the "matrix of human selfhood," whether gently or disruptively, they always enlarge, expand, and enrich consciousness. It is "an encounter of depth and spirit."[30]

The encounter with the beautiful, whether as an observer or a creator, thus has a healing aspect to it. It is capable of facilitating a feeling of "harmony, balance, and wholeness,"[31] better ways of experiencing and engaging the self and world. Moreover, it can "repair the feared fragmentation or damage done to internal objects by aggressive wishes." (Internal objects are "that towards which action or desire is directed; that which the subject requires in order to achieve" sexual or aggressive "satisfaction; that to which the subject relates himself.")[32] Put more simply, beauty helps the person subdue, transform or undo the aggressive fantasies that we all consciously or unconsciously periodically have toward others. It can also reduce the anxiety associated with death by putting the person "in touch" with a transcendent belief, value and self-experience that is regarded as definitively, overwhelmingly and eternally truthful and good.[33] As Hagman notes, "Beauty is not illusory, nor does it stand in or cover up something else" (though it can). Rather, beauty may express "man's search for perfection, transcendence and hope...." It is "one of the most exquisite forms of human

29   O'Donohue, *Beauty. The Invisible Embrace*, p. 23.

30   Ibid., pp. 21, 23.

31   Hagman, *Aesthetic Experience. Beauty, Creativity, and the Search for the Idea*, p. 99.

32   Rycroft, *Dictionary of Psychoanalysis*, p. 113.

33   As Gabriel Marcel has indicated, the denial of the transcendent reflects the "brokenness" of the self (e.g., the incapability or unwillingness to imagine and to wonder) and the world (e.g., the overvaluation of functionality, technical reasoning and so-called objectivity in everyday life). See Treanor, *Stanford Encyclopedia of Philosophy*, http://plato.stanford.edu/entries/marcel/#13, pp. 3, 5.

meaning that exists."[34] Actress and master acting teacher, Uta Hagen, put the point well when she wrote that "I believe in…. the redemption of all things by Beauty everlasting, and the message of Art. …."[35] Finally, as already insinuated, the experience of beauty is intimately related to truth in that beauty, following Hegel, can be conceptualized as the expression of truth in sensuous form.

FIDELITY TO THE TRUTH

Truth has a wide range of meanings and usages. Scholars widely differ in how they define and conceptualize what truth is. We have discussed the differing notions of truth in the theater context throughout this book in that the capacity to act truthfully is crucial for the actor to perform well. As Sanford Meisner said, following Stanislavski, acting is "living truthfully in imaginary circumstances," and Stanislavski noted in his discussion of scenic truth that "The actor must recreate his work each time he repeats his part, with sincerity, truth and directness."

Michael Chekhov, the teacher of Gregory Peck, Anthony Quinn and Marilyn Monroe, among other famous actors and actresses, says that there are many aspects and types of truth within the stage context that we believe have varying degrees of bearing on what it means to live the "good life." For example, there is psychological truth, the kind of truth of which psychoanalysts are most aware, where one's words and actions are "true to myself." There is also "being true to the given circumstances" of the playwright's script, what is called scenic truth or, in psychological language, context-dependent, setting-specific behavior. "Historical truth" refers to the sense of style of the age, capturing the details of the period aspect of the play, including the style of the country where the action occurs. "Stylistic truth" refers to the need for the actor to experience and convey the style of the play, whether it is a tragedy, drama, comedy or farce (as well as such categories of theater as Shakespearean or Brechtian). Perhaps most importantly for our book is "being true to the character," which will differ depending on the role one has to play. According to Chekhov, "the character dictates

34 Hagman, *Aesthetic Experience. Beauty, Creativity, and the Search for the Idea*, p. 101.

35 Uta Hagen, *A Challenge for the Actor* (New York: Charles Scribner's Sons, 1991), p. 20.

it, and you must become more and more receptive to what the character is showing you about itself." Finally, says Chekhov, there is "the truth of relationship," that is, "the often subtle differences and attitude of one character to each of the other characters around him." Perhaps the main thrust of having a feeling of truth both on the stage and in real life is the capacity for "opening yourself," "developing your sensitivity to truthful behavior."[36] Put somewhat differently by acting teacher Eric Morris, "You cannot create truth on the stage unless you come from a place of truth."[37]

Extrapolating from Chekhov and other acting teachers, the point we are making is that to live truthfully, that is, authentically in the circumstances of one's life, is essential to living the "good life." What the Russian actor I. Sudakov said in his essay "The Creative Process," about the actor is also true of the social actor striving to live the "good life": "an actor who loses his sense of truth is like a blind man." Likewise, Stanislavski noted, "the person you are is a thousand times more interesting than the best actor you could ever hope to be." By living truthfully we mean, in part, acting in a way that is in "good faith," true to the "true" self as opposed to acting in "bad faith," in self-deception, the "false" self. As Shakespeare famously wrote in *Hamlet*, "This above all: to thine own self be true. And it must follow as the night the day, Thou canst not then be false to any man." Most importantly, the quality of being true, of being a passionate truth bearer, requires that one's overall, everyday comportment is characterized by sincerity, genuineness, honesty, loyalty and trustworthiness, among other admirable personal qualities. To live truthfully and authentically centrally involves what neo-Socratic Christian philosopher Gabriel Marcel called "creative fidelity," being loyal and faithful to the truth as one knows it, especially in making truthful, "for the Other" connections to and with others. Creative fidelity, "a belief in someone," continues Brian Treanor, "consists in" humbly and "actively maintaining ourselves in a state of openness and permeability, in willing ourselves to remain open to the other and open to the influx of the presence of the other." Spolin characterizes this kind of openness as "not *waiting*

36   Michael Chekhov, *On the Technique of Acting* (New York: HarperCollins Publishers, 1991), p. xxxix.

37   Eva Mekler (Ed.), *The New Generation of Acting Teachers* (New York: Penguin Books, 1987), p. 196.

for, but *in waiting*" [emphasis in original]. Moreover, "the truest fidelity is creative, that is, a fidelity that creates the self in order to meet the demands of fidelity,"[38] that is, loyalty, allegiance, a promise, a vow, to serve the Other. Thus, living truthfully, conceived as a kind of dynamic openness and lively receptivity toward the Other, involves respectfully committing oneself to the reasonable needs and desires of the Other, of putting oneself at their disposal often before oneself, what Levinas calls "Goodness." Says Marcel, "Beings can only be in harmony in the truth, but truth is inseparable from the apprehension of that great mystery which envelops us, in which we have our being," that is love.[39] This leads us to the last and perhaps most important aspect of the self and Other-ennobling valuative triad of Beauty, Truth and Goodness. Before proceeding to discussing goodness, one should bear in mind Tolstoy's cautionary words, "What a strange illusion it is to suppose that beauty is goodness." The same could probably be said of truth. For in some contexts, beauty and truth can be slaves to evil taskmasters.[40] Likewise, being brutally truthful to someone can hurt, undermine, and even devastate one's sense of self. It is not surprising that the Rabbis of the Talmud indicated that sometimes a lie is ethically superior, as it has more practical wisdom than telling the truth. As J.H. Heertz notes in a different context, on and off the stage, the beautiful truth must be spoken in love, it must be moral. That is, the intention of the truth-telling must be ethical. Said Blake, "A truth that's told with bad intent/ Beats all the lies you can invent." Lovingkindness, the essence of Goodness and itself beautiful, conclude the ancient Rabbis, must always precede truth.[41]

---

38 Treanor, *Stanford Encyclopedia of Philosophy*, http://plato.stanford.edu/entries/marcel/#13, p. 16.

39 Gabriel Marcel, *Creative Fidelity*, Robert Rosthal (Trans.) (New York: Noonday Press, 1964), p. 151.

40 "Goodness," under certain definitions and usages, can also be used for evil purposes. For example, the Nazis believed that they were serving the "good," a "higher good" of their nation by murdering Jews, Gypsies and others.

41 J.H. Hertz (Ed.), *The Pentateuch and Haftorahs*. Second Edition (London: Soncino Press, 1960), p. 499.

THE GOODNESS OF GOODNESS

At first glance, it may seem a bit of a stretch to assert that there is a strong ethical thrust to acting and acting theory, but there clearly is. Some illustrative quotes from some of the greatest acting teachers, those discussed in this book, will be helpful in setting the tone of our discussion of the role of Goodness in acting and living the "good life." By Goodness we mainly mean a comportment that is characterized by a broadly conceived responsibility for the Other, often before oneself, or at least as much as oneself, as exemplified in love at its best. Through the "gift" of love, truth, beauty and goodness become one. Below are some quotations that strongly suggest that great acting demands an other-directed, other-regarding orientation—to one's craft, fellow actors, director, the audience and the script.

1. *Stanislavski*: "The service to art consists in the ability to make selfless sacrifice to it"; "Your first duty is to adapt yourself to your partner"; "Learn how to love art in yourselves, not yourselves in art."

2. *Strasberg*: "The actor becomes completely responsive [i.e., to the Other, especially the otherness in himself]. His instrument gives forth a new depth of resonance. Emotion that has been habitually held back suddenly rushes forth. The actor becomes real—not merely simple or natural."

3. *Adler*: "The actor shows special generosity in saying to the audience: 'I am going to give you ideas.' 'I am going to give you pleasure.' 'I am going to dance for you.' 'I am going to tell you the aches of my heart.'"; "The whole thing about acting is to give. The actor must above everything be generous, he doesn't hoard his riches. He has to say, 'I want you to hear this essay. It has wonderful ideas'"; "Artists are together, helping each other's soulfulness to emerge." The actor must be "compassionate"; "All of this is a form of artistry, of giving. It is a love affair with the audience."

4. *Meisner*: "What you do doesn't depend on you; it depends on the other fellow."

5. *Spolin*: "Acting requires presence. Being there....the very act of seeking the moment, of being open to fellow players, produces a life force, a flow, a regeneration for who participate....If our openness is more than just a hope, a sentiment, a word, certain conditions must be met. The first of these we would call mutuality or trust. True playing

will produce trust"; "Theater games do not inspire 'proper' moral behavior (good/bad), but rather seek to free each person to feel his or her own, out of which a felt, experienced, actual love of neighbor will appear."

6. *Brecht*: "The smallest social unit is not the single person but two people. In life too we develop one another."

7. *Suzuki*: "Yet, if the initial energy involved consists not in the emotion itself but in a belief in the importance of emotional attachment, then perhaps the individual can indeed come to feel that the emotions of others are genuine as well."

8. *Grotowski*: "A complete stripping down, by the laying bare of one's own intimacy—all this without the least trace of egotism…the actor makes a total gift of himself"; "A question of giving oneself. One must give oneself totally, in one's deepest intimacy, with confidence, as when one gives oneself in love."

9. *Comedians*: Jerry Seinfeld: "You have to love those people out there for some unexplainable reason, and be willing to take a chance on perhaps embarrassing yourself so that they have a good time"; Richard Belzer: "The idea of making a bunch of strangers laugh and share the same thing at the same moment is a very profound metaphysical and physical force. To be able to do that can be taken for granted or it can be thought of as a responsibility. Let's put it this way—it's my religion"; Jamie Masada: "My goal came from something my father told me when I was a kid, which was [that] the greatest *mitzvah* or greatest good deed you could do for people was to make them laugh."

10. *Mamet*: "A life in the theater is a life spent giving things away," "it is an act of selfless spirit."

Being a great actor thus requires having many of the personal qualities and an overall sensibility of someone who is deeply in love. Not only romantically with the idealization of the significant other and the sense of passionate unfoldings, but in addition, and most importantly, love as we conceive it following Levinas, Stanislavski and others, is a commitment to "serve" the broadly defined Other. Indeed, the above quotations point to the qualities we associate with adult love at its best: "selfless sacrifice," "responsiveness," "to give," "generosity," compassion," "trust," "freedom'," "'develop one another'," "emotional attachment," "feel that the emotions of others are genuine," "laying bare of one's intimacy" and "responsibility." As we have quoted in the Stanislavski chapter, and it is worth repeating, Stanislavski used the love metaphor to describe aspects of acting technique and this metaphor has turned up among actors in our time, including the late Paul Newman and Ralph Richardson. Wrote Stanislavski:

> Whereas the first period of work on a role was only one of preparation, this second period is one of creation. If the first period could be compared to the early courtship between two lovers, the second represents the consummation of their love, the conception and the formation of the fruit of their union.[42]

Stanislavski further elaborates the acting/love metaphor:

> If you will carry out in your imagination—with the right basis of detailed circumstances, proper thinking, sincerity of feeling—each step in the series of actions, you will find that first externally and then internally you will reach the condition of a person in love. With such preparations you find it easier to take on a role and a play in which this passion figures.[43]

Paul Newman also expressed similar sentiments to the words of Stanislavski quoted above: "Every time I get a script it's a matter of trying to know what I could do with it. I see colors, imagery. It has to have a smell. It's like falling in love. You can't give a reason why." Likewise, one of the greatest British actors, Ralph Richardson, described acting in ways that conjure up the all-important empathic immersion that in part constitutes the basis of great performing and the capacity to deeply love:

> No one can show, no one really act what the audience sees a great actor do. He doesn't in point of fact do it. He suggests it to you and you do the work in your imagination. This is complete contact with the deep imaginative subconscious inside the mind of the beholder.[44]

The upshot of this analogy—that the capacity to be a great actor requires an equally great capacity to love the Other—has been succinctly suggested by Hagen: "We must serve the play by serving each other;

42   Stanislavski, *Creating a Role*, p. 44.
43   Stanislavski, *Building a Character*, p. 280.
44   John Miller, *Ralph Richardson. The Authorized Biography* (New York: Pan Books, 1995), p. 4.

an ego-maniacal 'star' attitude is only self-serving and hurts everyone, including the 'star.'"⁴⁵ The reason for this category mistake, confusing the wish to "play" to the audience rather than "serve" the audience—on the part of the non-impressive actor is often related to the fact that rather than give love through their performance, they are seeking love through the audience and other forms of approval. Such a shallow dependence on the outside world for self-validation inevitably impairs one's ability to give a great performance as it closes one off from the potentiating, individuating and deeply creative forces emanating from the Other that one is serving; it is also an incredibly dicey way of doing one's craft and life. As Dustin Hoffman noted, "A good review from the critics is just another stay of execution." In other words, ironically, for a profession in which its members are often overly self-absorbed—"It's a business you go into because you're an egocentric," said Katherine Heburn—to be a great actor requires that they radically reduce, and in other ways downwardly modify their inordinate and infantile narcissistic ways of being, certainly on the stage, but probably also in real life. As Hagen wrote, "self-involvement deadens the senses, and vanity slaughters them until you end up playing alone—and meaninglessly."⁴⁶ Stanislavski asserted that "self-admiration and exhibitionism impair and destroy the power to charm."⁴⁷ The great actress Sarah Bernhardt

45 Uta Hagen, *Respect for Acting* (New York: Macmillan Publishing Company, 1973), p. 19.

46 Hagen, *Respect for Acting*, p. 60. This is not to say that all forms of self-involvement are bad. For example, as Marcel noted, "self-love" that is a manifestation of "self-divinization" is an "idolatrous love." In contrast, there is what he calls "charity towards oneself, which far from treating the self as a plenary reality sufficing to itself, considers it as a seed which must be cultivated, as a ground which must be readied for the spiritual or even for the divine in the world" (Marcel, *Creative Fidelity*, pp. 46-47, 30). Freud and psychoanalysts Otto Kernberg and Heinz Kohut have also described healthy as opposed to pathological forms of narcissism such as in creativity, a sense of humor and wisdom.

47 Stanislavski, *Building a Character*, p. 246. Stanislavski actually advocated a kind of "self-oblivion" (p. 296), though what he actually meant is not clear. Perhaps he was referring to the need for the actor not to cling, often out of safety, to the part of himself that prevents him from fully inhabiting a character. It may also be a reference to the obligation of the actor to firstly serve the play and not one's own narcissistic needs. Adler probably picked up on Stanislavski's point when she wrote "Always, always keep yourself

indicated that to be a great actor one must have the capacity to "forget himself."[48] Spolin noted that it is "ego-centeredness" that is the actor's biggest problem.[49] And finally, actor/comedian Billy Crystal cutely said, "Gentlemen, start your egos!" Needless to say, what is usually true for great actors is also usually true for those who are with mind, heart and spirit working at creating the "good life," a life whose energizing, creative and structuralizing source is the Other. That is, like the great actor on stage, one must act in real life according to a "for the Other" calculus, a way of being in the world that moves toward the "perfection of love" as Levinas calls it, the goodness of Goodness. Then, and perhaps only then, will one paradoxically be graced with the personal benefits that go with aesthetic (Beauty), epistemological (Truth) and ethical (Goodness) excellence, that is, greater internal richness and external freedom. As Stanislavski said, "there are no small parts, only small actors."

out of it. Say to yourself: I myself don't count. The world counts" (Adler, *The Art of Acting*, p. 130). Elsewhere, again emphasizing the other-directed, other-regarding nature of great acting, she wrote, "Your professional obligation from the stage is to make your partner and the audience understand" (Stella Adler, *The Technique of Acting* (New York: Bantam, 1988), p. 11). Lawrence Olivier concurred with Adler when he wrote, "the actor, above all, must be a great understander."

48   Cole and Chinoy, *Actors on Acting*, p. 212.
49   Viola Spolin, *Theater Games for the Lone Actor. A Handbook* (Evanston, IL: Northeastern University Press, 2001), p. 9.

INDEX

Von Berg, Peter, 62

W

warm heart, cool mind (Strasberg),
    37–39
Watson, Burton, 27, 149
Watts, Alan, 28
The Way of Acting (Suzuki), 125
Weigel, Helen, 108–9
Westbrook, Mark, 182
Wiener, Daniel J., 80
Willet, John, 121
Wilson, Glenn, 163
Winnicott, Donald, 48–49, 81, 88,
    241
Wolford, Lisa, 148, 152–53
Word Repetition Game (Meisner),
    65, 68–70
wu-wei, 27–28, 149

X

"X-area, the" (Spolin), 78

Y

Yalom, Irvin, 15
Yasunari, Takahashi, 124